The Final Curtain:
Burma 1941–1945

The Final Curtain: Burma 1941–1945

Veterans' Stories

Jeremy Archer

Pen & Sword
MILITARY

First published in Great Britain in 2022 by
Pen & Sword Military
An imprint of
Pen & Sword Books Ltd
Yorkshire – Philadelphia

Copyright © Jeremy Archer 2022

ISBN 978 1 39907 041 6

The right of Jeremy Archer to be identified as Author of this work has been asserted by him in accordance with the Copyright, Designs and Patents Act 1988.

A CIP catalogue record for this book is available from the British Library.

All rights reserved. No part of this book may be reproduced or transmitted in any form or by any means, electronic or mechanical including photocopying, recording or by any information storage and retrieval system, without permission from the Publisher in writing.

Typeset by Mac Style
Printed and bound in the UK by CPI Group (UK) Ltd, Croydon, CR0 4YY.

Pen & Sword Books Limited incorporates the imprints of Atlas, Archaeology, Aviation, Discovery, Family History, Fiction, History, Maritime, Military, Military Classics, Politics, Select, Transport, True Crime, Air World, Frontline Publishing, Leo Cooper, Remember When, Seaforth Publishing, The Praetorian Press, Wharncliffe Local History, Wharncliffe Transport, Wharncliffe True Crime and White Owl.

For a complete list of Pen & Sword titles please contact

PEN & SWORD BOOKS LIMITED
47 Church Street, Barnsley, South Yorkshire, S70 2AS, England
E-mail: enquiries@pen-and-sword.co.uk
Website: www.pen-and-sword.co.uk

Or

PEN AND SWORD BOOKS
1950 Lawrence Rd, Havertown, PA 19083, USA
E-mail: Uspen-and-sword@casematepublishers.com
Website: www.penandswordbooks.com

In memory of my late father-in-law, Major General John David Whitlock Goodman CB, only son of Brigadier Eric Whitlock Goodman DSO MC, BRA Malaya Command, who was a Japanese prisoner of war for three-and-a-half years.

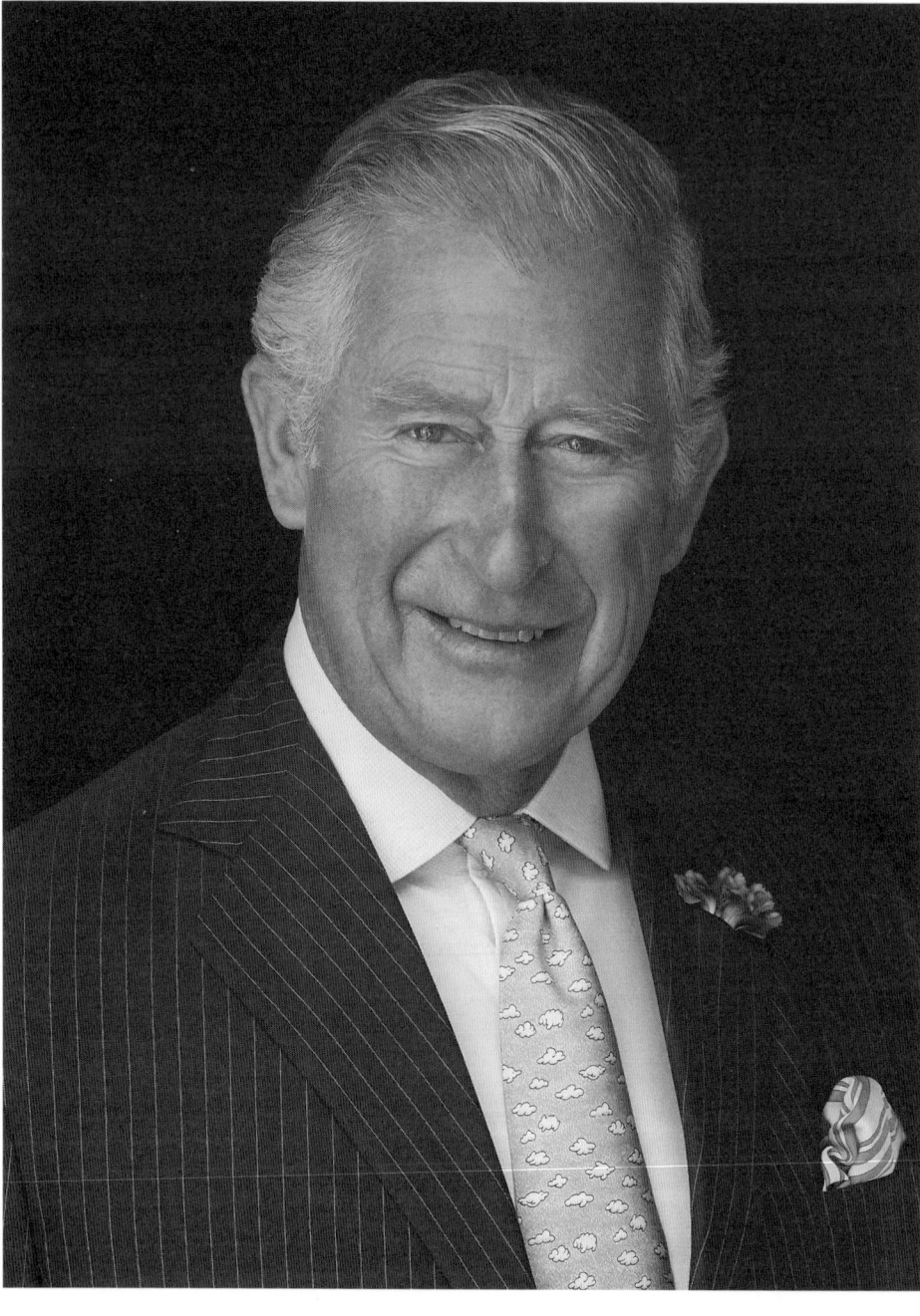

CLARENCE HOUSE

Some of my most vivid and special memories are from time spent with many Burma Veterans, often alongside my great uncle, Lord Mountbatten, and my father who was Patron of the Burma Star Association for some forty years. I was therefore touched and delighted to be asked by the current Viscount Slim to become Patron of the Burma Star Memorial Fund in early 2020 and to continue my close association with this most remarkable group of veterans. It is through the Memorial Fund and its Scholarship Programme, which assumed the mantle of the Association, that a lasting memorial has been created to the veterans of the Burma campaign through the provision of Scholarships to young people from any nation that served on the Allied side in Burma – reflecting the multi-national nature of Field Marshal Slim's Fourteenth Army.

Despite the prevailing uncertainties at the time on 15th August 2020, the Seventy-Fifth Anniversary of V.J. Day was commemorated by a socially distanced gathering at the National Memorial Arboretum in Staffordshire, during which my wife and I had the great pleasure to be reunited with a number of Burma Veterans, as well as to meet the first two Burma Star Scholars.

Although, sadly, very few Burma Veterans are still with us today, I am delighted that their recollections have been recorded in this splendid book, which compellingly recalls the indefatigable spirit of those who took part in that most arduous of campaigns. I can only pray that through these moving stories, along with the legacy of the Memorial Fund, those who served this nation most gallantly are never forgotten.

Burma Star Association Reunion, Royal Albert Hall, 29 April 1978: (left to right) Earl Mountbatten of Burma, HRH The Prince of Wales and Colonel The Viscount Slim.

Contents

Dedication	v
Foreword by HRH The Prince of Wales	vi
Acknowledgements	xi
Burma Star Memorial Fund	xiii
The Burma Campaign 1941–1945	xvi
The Final Burma Star Reunion	xix
Maps	xx
Glossary of Terms/Names	xxii
L/FX 95053 Petty Officer Harry Aitken, Royal Navy	1
5618787 Sergeant George Bastone, Devonshire Regiment	5
1715951 LAC Fred Behagg, Royal Air Force	17
14244284 Gunner Alan Bevan, Royal Artillery	25
1535378 Corporal Neil Bullock, Royal Air Force	29
1836374 Corporal Eric Davis, Royal Air Force	38
14867839 Fusilier Richard Day, Royal Welch Fusiliers	45
14315501 Lance Corporal Ted Downs, 3rd Carabiniers	50
14783968 Lance Corporal Mervyn Ellicott, Queen's Royal Regiment	55
3034775 LAC Brian Foster, Royal Air Force	58
315629 Captain Stuart Guild, Royal Artillery	66
353446 Major Patrick Hamilton, 18th Royal Garhwal Rifles	74
GC 63688 Private Joseph Hammond, Gold Coast Regiment	77
2010594 Corporal Peter Heppell, Royal Engineers	84
Captain Richard Hilder, 3rd Carabiniers	92
14524981 Private Idris Jones, Suffolk Regiment	98
ZBK 13224 Colour Sergeant Maxmos Kettle, King's African Rifles	107

x   The Final Curtain: Burma 1941–1945

14429428 Sergeant Vic Knibb, Queen's Own Royal West Kent Regiment	110
Lance Corporal Wisdom Kudowor, 26th West African Artisan Works Company	114
EC 12735 Lieutenant Ted Luscombe, 19th Hyderabad Regiment	116
1820545 Bombardier Neil McInnes, Royal Artillery	121
14318391 Private Sid Machin, King's (Liverpool) Regiment	127
14532305 Sapper Arthur Massey, Royal Engineers	133
265871 Major Charles Mercer, Nigeria Regiment	137
PJX 298234 Warrant Officer Roy Miller, Royal Navy	144
14532998 Corporal Victor Mock, Devonshire Regiment	150
IA 584 Major Drogo Montagu, 2nd Punjab Regiment	154
3608538 Sergeant Vincent Murphy, Border Regiment	158
14580396 Signaller Dennis Newland, Royal Signals	164
14408980 Sergeant Ian Niven, Lancashire Fusiliers	176
14821064 Private Lawrie Powers, King's Own Scottish Borderers	182
269213 Maurice Ramsay MC, Royal Norfolk Regiment	186
EC 3877 Captain John Randle MC, 10th Baluch Regiment	196
575568 Sergeant George Rice, Royal Air Force	204
109503 Captain John Riggs, Bedfordshire and Hertfordshire Regiment	212
Gunner Stanley Seymour, Royal Artillery	220
126426 Major David Shirreff MC, King's African Rifles	224
273680 Captain Gordon Short, Queen's Own Royal West Kent Regiment	239
3064464 LAC Alan Sier, Royal Air Force	248
JX 730343 Telegraphist (S) Ken Tomkinson, Royal Navy	255
579013 LAC Thomas Tuer, Royal Air Force	259
Footnote: A Hill called Melrose	266
Index	272

Acknowledgements

To begin with, I would like to thank HRH The Prince of Wales, Patron of The Burma Star Memorial Fund, for writing a Foreword. The principal credit for this book goes, of course, to those who agreed to be interviewed in the first place and then took the trouble to correct any mistakes or misunderstandings that may have arisen from the interview. In most instances, this involved either a follow-up conversation or an exchange of emails or both. Many of the veterans were assisted by close members of their family, not only because of hearing difficulties but also with illustrative material. In a small number of instances – George Bastone, Richard Hilder, Drogo Montagu and David Shirreff – families shared with me recordings of interviews conducted as part of the Imperial War Museum's Sound Archive project. These proved to be invaluable, not only as a resource but also as a memory prompt.

On that basis, I am most grateful to the following, with the date of the first interview in brackets: Harry Aitken (14 December 2020); George Bastone and his daughter, Fiona Peters (1 March 2021); Fred Behagg and his eldest son, Brigadier Alan Behagg (24 March 2021); Alan Bevan (24 May 2021); Neil Bullock and his daughter, Annette (1 September 2021); Eric Davis (3 March 2021); Richard Day (21 April 2021); Ted Downs and his daughter-in-law, Janice Stephenson (14 February 2021); Mervyn Ellicott (26 April 2021); Brian Foster (15 May 2021); Stuart Guild (1 February 2021); Peter Heppell and his daughter, Sally Lockhart (12 March 2021); Richard Hilder and his younger son, Nick (11 March 2021); Idris Jones (15 February 2021); Ted Luscombe (1 May 2021); Sid Machin and his son, Trevor (7 March 2021); Arthur Massey and his daughter, Julie Birrell (16 March 2021); Charles Mercer (18 March 2021); Roy Miller and his daughter, Gill Nokes (29 March 2021); Victor Mock (10 May 2021); Vincent Murphy and his son, Tim (21 February 2021); Dennis Newland (6 May 2021); Ian Niven (7 June 2021); John Norton (2 November 2021); Lawrie Powers (17 February 2021); Maurice Ramsay

(15 May 2021); George Rice (31 May 2021); Gordon Short (11 May 2021); Alan Sier and his son, Chris (5 March 2021); Ken Tomkinson (30 January 2021); and Tommy Tuer (28 May 2021).

There are also a number of veterans whom I knew well but never formally interviewed, as well as a handful whom I never met. In respect of these individuals, I would like to thank Reeta Chakrabarti, who committed the story of her late father-in-law, Patrick Hamilton, to paper at my request; Derrick Cobbinah of RCEL and Tom Garner of *History of War*, who, respectively, facilitated and interviewed Joseph Hammond in Ghana while Derrick also assisted with Wisdom Kudowor's story; Denis Lewis, who interviewed Maxmos Kettle in Malawi; Robin and Roy, the sons of Vic Knibb, who gave a number of interviews at the time of the 70th anniversary of VJ-Day; Betty Macey, daughter of Neil McInnes; Mike Montagu and Crispin Ellison, contemporaries of mine at Sandhurst and son and son-in-law respectively of Lieutenant Colonel Drogo Montagu; Will, only son of Brigadier John Randle; the late John Riggs, who gave me a copy of his Burma Campaign memoirs in 2016; Sue Thompson, stepdaughter of Stanley Seymour, who helpfully liaised with Stanley's daughter, Hillary, so that we were able to acknowledge more fully her late mother's extremely generous legacy to the Burma Star Memorial Fund; and my old friend, General Sir Richard Shirreff, who kindly made his father's wartime papers available to me. Unfortunately, strenuous efforts to contact Dr Yashwant Thorat proved unavailing.

The excellent maps were produced by Isobel Rae, who recently graduated from the University of Manchester with a Masters in Environmental Monitoring, Modelling and Reconstruction. Paul Corden, with whom I participated in Ex Chinthe Endeavour, a 77th Brigade Chindit Battlefield Study in Myanmar in March 2016, sourced a number of the illustrations and also negotiated with David Rowland over the permission he generously granted to use his painting, 'Operation BROADWAY, Burma, 5/6 March 1944'. Wendy Aldiss had previously photographed a large number of Burma veterans and generously allowed me to use relevant images in the book. At Pen & Sword, Henry Wilson was the supportive commissioning editor, Jon Wilkinson designed the jacket while the late Barnaby Blacker was an outstanding copy editor until his untimely death, after which he was succeeded by Matt Jones, who capably guided the book through to publication. It was a real team effort: Betty Macey, daughter of Neil McInnes, compiled the index.

Burma Star Memorial Fund

The Burma Star Association (BSA) was merged into the Burma Star Memorial Fund (BSMF) on 15 August 2020, the seventy-fifth anniversary of VJ-Day. In the early days, the BSA, which was founded in 1951 and attracted more than 50,000 members, was comfortably able to fill the Royal Albert Hall to capacity for the annual London reunions. There are 52,482 digitised membership records on the newly-created BSMF website, www.burmastarmemorial.org. While the relief of hardship for veterans and their families remained a London head office responsibility, comradeship was managed locally, through an extensive branch network. Sadly, due to the declining numbers of veterans, the BSA branch network has now ceased to operate.

While the BSMF retains responsibility for benevolence work, its core objective is to raise funds to enable Burma Star scholars to study for one-year, post-graduate, degrees at University College London. The BSMF encourages applicants from any nation which fought on the Allied side during the Burma Campaign 1941–45. They are open to those studying for a master's degree in Global Health and Development, Applied Infectious Disease Epidemiology or Engineering for International Development.

When considering the most effective way in which to communicate with our generous financial supporters, the trustees of the BSMF alighted upon the idea of a quarterly newsletter, which would include, among other things, a 'veteran's corner' feature. It soon became clear, however, that it was simply impossible to do justice – in just 400–500 words – to the stories, reminiscences and hugely impressive memories of veterans ranging in age from 94 to 101. With that realisation, the interview process evolved and gathered momentum; after all, time was hardly on our side.

Without a centralised database, contacting surviving veterans proved to be a challenge. The starting point was the mailing list for *Dekho!*, the BSA Journal, of which number 195, the final edition, was published in the summer of 2020. Unfortunately there were no telephone numbers – just postal addresses – so some detective work was required. Slowly, surviving veterans were identified and, furthermore, most were delighted to share their wartime experiences. Due to the prevailing epidemic and the age of the veterans, the interviews were conducted on the telephone, often with veterans' children in attendance to act as intermediaries.

Poor hearing was the greatest problem and one veteran insisted on submitting no fewer than fourteen pages of reminiscences – in two batches and in block capitals – in response to a list of focused questions. Unhappy with the initial interview notes, two veterans took the trouble to rewrite their stories completely so that they more accurately reflected the points that they wished to make. One of them said: 'I enjoyed doing it. It was a bit of trouble but it brought back many memories and has given me something to do.' A son wrote that his father 'has really enjoyed reminiscing about his time in Burma', while a daughter thoughtfully offered 'many thanks for providing me with a bit of a project to see me through lockdown'. All the photographs have been provided by the veterans or their families, often by removing them from personal photograph albums and putting them in the post.

The format of the interviews was simple: every story should have a beginning, a middle and an end. The beginning covered parentage, schooling, enlistment and training; the middle – the heart of the matter – encompassed wartime service, with a particular focus on stories still seared into the memory after more than 75 years; the end typically covered post-war employment, marriage and family life. The interviews took place between December 2020 and June 2021.

None of those interviewed considered themselves to be heroes, although they can count two Military Crosses and six mentions-in-despatches between them. As far as they were concerned, they were fighting for their country in a faraway place. One or two of them found the fact that they had been awarded the Burma Star slightly embarrassing, not feeling for a moment that they deserved such recognition. What came over most strongly, though, was the sense of wartime camaraderie, for which the BSA had provided a strong focus in the post-war years. They had all been through something together and all, therefore, 'belonged'.

Against that background, there was no question of selecting interviewees with a view to expanding on particular aspects of an extraordinarily complex campaign. One simply had to work with the surviving veterans, together with a handful of others who had left oral or written records of their experiences in Burma. Nevertheless, they proved to be an extremely varied group: although most were either British or Indian Army, there were six from the Royal Air Force (one of whom was attached to the Indian Air Force) and three from the Royal Navy. Most importantly, there were four who had served with Indian Army regiments and six with the large East and West African contingents. Those who served in the army included men from the Royal Armoured Corps, the Royal Regiment of Artillery, the Corps of Royal Engineers, the Royal Corps of Signals, the Infantry and the Royal Army Service Corps.

The range of wartime roles represented is remarkable and serves as a timely reminder that the 14th Army comprised so much more than soldiers serving on the front line. The ratio of 'teeth-to-tail' was always small but everyone had a crucial role to play, whether it was signalling, supplying or salvaging. These are not tales of successful submarine commanders, of Victoria Cross winners or of Spitfire aces; instead, invariably modest veterans of the Burma Campaign tell their own stories, in their own words. For the interviewer, it has been a marvellously privileged and uplifting experience.

The Burma Campaign 1941–45

Field Marshal The Viscount Slim, commander of the victorious 14th Army, chose *Defeat into Victory* as the title for his account of a campaign with the distinction of being the only land campaign in the Far East which lasted from the outbreak of hostilities until the end of the war. Burma was a vital battleground for two reasons: the availability of oil and other natural resources and the newly-constructed Burma Road, which linked Lashio with the Chinese province of Yunnan. Having seized Victoria Point, in the far south of the country, on 14 December 1941, the Japanese army attacked in force in mid-January 1942. Early on 23 February, two brigades of the Burma Corps were stranded the wrong side of the river when the Sittang Bridge was blown prematurely, while Rangoon was evacuated on 7 March, and every Allied aircraft had either been destroyed or driven out of Burma by the end of that month.

When the monsoon rains brought campaigning to a halt in late May, the repeatedly-outflanked survivors of 17th Indian Division and 1st Burma Division had retreated more than 1,000 miles through mosquito-infested jungle and over mountainous terrain, all the way back to the Indian frontier, closely pursued by a relentless and determined enemy. They were exhausted and had lost most of their transport and equipment. Nevertheless, this heavily-outnumbered force had at least gained invaluable time for the preparation of the defences of India itself. Lord Mountbatten later wrote that 'it was a military defeat, but not a major disaster'.

As they advanced, the Japanese acquired not only a well-deserved reputation for fanaticism but also a far more questionable one for invincibility in jungle fighting, as they put into effect their proven tactics of bypassing strong resistance points and infiltrating deep behind Allied lines. Lord Mountbatten wrote of the importance of breaking 'the myth of the "Invincible Jap"'. It was clear that new tactics and skills had to be learned if Burma was to be reconquered. Jungle training was stepped up to restore confidence in the individual soldier while General Slim focused on imbuing a sense of identity in the 14th Army, too often referred to as 'The Forgotten Army'.

A makeshift fleet of light craft was assembled to protect the vulnerable waterways that linked with Calcutta. With the road networks often so poor and defensive positions frequently surrounded by the enemy, the ability to resupply by air was of great importance. Another crucial innovation was Special Force – also known as the Chindits, after the Chinthe which guard the entrance to Burmese temples – which practised long-range penetration, threatening Japanese lines of communication and supply, thus destabilising and disorientating the enemy.

The force assembled for the reconquest of Burma was uniquely multinational. As well as the British, it comprised Gurkhas, Garhwalis, Pathans, Dogras, Jats and Sikhs from the Indian subcontinent (of the 29 Victoria Crosses awarded in Burma, 20 were won by members of the Indian Army); Karens, Kachins and Chins from Burma itself; Chinese, Americans, Canadians, Australians, South Africans, East and West Africans, Ceylonese, French and Dutch; and even a Belgian medical unit.

As Dennis Newland explained: 'The 14th Army and the Air Force in Burma were very cosmopolitan: roughly made up of 100,000 British and other white Commonwealth personnel; 340,000 Indians, including Gurkhas; 90,000 East and West Africans; 65,000 Chinese; and 60,000 Americans. The majority of the British must have been Territorials or wartime conscripts, with a core of Regulars and Reservists; while all the Indians and Africans were volunteers. While it was normal for different races to have their own messes, all were equal when it came to fighting and dying!'

The provision of medical services in such unfavourable climatic conditions was tackled with increasing success, as the average proportion of sick admissions to battle casualties fell from 1 in 10 in 1943 to 1 in 120 in 1945. During the dry season of 1942/43, an Allied offensive in the Arakan, on the Bay of Bengal, was defeated by the Japanese. The principle behind the offensive/defensive strategy then adopted by the 14th Army was to encourage the Japanese to attack under circumstances favourable for the defenders. Forward troops would stand fast, resupplied from the air if necessary, thus cutting off the retreat of the infiltrating Japanese, who would then be destroyed by reserves moving forward.

Burial service in Burma.

Pacific Post VJ-Day 1945 issue.

In early 1944 this strategy was put to the test, as the Japanese attacked, initially in the Arakan, and subsequently during an epic and prolonged struggle in the Imphal Plain and at Kohima. As his biographer wrote, 'The steadiness of his forward troops provided an anvil against which Slim could destroy the Japanese with the sledge-hammer of his reserves.' The 14th Army next outflanked the Japanese defenders of Mandalay, capturing Meiktila on 4 March and then Mandalay on 20 March, before the Japanese withdrew from Rangoon, which was occupied on 1 May 1945. A Japanese 'break-out' operation in late July was a disaster for them and the campaign in Burma had been brought to a successful conclusion.

The Final Burma Star Reunion

Battle of Britain Memorial Flight Spitfire flypast.

The National Memorial Arboretum, 22 August 2021: (left to right) Ian Niven, George Rice, Richard Day, Fred Behagg, Eric Davis, Idris Jones, Roy Miller and Lawrie Powers.

Maps

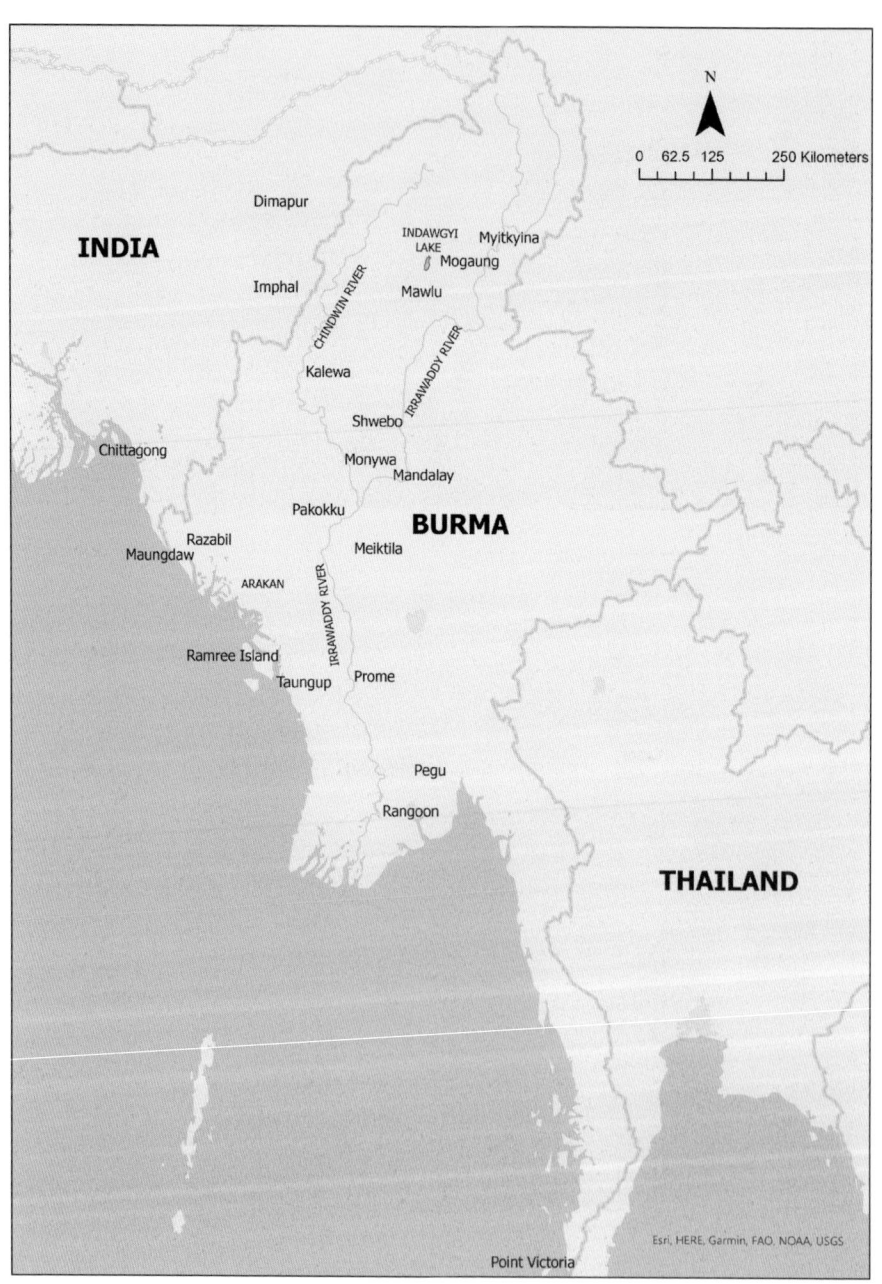

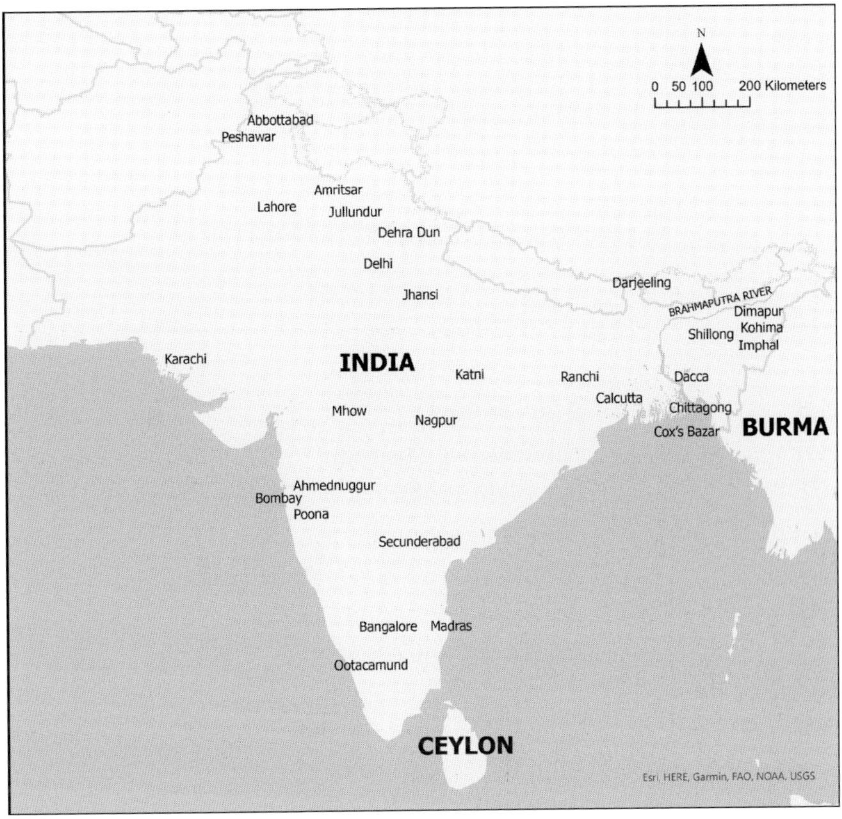
N
0 50 100 200 Kilometers
Abbottabad
Peshawar
Amritsar
Lahore
Jullundur
Dehra Dun
Delhi
Jhansi
Darjeeling
BRAHMAPUTRA RIVER
Dimapur
Kohima
Shillong
Imphal
Karachi
INDIA
Katni
Ranchi
Dacca
Calcutta
Mhow
Nagpur
Chittagong
Cox's Bazar
BURMA
Ahmednuggur
Bombay
Poona
Secunderabad
Bangalore
Madras
Ootacamund
CEYLON
Esri, HERE, Garmin, FAO, NOAA, USGS

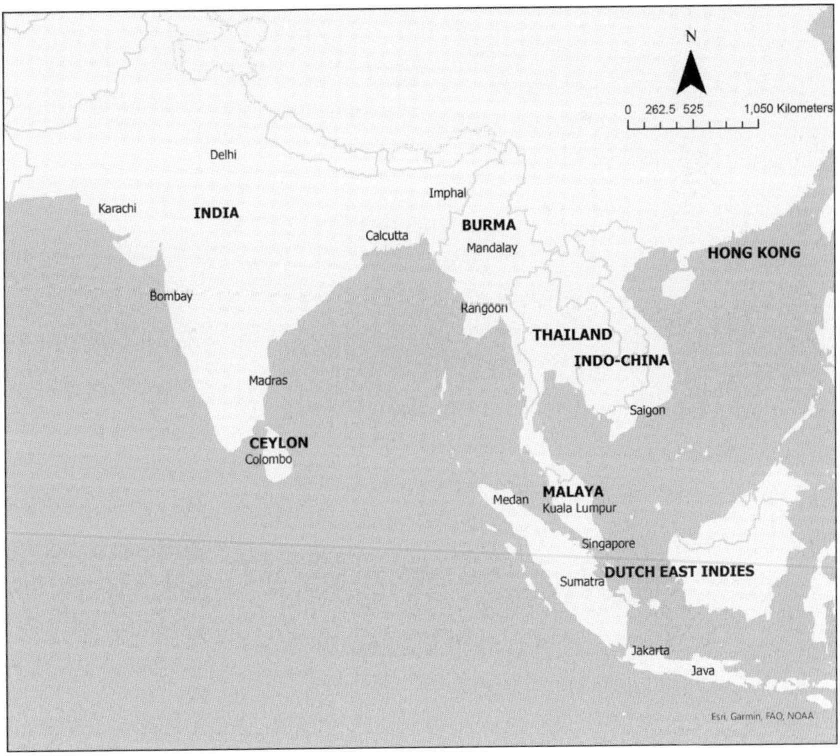
N
0 262.5 525 1,050 Kilometers
Delhi
Imphal
Karachi
INDIA
BURMA
Calcutta
Mandalay
HONG KONG
Bombay
Rangoon
THAILAND
INDO-CHINA
Madras
Saigon
CEYLON
Colombo
MALAYA
Medan
Kuala Lumpur
Singapore
DUTCH EAST INDIES
Sumatra
Jakarta
Java
Esri, Garmin, FAO, NOAA

Glossary of Terms/Names

ADC	Aide-de-camp
ADP	Air Defence Position
AFDS	Air Fighting Development Squadron
Air OP	Air Observation Post
A&Q	Administrative & Quartermaster
ARP	Air Raid Precautions
ATC	Air Training Corps
AWOL	Absent without leave
BAS	British Attached Section
Bombay	Mumbai
BOC	British Oxygen Company
BOR	British Other Rank
Burma	Myanmar
Calcutta	Kolkata
CDL	Canal Defence Lights
Ceylon	Sri Lanka
Char	Tea
Chargul	One-gallon water bags tied with string at the top
Charpoy	Bed
Charwallah	Tea-maker
Chaung	Stream or small river
Chittagong, India	Chittogram, Bangladesh
CO	Commanding Officer
CP	Command Post
CQMS	Company Quartermaster Sergeant
CSM	Company Sergeant Major
Dhobi	Washing
DSO	Distinguished Service Order
East Bengal	Bangladesh
ENSA	Entertainments National Service Association

Glossary of Terms/Names xxiii

EOKA	Ethniki Organosis Kyprion Agoniston
ES	Electrician Signals
Fakir	Religious ascetic
FAP	Forward Aid Post
FDO	Fire Direction Officer
FEU	Forward Equipment Unit
FM	Frequency Modulated
FOO	Forward Observation Officer
French Indo-China	Vietnam
Gold Coast	Ghana
GPO	General Post Office
Gunners	Royal Artillery
Havildar	Sergeant
HF/DF	High Frequency/Direction Finding
HLI	Highland Light Infantry
HMT	His Majesty's Transport
HQ	Headquarters
IAF	Indian Air Force
ICI	Imperial Chemical Industries
IEME	Indian Electrical & Mechanical Engineers
IS	Internal Security
Jemadar	Viceroy Commissioned Officer
JSP	Japanese Surrendered Personnel
KOSB	King's Own Scottish Borderers
LAC	Leading Aircraftman
LCA	Landing Craft Assault
LCI	Landing Craft Infantry
LCT	Landing Craft Tank
LDV	Local Defence Volunteers
LILOP	Leave In Lieu Of Python
LMG	Light machine gun
Madras	Chennai
Maidan	Open space where meetings take place
MBE	Member of the Most Excellent Order of the British Empire
MC	Military Cross
MCC	Marylebone Cricket Club

MM	Military Medal
MMG	Medium machine gun
MO	Medical Officer
MONAB	Mobile Overseas Naval Airbase
MT	Motor Transport
MTB	Motor torpedo boat
MU	Maintenance Unit
Munshi	Teacher
NAAFI	Navy, Army and Air Force Institutes
NCO	Non-commissioned officer
NPC	NATO Programming Centre
OBE	Officer of the Most Excellent Order of the British Empire
OC	Officer Commanding
OCTU	Officer Cadet Training Unit
O Group	Orders' Group
OP	Observation Post
OTC	Officer Training Corps
OTU	Operational Training Unit
Pegu, Burma	Bago, Myanmar
P&O	Peninsular & Oriental
Poona	Pune
PoW	Prisoner of war
PT	Physical Training
Punkah	Fan
PVR	Premature Voluntary Release
QARANC	Queen Alexandra's Royal Army Nursing Corps
QF	Quick Firing
RA	Royal Artillery
RAC	Royal Armoured Corps
RADAR	RAdio Detection And Ranging
RAF	Royal Air Force
RAMC	Royal Army Medical Corps
Rangoon, Burma	Yangon, Myanmar
RASC	Royal Army Service Corps
Redcap	Military policeman
RN	Royal Navy

RNVR	Royal Navy Volunteer Reserve
R&R	Rest and Recuperation
RSM	Regimental Sergeant Major
RSU	Repair & Service Unit
RT	Radio Transmission
RTO	Rail Transport Officer
RV	Rendezvous
RWAFF	Royal West African Frontier Force
SAA	Small arms ammunition
Sappers	Royal Engineers
SD	Special duties
SEAAF	South East Asia Air Forces
SEAC	South East Asia Command
Simla	Shimla
Subedar	Captain
Sweeper	Indian lavatory attendant
TA	Territorial Army
UAC	United Africa Company
VAD	Voluntary Aid Detachment
VC	Victoria Cross
VCO	Viceroy Commissioned Officer
VE-Day	Victory in Europe Day
VJ-Day	Victory over Japan Day
WO	Warrant Officer
WS	Writer to the Signet
WVS	Women's Voluntary Service
2IC	Second-in-Command

L/FX 95053 Petty Officer Harry Aitken, Royal Navy

Harry Claude Aitken – who was, perhaps inevitably, known as 'Max', after the wartime Minister of Aircraft Production – was born at Cardington, Bedfordshire, on 10 December 1921, son of Alexander Smith Aitken of 5 Eastcote, Shortstown, Bedfordshire and his wife Mary, daughter of Richard Bayes, who, with his wife, Mary Ann, managed the village grocery stores in High Street, Sharnbrook, some ten miles north of Bedford. Shortstown was the dormitory village for the airship works developed by Short Brothers at Cardington during the First World War. After the *R-101* disaster in October 1930, work on airships abruptly ceased, to be replaced by the manufacture of barrage balloons. The air was clearly in the Aitken family's blood. Alexander, who was born at Cluny in Aberdeenshire, enlisted in the Royal Naval Air Service on 20 April 1915, for the 'duration of hostilities'. Sailing in HMS *Manxman*, an Isle of Man ferry converted into a seaplane carrier, Chief Petty Officer Aitken served with the Grand Fleet and the Mediterranean Fleet. On 1 April 1918, Flight Sergeant A.S. Aitken became a founder member of the Royal Air Force. After the war he became foreman in the machine shop at Cardington.

'Rookie', May 1942.

Having left Cardington Village School on his fourteenth birthday, Harry embarked on a seven-year indentured apprenticeship in electrics with W.H. Allen of Bedford. Although in a reserved occupation, he was eventually permitted to enlist. His elder brother, Richard, had already joined the RAF while his three surviving younger sisters – June, Trixie and Nora – all married into the RAF. Since they had no children of their own, he often stayed with his mother's youngest sister, Mabel, who was married to Warrant Officer George Arthur Chandler. His uncle transferred from the Northamptonshire Regiment to the RAF after the

2 The Final Curtain: Burma 1941–1945

First World War and was mentioned in despatches for 'distinguished services' in the Middle East on 11 June 1942. After three months' basic training at HMS *Duke*, a requisitioned girls' school in Malvern, and a further year of specialist training, Harry joined HMS *Begum*, a Ruler-class escort carrier, in Liverpool. Having embarked four squadrons, she set sail with Convoy KMF29A on 3 March 1944, as a reinforcement for the Eastern Fleet. A specialist in aircraft electrics and cockpit instruments, Harry was responsible for the four Wildcats of 'C' Flight, 1832 Squadron, Fleet Air Arm. He described Captain Jack Broome, whose reputation was adversely affected by the scattering of Arctic Convoy PQ17, as 'efficient and fair – but don't cross him!' Between June 1944 and the end of the year, *Begum* was engaged in a series of anti-submarine sweeps in the Bay of Bengal, in the process assisting in the destruction of *U-198* off the Seychelles on 10 August 1944.

L/FX 95053 Petty Officer H.C. Aitken, Royal Navy, Mombasa, August 1944.

After HMS *Begum* sailed for the United Kingdom, prior to conversion to a ferry carrier, Harry was transferred to HMS *Unicorn* (I72), an aircraft repair ship and light aircraft carrier: 'She was the tallest in the fleet, with two hanger decks, one above the other, which ran right through the ship.' The specialist maintenance teams in HMS *Unicorn* were responsible for many types of carrier-borne aircraft: Avengers, Wildcats, Hellcats, Corsairs, Barracudas, Seafires and Fireflys. While in the Pacific theatre, they provided no fewer than 686 aircraft and 283 engines. Despite serving with the British Pacific Fleet during Operation Iceberg, the Kamikaze-threatened invasion of Okinawa in May 1945, Harry described his war as 'nothing hairy: we were never exposed to any degree. Compared to the Army who went to Burma, we got away with it pretty well. I have a lot of respect for those guys – especially those who fought in the Battle of Kohima.'

As the Pacific war drew to a close, he remembers clearly that Admiral William F. 'Bull' Halsey, Commander South Pacific, sent a signal: 'It is likely that Kamikazes will attack the Fleet as a final fling. Any

HMS *Unicorn*, San Pedro Bay, Philippines, May 1945.

ex-enemy aircraft attacking the Fleet is to be shot down in a friendly manner.' Anchored off Manus in the Admiralty Islands, just south of the equator, the ship's company celebrated VJ-Day with a dinner that had been stored in the freezer for Christmas: cream of tomato soup, turkey with roast potatoes and peas, followed by plum pudding. Harry elaborated: 'The thought on VJ-Day was that the war was over: I'd been away from home for four years, but there was no great outpouring of joy. There was still much to do. But what we did do was "splice the mainbrace" – we celebrated with a double issue of rum.' It had been quite an odyssey for Harry: from Ceylon in May 1944; to Aden and Mombasa in August 1944; to the Gulf of Leyte in the Philippines in May 1945; and, finally, shore leave in Brisbane in September 1945.

Following demobilisation in June 1946, Harry – according to the stipulations of the newly-elected Labour government – was re-offered his pre-war job. Within months,

Harry Aitken, St George's, Arreton, Isle of Wight, VJ-Day, 2016.

4 The Final Curtain: Burma 1941–1945

VJ-Day, St George's, Arreton, Isle of Wight, 2021: (left to right) Jeremy Archer and Harry Aitken.

though, he accepted a job with Frigidaire. On 1 April 1950 at Elstow in Bedfordshire, he married Edna, only daughter of Fred Williamson of 66 Wilstead Road, Bedford, a worker at a crayon factory who served as an air raid warden during the Second World War, and his wife Mabel (née Faulkner). Given his expertise, Harry was called up once again for the Korean War; this time, though, he was sent to Northern Ireland. Between 1953 and 1962, having spotted a job advert, Harry worked in Luton for D. Napier & Son as an 'aircraft fitter for development work'. With 'itchy feet', the family moved to Carisbrooke on the Isle of Wight and he worked briefly for an American boat builder, which went bust, before joining Plessey and working as a quality engineer doing final inspections, until his retirement. Suffering from dementia, Edna died in 2017, leaving one son, Roderick, and two grandchildren, Andrew and Nicola. He became a life member of the Isle of Wight branch of the Burma Star Association on 10 January 1975 (membership number A/790/74). From a once-impressive and active branch that once numbered 325 members, Harry is now the sole survivor.

5618787 Sergeant George Bastone, Devonshire Regiment

Leonard George Bastone was born on 23 April 1920, youngest twin son of John (Jack) Bastone, gardener and groundsman for Seaton Cricket Club, of Couchill Cottages, and later of Sunnyside, New Road, Beer, Devon, and his wife Margaret Jane, second daughter of William Huntley, agricultural labourer, of Little Bedwyn, Wiltshire. Born on St George's Day and always known as George, he remembered that Couchill Cottages 'was a two-bedroom cottage with an outdoor toilet across the yard, all covered in'. Bastone is an old South Devon surname, centred on Ottery St Mary, Honiton on Otter and Salcombe Regis. It was a large family: as well as his twin brother, Jack, George had three older brothers and three older sisters. 36183 Private John (Jack) Bastone served on the Western Front with the 7th and 11th Battalions of the Leicestershire Regiment during the First World War. George's 'Uncle Bill', 596 Temporary WOI William John Bastone, served with the Royal Army Medical Corps and his award of the Military Medal was gazetted on 11 November 1916. Soldiers with the name John Bastone also served with the 19th (Green Howards) Regiment of Foot in Ceylon in 1814, fought with the 33rd (Duke of Wellington's) Regiment of Foot at the Battle of Waterloo (where he was severely wounded), and was present with the 20th (East Devonshire) Regiment of Foot at the relief of Lucknow in March 1858, while W. Bastone died at Kandahar in Afghanistan on 28 November 1880 when serving with the 2nd Battalion, the Devonshire Regiment. There is clearly a longstanding tradition of military service in the family.

George explained: 'When I turned fourteen, I left Beer Church School at Easter on a Friday and, the following Tuesday, I started at Eastman's, the butchers in Seaton, as an errand boy. There were five or six of us and we used to go out and take orders, the chaps would put the orders together and we would then go out again to deliver them.' At 16, George joined the Territorial Army, explaining that 'my friends joined the TA and I went with the crowd. I had a medical, was sworn in and joined B Company, 4th Devons, which covered the Axminster area. They taught us the importance of maintaining and cleaning our kit, about discipline and obeying orders and drill. We also had weapon-training instruction: on rifles, Bren guns, hand grenades and mortars. I used to like the camps every year. There were rows and rows of bell tents and marquees for food and we used to go on schemes, which were hard work. We went to Honiton Common and Aylesbeare Common; we just had ourselves, no tanks and one company was the enemy.

'One day, the company commander summoned me and asked me to be his batman: I used to clean his gear, wait on him and pack his kit. He was a real gentleman. You could speak to him without shaking in your boots. I have never known an officer as well liked as he was and he really stood up for the chaps.' The company commander in question was Major Cecil George Percy-Hardman, an architect in civilian life, who later served with the 1st Battalion, Oxfordshire and Buckinghamshire Light Infantry, in northwest Europe. He was awarded an immediate DSO (upgraded from an MC recommendation, which is unusual) but was killed in action at Mook-en-Middelaar in Holland on 8 March 1945, four weeks before the award was gazetted.

A few weeks before war was declared, 'Mum opened my call-up papers and Dad came down to Eastman's and told me that I had to come home, before I reported to the Drill Hall in Honiton, ten miles away. The furthest I had ever been before was Exeter, once a year. I spent a couple of weeks in a Key Party, sending out call-up papers – it was quite exciting for us and we used to go to a local café in Honiton, Gill's Café. I was on guard at Eastern Kings Fort, Plymouth, when a marine walked behind me: "War's been declared, mate!" My father said: "Just keep your head down." The Battalion moved to Eastbourne for coastal defence duties and we took over a girls' school: a lot of stuff was left there by the school and a lot of stuff went when we went! We were stationed in the redoubts, as they called them, and used to go on patrols all night, but I was a batman so I didn't do them. Then we went to Shoeburyness, where we had little schemes against the Home Guard, which were good fun. They were fine chaps but a little elderly though. We took it in turns to be the enemy – nothing too strenuous, otherwise the Home Guard wouldn't be able to keep up.

'They had split the 4th Battalion and formed the 8th Battalion [8 Devon], which I joined with some old friends from Colyton, Beer, Branscombe and Seaton. We got on so well together. One of them was Dickie Santer, a bolshie little chap but a good friend and we went right through the lot together. Five of us mucked in and we used to volunteer for everything.' 8 Devon was frequently milked to provide reinforcements for the three battalions of the Regiment which saw active service overseas: the 1st, 2nd and 12th Battalions: 'One day at Shoeburyness, the Orderly Sergeant came round and asked if anyone wanted to volunteer for overseas service. I didn't answer. My mate Dickie came up and asked: "Did you put your name down? All the rest have." So I put my name down – I thought we'd go nowhere.

'To my amazement, two days later we were on embarkation leave before reporting to Dorchester. We were there for a couple of weeks before packing everything up and marching to the station. We learnt that we were going to India as a draft to 1st Devons [1 Devon]. We sailed from Southampton in the *Duchess of York*. It was a terrible journey and so crowded that there was hardly any room to sleep. You had to grab a space where you could and you had to watch your kit. It was all new and exciting though. A lot of the chaps used to go up on deck to sleep but the trouble was you had to get up early because the ship's crew were hosing down the decks and you just got wet. First up was Durban, which was really good: the locals would come down to the docks and take us out to dinner and different things. We had oranges, bananas and all sorts of things we hadn't seen for a long, long time. The divisional badge was "Drake's drum" and they thought that I was a drummer boy and I had a good time and a couple of nights out – lovely it was. There was a lady who sang: whenever a troopship came in or went out, you could hear her singing.' She was the 'Lady in White', Perla Gibson, who stood on the dockside, singing through a megaphone as convoys sailed in and out of the harbour. When she saw that a convoy was on the move, she drove the short distance from her home in Berea, on a ridge above the city, overlooking the Indian Ocean. Amongst the soprano's repertoire were, inevitably, *There'll Always Be An England* and *Land of Hope and Glory*. A plaque on the North Pier at Durban marks the spot from which she serenaded the gallant soldiery.

George continued: 'Bombay was a shock really but we weren't there long and sailed to Karachi in a banana boat and joined the Battalion. I was in B Company again. I was a bit wary and a bit nervous. All the regulars had been in India for four or five years already but they didn't look down on us and we all mucked in. We were in camp under canvas; it was pretty hard going and that is where the training really started. I liked the heat; if it had been cold, I should have run away. We knew all about the new Bren guns but they had had Lewis guns, so we had an advantage. We completed terrible assault courses and had to climb walls and there were machine guns firing over our heads to teach us to keep our heads down as we came out of the tunnel. We had a bit of fun one night. The officers went through separately and a couple of us dug a trench across the tunnel and filled it with water. They had a rough time and got wet and muddy and there was a bit of a fuss. We then went to a barracks in Secunderabad and I had a boy who cleaned my kit, did my *dhobi* and brought me a cup of tea in the morning. I paid him 8 annas a week, about eight pence.'

Few battalions were more affected by rapidly-changing wartime circumstances than 1 Devon. They were posted to Abbottabad on 22 July 1940 for intensive training in mountain warfare techniques prior to service on the unsettled North-West Frontier. The region was as lawless then as it is today, and that November the Battalion lost an officer and five men in four separate incidents. In April the following year, 1 Devon was posted to Jullundur, fifty miles south-east of Amritsar, in the Punjab, for desert warfare training in the expectation that they would be sent to North Africa. The outbreak of war in the Far East then changed everything. Warned off for service in Burma, Rangoon was evacuated on 8 March 1942, before 1 Devon had embarked for the country.

From India, 1 Devon moved to Kalutara, on the west coast of Ceylon, some twenty miles south of the capital, Colombo, for jungle training. This was very different from what had gone before, as the Regimental History emphasises: 'Soldiers were trained to carry heavy loads over rough country: movement – silent movement – rapid deployment in defence and attack where there was little or no communication between sub-units, and techniques for river crossing using makeshift materials were all studied.' George said: 'It was a bit scary. You had to hack your way through and they used to set traps for us, tripwires and things like that. It was important to make as little noise as possible and we had to be alert all the time.' Rivers held particular terrors for him: 'I couldn't swim for a start and we often had to pull ourselves across using ropes. Once I caught the tail of a mule and it pulled me across. Once again, I was asked to report to the company commander and same thing, Major Braun, an old regular soldier, said: "You will be my batman." The batmen used to lay up and wait at table in the Officers' Mess: we were paid extra and there were no guard duties.

'One day, I read in Battalion Orders that Private Bastone had been promoted to lance corporal, which I knew nothing about and it shook me. I went to see Major Braun, who asked if I was alright. I replied: "No, I don't want to be a lance corporal." He said: "It's not what you want, it's what I want." I had to go back to duty then. I remember the first time I put my stripe on, they made me call the roll for the company. I'd never been so nervous in my life. It was awful but I got used to the rank. They used to call us lance corporals, unpaid and unwanted. I had learnt a lot from Major Percy-Hardman. We went to Ranchi [in the Indian State of Bihar] for a bit more training, and then from there we went to Imphal. We were in 20th Indian Division [20 Division] and were dug in on the high ground – it's very hilly there. We were always sending out patrols: in the beginning it wasn't too bad, but as we went further into Burma, it became more frightening. There were defensive positions all the way round. A couple of chaps used to go out at night, sit quiet and just listen.

'Then we gradually went into Burma along the Tamu Road: it was quite difficult for map-reading because it was only tracks. You'd go up a track one day and next week it would be gone. The Japs would send out 'jitter parties': they'd shout "Hello, Johnny", and used to rattle the tins on our barbed wire to draw fire so they could pinpoint our positions – but we were well trained. They were dedicated soldiers: it was a job to kill them and they'd fight to the finish and never gave in. We never heard them coming because they used to wear soft shoes, like plimsolls. They used to come in behind us, but we had the advantage because from where we were to Rangoon was a long way and they were stretched for supplies. I always found that, unless they had an officer with them, they were a bit lost. They had to have someone in command.

'I was taken ill at Imphal. Well over a hundred of us had scrub typhus fever [spread by the intracellular parasite *Orientia tsutsugamishi* that infested the thick vegetation]. We lost a lot who died through it: terrible, awful it was, fever and I didn't know where I was for a week or more, I suppose. 126 of us went down in one go to a field hospital at Karachi. It had strange effects: the mule leaders, they'd get up in the night looking for their mules because they were hallucinating.' Meanwhile, the battalion embarked on a two-day march to a position known, after the commanding officer (CO), Lieutenant Colonel Gerard Augustine de Vere Harvest, as 'Harvest Home'. His nickname was 'Mahsud', after the Pathan people on the North-West Frontier, because of his enthusiasm for long marches over difficult country. Soon after George returned from hospital, he was appointed platoon sergeant. Despite initial nervousness about the additional responsibility, he clearly performed well in the field and therefore enjoyed rapid promotion through the ranks.

When the Japanese Fifteenth Army launched Operation U-Go on 6 March 1944, 20 Division was separated by almost eighty miles of very difficult terrain from the Imphal Plain. Furthermore, the hot season was almost upon them. As 1 Devon retreated towards relative security, George emphasised the importance of patrolling: 'We had silent patrols, listening patrols, recce patrols and fighting patrols. Recce patrols involved going ahead and finding out where the Japs were, before reporting back. We sent scouts ahead in case of running into ambushes, which we did all the time.' The 14th Army benefited from overwhelming air superiority: 'The tracks were unsuitable for vehicles and we had to be supplied from the air by Dakotas. They were marvellous and we would be notified when there was going to be an air supply drop and would send out patrols to secure the area and recover the supplies. They dropped all sorts of supplies by parachute in metal containers, which sometimes split open: food, mostly tinned stuff, ammunition which had red parachutes and clothes. Our uniforms used to get so wet and torn that we often needed replacements.

'Our food was good but not very plentiful: we had stewed corned beef and powdered potatoes, eggs and milk. We had to be very careful with the water because the Japanese poisoned the village wells. We all had water purification tablets and every day we used to drink a little salt water to stop heat exhaustion. On a long ambush patrol, I was once caught without water so I asked one of the chaps for a drink of his. "Well, you can't, Sarge." "Why not?" "Because I haven't got any, Sarge." I really let rip so he said: "I've got some rum though." He must have been on a drop and his water bottle was full of rum! At that time I had renal colic but couldn't go sick. Another time we came across a field of watermelons and the chaps went round eating them. Several of them came down with dysentery.'

Anything that could not be brought back to Imphal was destroyed and 1 Devon slowly retreated north-west via a series of features, to which names were soon given: Devon Hill, Nippon Hill and Patiala Ridge. The key ground of tactical importance, dominated by 4,900-foot high Nippon Hill, was the Shenam Pass, on which were situated yet more features not named on the local maps: Cyprus, Crete East and West, Lynch, Scraggy, Malta, Gibraltar, Recce Hill, Brigade Hill and Punjab Hill. For five weeks 20 Division fought to defend these positions, with battalions regularly rotating in and out of the forward positions. George remembered: 'Nippon Hill was a very high point overlooking the road and it had to be captured at all costs. The Punjabis attacked and failed. The Gurkhas had a go and they took it but the Japs retook it. Then the Devons took the hill and it took days to clear it because the Japs had dug in so well. There were lots of tunnels and they kept popping up everywhere.' The successful assault on Nippon Hill on 11 April 1944 cost 1 Devon three officers and seventeen other ranks killed in action or died of wounds and six officers and sixty-two other ranks wounded. The battalion suffered some two hundred casualties between 1 April and 10 May.

In the middle of that month, 20 Division was relieved by 23 Division and moved back to the Ukhrul Road, north-east of Imphal, for what was described as a 'deep penetration' operation behind Japanese lines: '5 Platoon was without an officer and I was the platoon sergeant, so I took command. I had to send a corporal and three men to contact a Scottish regiment which was coming towards us to cut the Japs off. The corporal returned, saying that he hadn't seen any Japs or anything so I took out three men. We had hardly gone a hundred yards when we heard some talking and crept forward. I sent one of the men back: "Should I bypass them or stay there?" The message came back: "We're sending a fighting patrol out to you." It turned out there was a lorry with about twenty Japs, all on their last legs and in a terrible state. They opened fire on us. You could hardly say that you wouldn't shoot at them just because they weren't well. The officer in the fighting patrol dealt with them. When we met up with the Scots, they gave us porridge with salt – ugh! – and I got a new pair of boots because the sole of one of my boots was hanging off. Very good to us they were. On the Ukhrul track trying to cut off the Japs, we marched by night and hid up by day, although we gradually changed to daylight patrols. We kept on having little attacks or being attacked or having 'jitter parties' come out. We were getting accustomed to it then and to their habits. The Japs might have been withdrawing, but they still fought to the end.

'The CO was very keen on getting prisoners so we could find out information from them: who they were and where they were. He said that if you bring back some Jap prisoners you would get the MC – that's how badly they wanted them. An officer, a sergeant and a private soldier went out on patrol and spotted two of the enemy sitting under a tree. They shot one and the other got away: the one they shot was a Burmese who sided with the Japs while the one who got away was Japanese, which was a bit disappointing really. For ambush patrols, we looked for a suitable spot on a bend or somewhere with a good view down the valley. One day I had some chaps who'd just joined and had never been in action before. We saw a Jap coming up the track. All of us shot at him – and all of us missed! He just vanished. We waited half-an-hour and nothing happened so I said we'll go down and have a look for him. We went back along the track and they were very good at camouflage. "You chaps find anything yet?" I asked. I then spotted a groundsheet over a gully, aimed my rifle and said, "Pull that back!" Tall chap he was, but spent out I think. He asked me for a cigarette but didn't get one because I didn't have any. I had a nice revolver off him though. One day a party of civilian American ambulance drivers came up to our position and they were mad to get original Jap rifles. We had plenty of those and they gave us a case of beer for a rifle, which was very acceptable, I have to say.

'We learned to cope with leeches, mosquitos, swamps and bogs. Take off your boots and there would be blood everywhere: leeches could get in anywhere. To remove them we used to touch them with a cigarette or squeeze some lime juice on them. We didn't have mosquito nets because we couldn't carry them. Jungle sores were like an ulcer and sometimes they were 2–3 inches across. They were nasty things which took a long time to heal, that was the trouble. There were not a lot of animals like you see in those storybooks, with lovely orchids, flowers growing and butterflies; because of all the shells, nothing much was there. The baboons were nasty and would pinch your kit – anything shiny – while the hawks would eat your grub. During the monsoon, we got soaking wet during the day and it was very cold at night. I was very fortunate with 5 Platoon, damned good chaps they were. If there was a patrol, I always used to ask for volunteers and they just stepped forward. We dug shallow trenches, so that we had a little shelter and could keep out of sight. The safety of the men was the most important thing.

'We always had to watch out for punji stakes made from bamboo sharpened to a point. They would stick them in a sandbag, which looked like a hedgehog, and then attach it to a tree with a length of rope, with a tripwire attached. If you tripped the wire when walking past, it would swing across at head height. They sometimes pinned notices on trees. Chaps would go up to read them and, if they weren't careful, they'd fall into a well-camouflaged trench full of punji stakes. I once went out on a patrol with the Gurkhas. They were wonderful soldiers, set up an ambush and wouldn't let me do a thing. I slept right through it. I remember that they drank very sweet tea, made with condensed milk. On one occasion, I had to go back to company headquarters past a platoon commanded by a lieutenant. He said: "Sergeant Bastone, some bugger's stole my boots. If you find them, let me know, I'll have him court-martialled." I replied: "If I was you, Sir, I wouldn't say a thing about it. Battalion Orders: no boots to be removed." So that was that.'

From the beginning of August until mid-November 1944, 1 Devon was out of the line at Wangjing in the Imphal Plain. On 15 November 1944, 80th Brigade drove past the recent battleground in the Shenam Pass and the soldiers were astonished to see that the resurgent jungle had reclothed the shell-blasted hills. On 1 January 1945, 1 Devon crossed the Chindwin at Kalewa, over the longest Bailey bridge built during the Second World War. Although the next three months, until the battalion withdrew to Pyabin to reorganise and rest, lacked the intensity of the fighting at Imphal, because, in the words of one regimental officer, the Japanese were by then 'disorganised and defeated', there were some testing encounters with the retreating Japanese. George explained: 'It was just continuous really. You'd come across these roadblocks and attack them. They were very artful the Japs: they'd do all sorts because they weren't afraid of dying. They all carried their little flags with their ancestors' signs written all over them. The further we got into Burma, the harder it got because the Japs were building up, but we kept them on the move.

'We crossed the Irrawaddy in canoes – you could easily capsize in them and had to be very careful. We didn't take canoes with us because you could always find them in the villages. We sent a lot of recce patrols across the Irrawaddy to find out what was on the other side. The Japs would leave suicide gangs behind who would fight to the finish. Once I led a contact patrol to find another platoon in our company which had been left behind.

I took my lance sergeant, a Bren gunner and the number two gunner. After about two hundred yards, we went over a little ridge and were crawling along the side of it when the Japs opened up and shot the Bren gunner through both arms. We got him back and put field dressings on him quickly but had to leave the Bren gun behind. I was worried about the Bren so dashed out to get it back – frightened to death I was. I sent the wounded chap back with one of the other chaps – he was later awarded an MM. Although Lance Sergeant Kiff and I were out all day, we never found the other platoon – they'd gone back another way. I always used to come back through A Company lines if I could, because a chap who lived in Seaton was a cook in A Company and if I could get back near his cookhouse I was guaranteed a mug of tea.

5618787 Sergeant George Bastone, Christmas 1945.

'We pushed on to a place called Meiktila and they were running 'liberty trucks' to Mandalay, but I didn't go because I was deadbeat. I regretted not going there because we soon flew back to India. We were in Dakotas: there were no doors but there was rope all round the inside. We had to sit down and catch hold of the rope but we didn't mind that. We rested, cleaned up and reorganised before going to Deolali [which gave the world the expression 'gone doolally' for mental illness, because conditions were so demanding]. I sailed home in the *Stirling Castle*, which was not so crowded this time, so I got plenty of sleep.' Excluding sick, the battalion suffered 122 killed, 307 wounded and 9 missing during the Burma Campaign. It is a measure of George's leadership skills that he was mentioned in despatches on 19 September 1946 'for distinguished service'. Entitling him to wear a bronze oak leaf on his war medal, this was a highly-regarded distinction. In what may have been the last such announcement for the Second World War, his was one of just nineteen names from the Devonshire Regiment who were mentioned in despatches: eight officers (including three lieutenant colonels), three warrant officers, one colour sergeant, four sergeants (two of whom were temporary) and three private soldiers.

B Company, 1 Devon, Wangjing, Manipur, India, autumn 1944: George Bastone is second from left in the front row, holding a Japanese flag.

After disembarking in Liverpool, George was issued with a rail warrant for the long cross-country journey to Seaton. No-one was expecting him – and he had no idea what he would find. In uniform, with a bulging kitbag over his shoulder, he walked out of Seaton station and spotted a friendly face peering out of the window of a fish lorry: 'Where have 'ee been, boy?' asked Ted Mutter. 'Oh, I've just returned from Burma, where I've been fighting the Japanese,' replied George. Before he was demobbed though, 'an officer, me and about forty men went to Chudleigh to help with the harvest. Working parties were sent to different farms and we picked potatoes. I wish I had signed on: I'm sure I would have been promoted, and I enjoyed army life but, on the spur of the moment, I just wanted to go home. My eldest brother had been in the Home Guard; I had one brother in India, another in France and my twin brother, Jack, also joined the Devons and was a prisoner in Germany for a couple of years.'

Muriel was the daughter of Garfield Williams, an employee of the London and South-West Railway Company who lived in Egloshayle Road, Wadebridge, Cornwall. She had worked as a supervisor at a munitions factory in Swindon during the war, before moving to live with her sister and brother-in-law, Gladys and Percival Westlake, who owned the Dolphin Hotel in Beer. George and Muriel met at the hotel and were married at Honiton register office on 14 December 1948. They made their home at 5 Underleys in Beer and soon had three daughters: Linda, Brenda and Fiona. After coming back home, George initially returned to his job at Eastman's. Once part of the Dewhurst empire, Eastman's is now independent and has recently been lovingly restored to its 1930s appearance.

Eventually, as Fiona explained, 'he got a proper job at last – without working overtime and not getting paid for it. He worked as a driver for Racal, based at the factory in Seaton, delivering products and ferrying people round the country.' George said: 'I was a minibus driver, taking the workers in and taking them home. Up and down to Reading, Maidenhead, Bracknell and Windsor – lovely it was.' Racal was once the third-largest electronics firm in Britain, but the Seaton factory, which manufactured communications equipment for the Ministry of Defence, closed its doors in 2000, a year after the subsidiary was sold to a US company. By then, though, George had long since retired. Although Muriel died on 7 July 2013, Brenda lives just a couple of miles away while Fiona visits Beer twice a week from her home in Wareham, Dorset.

George Bastone, Beer, Remembrance Day, 2019.

George Bastone died at home in Beer on 26 April 2021. Fiona wrote to me: 'I thought you would want to know, sadly Dad passed away peacefully at home yesterday. He managed to enjoy his 101st birthday on Friday with visitors and birthday cake, somehow I think he was just waiting for his birthday. He was very tired and ready and it was such a comfort to me that he remained in his own home. He will leave a huge hole in our lives.'

1715951 LAC Fred Behagg, Royal Air Force

Frederick Arthur (Fred) Behagg was born on 23 April 1921, the only son of Frederick Valentine Behagg, a porter at Covent Garden, of 106 Belmont Street, Chalk Farm, and his wife Edith Agnes, second daughter of Thomas Daniel Stanton, pressman, milkman and packer, of 19 Pancras Street and later of 30 Stanhope Street, St Pancras. Frederick senior enlisted in 1915, serving as a runner with B Company, 3/10th Battalion (Territorial Forces), The (Duke of Cambridge's Own) Middlesex Regiment, and seeing action during the battles of Polygon Wood, Broodseinde, Poelcapelle and Passchendaele. He told his grandson, Alan, just after he had been commissioned, 'I only fired my rifle three times on the range before going over the top.' After his baptism of fire at the Third Battle of Ypres, his son said: 'They were chasing the Germans back after Operation Michael [the German spring offensive that commenced on 21 March 1918] petered out and were at last getting into green fields when he was wounded in the thigh at a level crossing.' Fred was educated at Haverstock Central School, which he left at the age of 16, 'before taking Matric, much to my master's disgust – my father didn't believe in exams.' Nevertheless, he soon found a job as a junior cashier with Alfred Savills & Sons, then based at 51A Lincoln's Inn Fields in Holborn. The firm is now known simply as Savills, one of the country's largest firms of estate agents.

Fred explained: 'It was the last day of August 1939. War was imminent and everyone expected that London would be heavily bombed. I went to work as usual when, during the morning, Winnie Smith, the senior partner's secretary, came bustling into the office to say that the partners had just decided that our section, together with all the ledgers, were to be taken to the Guildford office for safety by three members of staff while the remaining three, of whom I was one, would go to Lord Wimborne's estate office in Lower Parkstone, between Bournemouth and Poole. We asked when we were to go and were told: "A train is leaving Waterloo at 12.30 – be on it." So we just went to the station and I never went home to live permanently until July 1946. Arriving in Parkstone I sent a telegram – there were no phones in those days – telling my mother and father where I was and asking them to put a suitcase on a train to Parkstone station. We booked into the one hotel and bought toothpaste at the local chemist near the office. Separated from the office by a small lane was a draper's shop, Knight's, where we purchased pyjamas. I don't remember who served me, but it could well have been someone called many years later 'Mum'.

'One of my colleagues made a date with one of the shop assistants and said he had also arranged a date for me that evening: I was to meet the young lady concerned under the clock at the bus stop in Lower Parkstone. So off I went and there was a young lady, Freda, standing there, so I assumed she was my date. We shook hands, went to the cinema and saw the film, *The Cisco Kid*. And the rest is history! She soon left the shop and volunteered for war work. After training, she was sent to a factory about six miles away, where she worked at a lathe, making 25-pounder shells. She worked long shifts, and because of the oil and grease on the floor she had to wear clogs. Meanwhile I lodged for three months in a thatched cottage owned by Lord Wimborne's agent, in the middle of a field in the village of Corfe Mullen. At the end of the year he was called up so I had to find new digs. I took lodgings with a colleague from the office, Dorothy (Dan) Gray, in her mother's house in Upper Parkstone. To begin with I had the use of the agent's car but I then got a bicycle. I did a lot of recreational cycling with Freda: I remember we cycled to Weymouth one weekend. Then came the disaster and miracle of Dunkirk. It was decided by the government to form a civilian arm to be called the Local Defence Volunteers – fondly known as Look, Duck and Vanish!

'I joined on the first day and was a member of a platoon that had no weapons or anything. Later we became part of the Dorset Home Guard [which formally came into existence on 14 May 1940] and my company was based at the Drill Hall in Upper Parkstone. We drilled a bit and eventually we were supplied with two rifles and four bullets. Patrolling the area, usually with a First World War veteran, I would carry the rifle and he the bullets. Then, wonder of wonders, we all received rifles with five rounds apiece and also two First World War Lewis machine guns, one of which was allocated to me. I had a magazine of, I think, 27 rounds and was promoted to corporal. Naturally, when Adolf saw what he was up against he called off the invasion and attacked Russia instead. If he hadn't, I doubt very much that I would still be here. With the memory of the trenches of the Great War, my father suggested the RAF was a better bet so I volunteered and had a medical. The RAF said they wanted wireless operators so they added my name and told me to wait for call-up, which eventually came at the end of 1941. It was a great wrench to be leaving Freda, with whom I was very much in love – but war was war.

'I went to Warrington to be kitted out and then on to Blackpool, which was then a town which had been taken over by the RAF: we drilled on the Promenade and often did arms drill in the streets. I also started to learn Morse code. On reaching a speed of ten words a minute, we were posted to Compton Bassett in Wiltshire where we were taught the rudiments of wireless technology. As far as I was concerned, Chinese would have been easier and I think it was only my ability at Morse that finally got me my 'sparks' badge. We now moved up from a speed of ten words a minute to twenty-two words a minute and on to a course on High Frequency Direction Finding (HF/DF). This was to help lost aircraft which wanted assistance with navigation. I was posted to Predannack – an aerodrome on the top of a cliff on The Lizard in Cornwall. We were based in a hut in the middle of a field of cows about three miles from the airfield. The cows seemed to like us: they would put their heads through the door and we would feed them with bread. The farmer said he had never seen anything like it before. He sometimes gave us rabbits which he'd snared and we cooked them with mushrooms picked from his fields.

'Life continued with regular watch-keeping duties. There were four masts outside our hut: north, south, east and west. Any aircraft seeking assistance would call up and ask for a bearing. We were callsign 'QQ6' and all transmissions were in Morse code. I would reply, asking him to hold down the key in the aircraft so that I could get a fix, using an instrument called a goniometer. In return I would indicate the direction he was in, which he would acknowledge before signing off. Predannack was an RAF Coastal Command station with Liberators, Blenheims and, latterly, Mosquitos based there. Things were quiet working in the HF/DF hut but one memory stands out. I received a call in the middle of the night from a Walrus aircraft from Air-Sea Rescue. The pilot had landed on the sea for a rescue but couldn't take off. The message was in plain language rather than Morse code, which was quite unusual. I was able to provide him with a bearing and he powered the aircraft along the surface of the sea and eventually arrived on the beach at Porthleven, immediately below the Predannack officers' mess. The pilot who had been rescued was Canadian and had been in the water for a number of days. There was a full press report about the rescue – but of course no mention of yours truly!

'I spent two years at Predannack, during which I proposed marriage to, and was accepted by, Freda. My mother was a great scrounger and there was more chance of a wedding feast in London, so the Huxfords came up from Parkstone. We had a few days' honeymoon at a relation of her mother in Banstead, Surrey. After our wedding, Freda came down to stay for a few days. After a horrendous journey down taking nearly ten hours, she arrived at midnight, although luckily there were some passengers going in the same direction so they all shared a cab. I obtained a 'sleeping out' pass and booked a stay in a house in the village of Cadgwith, on the east coast of The Lizard, less than five miles away. The landlady was not at all concerned about our late arrival and gave us a magnificent meal. During Freda's stay my colleagues were very helpful and thoughtfully took over some of my duties. On one occasion Freda actually came and sat on watch with me. Sadly the visit came to an end too soon – but it was lovely while it lasted.

'In late 1944, I received an overseas posting order – which was just one of those things that happened – and reported back to Blackpool, where we were all issued with tropical kit. We then went to Gourock in Scotland, where we boarded the troopship *Athlone Castle* [a commandeered Union Castle liner]. We soon learned that India was our destination. As we sailed down the Clyde, the workers from the factories came down to the water's edge and waved us on our way. We formed a small convoy with two other troopships and were escorted by destroyers to Gibraltar, and then through the Mediterranean to Suez, and then through the Suez Canal and the Red Sea, and finally across the Indian Ocean to Bombay. There were fatigues to do, of course. We had to carry crates of orange juice on our shoulders from the lower decks. On the way up people would help themselves, so by the time we got to the top we were often quite a few bottles short – although no-one seemed to worry.

'On arrival in Bombay [on 25 October 1944] we were taken by lorry to Worli transit camp, where after a week or so we received our posting orders. I was posted to 357 (SD) Squadron at Jessore in East Bengal, now Bangladesh. The train journey was something, I can tell you. I cannot for the life of me remember how we were fed during the two or three days' journey to Calcutta. I do, however, remember the toilet: a hole in the floor between the carriages, with no such thing as a seat. If the train was swaying a bit, it could make ablutions a bit tricky. It was a military train and we all had our rifles. Someone on the train fired a shot out of the window at something – I don't know what – and there was a terrible hoo-hah. All our rifles were inspected to see who had fired the shot. They never found out though, because the culprit switched his rifle with that of a chap who was sick. The whole saga delayed us for a couple of days. If you saw a train coming into a station, the people would charge straight through the windows and find any way they could to get on.

1715951 LAC F.A. Behagg, Jessore, East Bengal: 'To my Darling Freda with all my love Fred xxxx India 1944.'

'After arriving in Calcutta, we continued our train journey to Jessore, which is close to the Burmese border. The Indian railways were largely run by the Anglo-Indians. The real Indians didn't like the Anglo-Indians, who thought of themselves more as Europeans, and they didn't much like us either. I once had a brick thrown at me by someone shouting: "Quit India, quit India!" 357 (SD) Squadron was a special duties squadron, operating Liberators and Dakotas. It was all hush-hush and very secretive. They only flew on moonlit nights, dropping people behind the Jap lines. I worked in a bamboo hut, miles from anywhere and anyone, listening to Morse for twelve hours at a stretch and watching the ants crawling up and down the walls. It was very lonely. I wasn't in a very important position but was just providing direction-finding if any aircraft needed it. We were just sat in a paddy field, 200 yards from the main road, using callsign 'XG9'.

'At one stage I was granted seven days' leave and, on the recommendation of my friend Eddie Edwards, we decided, along with another friend, Robert Messenger, to spend it in the hill station of Ootacamund. We took the train to Madras and then on to the foothills – the starting-off point for the spectacular railway journey to the summit of the Nilgiri hills. 'Snooty Ooty', as it was known, was mainly inhabited by wealthy, white 'Sahibs'. Eddie had been on leave there once before and had made the acquaintance of an elderly lady who was looking after the two children of the brother of Sir Alan Brooke, Chief of the Imperial General Staff. We met her and one evening she invited us to dinner. There were lots of knives and forks on the table and we were served by servants in very formal attire. After the meal, we were taught to play mahjong. I was lounging in the park one day when I was approached by a young Sikh boy, who asked if he could read my fortune. We were not supposed to do this but he persuaded me to go ahead. He told me that I would have a long life and would have many sons. He also said that, although I was a peaceful man, I would roar like a lion if I was annoyed. Never – a kitten more like!

'When leave ended, it was back to the war again. The war was on the move as the Japs were being steadily pushed back and then came the two atomic bombs. Although many thousands of Japanese were killed, the bombs saved thousands of Allied lives. To be quite honest, it was a great relief to know that the war was over. It wasn't for a while that we realised the implications. We had no sympathy for the Japanese, although it was a terrible thing and a cruel way to do it. For us, the war was over and we'd be going home. Although I'm not a vindictive person, I will never, ever forgive them – I heard such terrible stories from prisoners of war. At that time we were stationed at Pegu in Burma. With the Japs beaten, it was planned that we would go to Hanoi in order to support the French, who were trying to re-establish themselves in French Indo-China; however, this move was overtaken by events and was cancelled.

'With the posting cancelled, my three close friends and I were more or less stranded in Pegu. We tried to keep a low profile in order to avoid guard duty and fatigues and, in this, we were largely successful. Then one of us, Wally, got his demobilisation number and had a formal interview with the CO, who asked what the four of us had been doing in Pegu. Wally told him and so it was that we found ourselves back in the signals section in a distant part of the airfield and back to watch-keeping which, because of the peace, meant very little traffic. However, one incident stands out – a very sad and tragic one. When coming into land, a Liberator crashed on the runway and burst into flames, killing all on board. We could only look on in horror. To survive the war – only to die like that – was truly terrible.

'Our stay at Pegu ended when our demobilisation numbers were confirmed and we were transported to a transit camp on the outskirts of Rangoon. The camp was right next to the enormous Shwedagon Pagoda, which we visited one day – it was amazing. Our duties were very light: just a couple of guards each week. Most evenings we spent at the local Forces Club, where we played 'housey housey', a form of bingo. We were quite lucky at this and always shared our winnings. Then, in late June 1946, the day to return home finally arrived and we packed our bags and embarked in the troopship SS *Orduna* in Rangoon. It was typical troopship life – but who cared? We were going home at last. Every morning we had to fold up our hammocks and often someone would nick them so we would have to nick someone else's – and so it went on. We called at Colombo in Ceylon, before sailing up the Red Sea and back through the Suez Canal. We all got very angry when another troopship overtook us in the Red Sea: we all thought they'd get the best suits and the best jobs! A huge cheer went up when the lighthouse off the coast of Pembrokeshire was spotted. We docked at Liverpool, where we were welcomed by the mayor, before being taken to the demobilisation centre. Of course we had no civilian clothes so were all kitted out in new 'civvies'. I was given quite a decent suit, a Raglan overcoat and a Trilby hat, as well as £60 'from a Grateful Nation'. I also got a good supply of petrol coupons, which were eagerly seized on by my father, who met me at Euston with the family.'

On 25 March 1944 at Holy Trinity, Camden, Fred married Freda Winifred, daughter of Frederick George Huxford, an employee of the General Post Office, of 31 Weymouth Road, Parkstone, Dorset, and his wife Emma Annie Alice (née Nicholls). During the First World War, his father-in-law served in the Queen's Regiment, disembarking in France on 5 July 1915 and rising to the rank of lance corporal before being gassed on the Somme and discharged on 22 September 1917. Although Fred returned to Savills after being demobilised, 'there seemed no prospects', so he went to work as a cashier for the National and Local Government Officers' Association (NALGO), which represented local government 'white collar' workers. He 'stayed happily for thirty years' with NALGO – which amalgamated with two other unions to form UNISON in 1993 – until his retirement.

Initially, Fred and Freda lived at 106 Belmont Street, in a then-typical family arrangement: his parents lived on the ground floor; they and their rapidly-growing family lived on the middle floor; while his sister, Edith, her husband, Sidney Stevens, and their three daughters lived on the top floor. In 1952, just before the birth of their third son, they moved into a council house in Hanson Green, Loughton, Essex, remaining there until Freda's death on 9 March 2013. Their eldest son, Alan, explained: 'Despite – or perhaps because of – his experiences with his own father, who was a rather stern and forbidding man, he became a real role model for us and fully recognised the importance of education. Although the three of us shared a bedroom, we all had our own desk.' Fred and Freda's three sons are: Brigadier Alan Behagg MBE, Royal Anglian Regiment; Professor Clive Behagg OBE, lately vice-chancellor of Chichester University; and Neil, the senior partner of Neil Behagg & Associates, a Bahamas-based architectural practice. Fred Behagg died on Christmas Eve 2021, at the age of 100.

Fred Behagg after his second Covid-19 jab, 25 March 2021.

14244284 Gunner Alan Bevan, Royal Artillery

Alan Sydney Bevan was born on 20 August 1923, only son of Sydney Thomas Bevan, an electrician for Swansea Corporation, of 18 Oakwood Road, Swansea, and his wife Bertha, daughter of John Allen, haulage contractor and licensed victualler, of Llansamlet, Glamorgan. He was educated at Brynmill School and later at Clark's College, both of which are in Swansea, before leaving school at 16 to work as a clerk for Lloyds Bank. He joined the St Helen's branch in Swansea, where the poet Vernon Watkins also worked, explaining: 'Dylan Thomas was a good friend of Vernon's and he used to come in and collect him once a week for lunch.'

After it had been explained that Burma veterans were being interviewed, Alan said: 'I thought they were all dead! There are things that I'll have to leave out of course. Beginning at the beginning, I was called up on 6 August 1942. After primary training at Bradford in Yorkshire, I was posted to Wakefield to learn Morse code, because signalling was my trade within the Royal Artillery. We also received training on mustard gas and were tested on the use of respirators, just before I was sent on embarkation leave. On 22 February 1943, I boarded a troopship in Liverpool for the voyage to Bombay. We sailed in convoy and, with U-boats about, the escorts dropped a number of depth charges. We suffered engine problems off the Gold Coast, and, although it took 24 hours to fix the problem, we still managed to re-join the convoy the following day. We spent a month in Cape Town, living in a tented camp and amusing ourselves by giving names to our tents: ours was called

Cape Town, South Africa, March 1943: 14244284 Gunner A.S. Bevan (left) and Gunner W. (Billy) Atkins.

'Upham Hall'! When off duty, we were not allowed to leave camp on our own but always had to make up groups of two or three.

'After disembarking in Bombay, I joined 455th Independent Light Battery, which was equipped with the QF 3.7-inch mountain howitzer. Initially we were sent to Goa to practise beach landing techniques because that was how we expected to go into Burma. From there we took a long train ride across India, to Calcutta. Lord Louis Mountbatten came to talk to us and, perhaps because I was one of the youngest, I was selected to meet him. He said, reassuringly: "The area will be softened up before you get there." We next went to Cox's Bazar [now the world's largest refugee settlement, after the exodus of Rohinga Muslims from Rakhine state], sixty miles south of Chittagong, where we practised more amphibious landings because we still expected to land behind the Japanese lines. The medics would come round trying to persuade me to take salt tablets, but they were horrible so I used to put salt on my food instead.

'Suddenly we were told that we weren't going in by boat after all but would go in overland instead. As a result, much of our equipment – particularly the vehicles – had to be modified. Although our guns could be carried on mules, we only used them once; we normally used American 4x4s and Bedford 3-tonners. I had nothing to do with the guns: I was

India, 1944: Gunner A.S. Bevan (top row, second from right).

based at Battery HQ, working with Captain Gibbs. My job was to listen to instructions from the FOOs [Forward Observation Officer], before relaying them to the officer in charge of the gun line. When rounds were fired, the FOOs provided corrections over the radio and the gun line would make the necessary adjustments. When we had straddled the target with successive rounds, we knew that we had found the target. Towards the end of the war, we had a couple of Sherman tanks attached to us.

'We used No. 11 wireless sets, which rarely worked properly. When there was a problem, we used to tip them over, which usually did the trick. A lot of our equipment was poor and cheaply-made. For example, we were issued with Sten guns, which had a switch – 'automatic' or 'single' – but mine would only fire on 'automatic'. I was once in the back of a 3-tonner and there was an officer in the passenger seat. We went over a bump and the damned thing went off: a round went through the driver's door. We were constantly on the move and I was always on the radio.

'We worked very closely with West African and Indian troops; the Africans were really good drivers. If volunteers were sought for missions, they always wanted to go, and they often stayed on patrol longer than expected, frequently returning with strings of Japanese ears to show how successful they'd been. The Japs often attempted to infiltrate our positions at night. They used to shout, "Help me, Johnny! Help me, Jack!" Of course, we used to lie low. If you gave yourself away, you were in real trouble. The Japs once walked into a gun emplacement and slaughtered the gun crew – all six of them. In April 1945 we became part of 208th Field (SP) Regiment, supporting 23rd Indian Infantry Division. You were just one of a group of people moving forward: most of the time you had no idea where you were or what was going on.

'When the Japanese surrendered, we were pretty exhausted so they sent us to Shillong for two months' R&R. After that we went to Ranchi and then to Poona, before boarding the HMT *Alcantara* for the voyage home to Woolwich, after which I was sent on disembarkation on 5 June 1946. When we came home we all had a bit of colour and certainly looked fighting fit. As a result, a lot of us were sent up to Fort William to act as extras in the David Niven film *Bonnie Prince Charlie*. We were dressed for the part and 'starred' as ravaging Scotsmen running up and down hills.'

Alan's wife, Sue, explained the very real sadness of his homecoming: 'At the end of 1943, Alan had received a short telegram: "Mum died Boxing

Day" [at the age of 52]. Coming home was the hardest part for him – even worse than the war in Burma. At the end of 1945 his father had married Beatrice and his new stepmother wouldn't have him in the house.' Alan returned to his job with Lloyds Bank but there were no vacancies in the St Helen's branch so he went instead to Canton, close to Cardiff city centre, where he lived in lodgings. Subsequently he worked for Lloyds at Tenby in Pembrokeshire and at Pontardawe, near Cardiff, becoming a sub-manager, specializing in securities. Sue said: 'He still watches *Bloomberg* three or four times a day to see what the markets are doing and continues to dabble in the stock market.' Having worked for Lloyds Bank for thirty-eight years, Alan has now been retired for longer than he worked for the bank.

Alan Bevan in costume for the film, *Bonnie Prince Charlie*, Fort William, Scotland, 1946.

In 1951 at St Paul's, Sketty, he married Elaine, only child of James Guppy and his wife Loen (née Weeks) and they had a daughter. Elaine died on 3 October 1987, aged 62, and on 17 July 1993 at Swansea register office he married Sue, daughter of Arthur Thomas Turley, who worked for Midlands Electricity Board. Alan became a life member of the Swansea & district branch of the Burma Star Association on 11 October 1995 (membership number B/5347/95).

Alan Bevan, Reynoldston, Swansea, Remembrance Day, 2018.

1535378 Corporal Neil Bullock, Royal Air Force

Neil Bullock was born at 74 Avon Street, Sparkhill, Birmingham, on 24 October 1921, the youngest of five children of William James Bullock, a wagon repairer with the Great Western Railway, and his wife Flora Sylvia, daughter of James Sheldon, coal merchant, of 27 Bordesley Street, Birmingham. Since his hearing is now very poor and he can't therefore use the telephone, his daughter, Annette, acted as an intermediary. She kindly persuaded her father that his story was worth telling and helped him along the way with memory prompts, dates and spelling. Neil explained: 'Avon Street was a cul-de-sac and was only a short walk from the Sparkhill shopping centre and just fifteen minutes from Golden Hillock School, which I attended at all three stages: Infants, Junior and Senior. I loved my school, which was next door to the famous BSA [Birmingham Small Arms] factory and was very happy there. I played in the school football and cricket teams and was also quite a good runner. We always ran to and from school. All my siblings were educated at the same school. I lived at Avon Street until 1932, when we moved to 443 Stratford Road, Birmingham, when my father was appointed caretaker of the neighbouring Primitive Methodist Church. After leaving school at the age of 14, I got my first job at the Midland Education Co, working in the warehouse supplying schools with books and equipment. It was here that I made two special friends, Jack Philpot and Peter Deeley, friendships that lasted until their deaths.

'Between 1936 and 1939, Jack and I cycled all over the place, in training for 25-mile time trials. Our favourite place at weekends was the Cotswolds and our very favourite place was Lower Slaughter, which I have loved ever since. I bought a new bike made by Joe Cooke – it cost me £9 and one penny. The bikes were called Imperial Petrel. In 1939, I got a new job when I took over as manager of the stores at the Reliance Telegraph Co, a subsidiary of GEC in New Meeting Street Birmingham, at the princely rate of two shillings an hour! It was while working there that I met Catherine, my wife-to-be [who was born on 3 December 1923, daughter of George Holman, bus conductor, of Vauxhall, Birmingham, and his wife Ann (née Clayton)]. Our first date was nearly a disaster. It was almost Christmas 1940 and we had arranged to meet outside the

Odeon cinema in New Street. It was snowing, Catherine was late and covered in snow. We went to see Jeanette Macdonald and Nelson Eddy in *New Moon*.

'1940 was a very bad year. My brother, Bill, died on 30 July from a heart problem, and on 19 November, during a heavy bombing raid, my sister, Hilda, was killed by a direct hit after the 'all-clear' had sounded. She is commemorated on a memorial in Birmingham near St Martin's Church and also in the Book of Remembrance in the Hall of Memory. Both are buried near my parents in Robin Hood Cemetery, Solihull. Prior to this we were not entitled to an Anderson shelter and we had to pop round the corner and take shelter in the cellar of a shop. During this time, and for the rest of the Blitz, Birmingham was the next most bombed city after London and the Liverpool Docks. While in the shelter one very bad night, our house was hit and became untenable. We got new accommodation at a friend's house at Warley on the outskirts of Birmingham.

'In 1941, I received my call-up papers and managed to get assigned to the Royal Air Force. On 5 July 1941, I reported to the 3rd Reception Centre, Padgate. There I got kitted out, 'inaugurated' and given the number 1535378 AC2, and on 8 July 1941 left by lorry and train to Filey Basic Training Centre. I was only too pleased to get away from Padgate. I was very lucky because I was put in civilian digs with another fellow and we were looked after very well. On 15 August, I moved to the Equipment Training School at Bridlington in Yorkshire. Here I and a couple of others were billeted with a Mrs Ireland: during our stay we were treated like sons and what wonderful food we had. I just don't know how she did it with the rationing. On 2 October, I passed out with a mark of 77% in the examination, as an AC1 Equipment Assistant, and had two weeks' leave, waiting for a posting to my unit, which turned out to be 938 Balloon Squadron at Hartburn, just outside Stockton-on-Tees. On 11 November 1941, I had a short leave, and during that time got engaged to Catherine. In late February 1942, I was sent to RAF Blackpool to await a posting overseas.

'On 4 March 1942, I reported to a very frozen-up 110 (Hyderabad) Squadron at Wattisham in Suffolk and was issued with tropical kit. On 16 March the squadron left by train for Liverpool and sailed the next day in a 22,000-ton Dutch ex-East Indies liner, *Johan van Oldenbarnevelt* [which became the Greek cruise liner TSMS *Lakonia* in 1962 and caught fire and sank on 29 December the following year with the loss of 128 lives]. We had real fun and games getting into crowded hammocks. As we got further south in the Atlantic towards the Equator, we started to sleep on the deck. You had to get up early though because the Dutch crew swabbed the deck around six o'clock, and if you were still there you would get drenched – they didn't wait for you to move. The convoy was absolutely huge: there were ships as far as you could see. We learnt later it was the biggest convoy to sail from Liverpool. It was very interesting watching the destroyers nipping around and the aircraft flying around from the aircraft carrier that was on station quite near us. We anchored off Freetown and natives in their boats came out trying to sell us fruit. When we left there, a lot of the Royal Navy escort left us. We crossed the Equator without the usual ceremony and saw sights like whales and flying fish.

'We finally arrived at Cape Town and what a lovely sight it was as we sailed into the harbour, with Table Mountain in the background. We were told that the clouds sitting on the top are called the table cloth. We had four days in Cape Town, including shore leave. I was very fortunate because a couple picked two of us up and took us to their home and vineyard. We were treated like long-lost family and they dropped us back at the ship in the evening. Then they picked us up again the following day. It was amazing to see shops that stocked everything that was rationed at home. The really bad thing was the segregation between blacks and whites. For example, when we went to the pictures, our seating in the restaurant at the interval was fabulous but all the blacks were seated on what looked like benches down at the front.

'After four days on shore, it was back to the *Johan van Oldenbarnevelt* and we departed Cape Town for Bombay, where we arrived on 19 May 1942. Once again, the approach was quite a surprise. The 'Gateway to India' stands proudly on the front, flanked by the Taj Mahal Hotel, a fantastic building. We marched across the docks to an old tramp ship and left for Karachi. I cannot remember how long we spent at Karachi but we soon left for Quetta by train across the sand desert. I recall that trip because it was so hot and dry that your nostrils seemed to be burning. We were billeted in an old barracks that had been vacated by the army. Quetta is a very barren place not too far from the Khyber Pass. We settled down into being a squadron again and getting to know each other. The stores were always busy so we quickly got into our routines. Here we waited to be allocated some planes and eventually some Vultee Vengeance dive-bombers arrived. On 1 July 1942, I was made up to Leading Air Craftman.

'On 11 October, we finally left Quetta: we couldn't go by train because of floods so we had to go by 10-ton trucks through the mountains. It was a hair-raising journey on roads with hairpin bends and a drop of hundreds of feet on one side. The trucks were driven by Sikh drivers who didn't seem to know where the brakes were! Eventually, we got to the railhead and took the train to Ondal near Asansol just outside Calcutta. We only stayed there until 11 November, when we moved on to Pandaveswar, which is not far from Asansol.

1535378 Corporal N. Bullock, Royal Air Force.

'The stores were kept in large wooden crates, tipped on their sides for easy access. These crates were very heavy and we had two young Indian lads, called 'camp followers', to assist us. Every time we moved, we had the major job of repacking for transport. These two lads, whose names I'm afraid I have now forgotten, were a great asset, not only keeping the place clean but also exchanging our spare cigarettes, for eggs etc, in the local village. They loved a joke and a good laugh. The stores were really the hub of the squadron, as everything came through the stores. Although I was always very careful with food and never bought anything at the local bazaars, I was rushed into the CMH hospital in Asansol with a serious bout of dysentery on 10 December. I spent that Christmas Day in hospital and, in a book written by one of the nurses, *The Maturing Sun*, there is a picture of the two of us on the ward. On discharge from hospital, I went up to the CMH hill station at Chakrata. It was lovely up there near the Himalayan mountains, with cool, dry, crisp air after the stifling heat of the plains.

'I eventually rejoined the squadron at a place called Madigan and then went on a detachment to Chittagong in the Arakan. It is on the coast and very near to Cox's Bazar, where we managed a dip in the sea. We stayed there until a move to Digri [near Midnapore], which involved yet more packing up of spares etc in the crates. We had become real experts at this by now. I think it was maybe October 1943 when we packed up again and entrained for the Brahmaputra, which was so wide that it looked like the sea. We crossed by ferry in three-ton lorries and then drove to Kumbhirgram, an RAF station near Silchar. We remained there while the battles of Kohima and Imphal were raging, carrying out regular bombing requests from the Army. The planes had to fly over a hump of mountains to get where they were wanted. After each bombing mission, the Army would send back a communication. If the word 'strawberry' was mentioned, this meant it was a success; if the word 'raspberry' was used, then the mission had been a failure. I am pleased to say that we never once received a 'raspberry'!

'This is an extract from one of the signals which we were pleased to receive: "General Grover commanding Kohima operations has asked that his appreciation be conveyed to you for air support. Particularly to crews of the *Vengeance* who operated successfully despite adverse weather over target." The Vengeance arrived at the right moment and the aircraft kept the Japanese heads down for the rest of the operation. During this time, we had a visit from three Japanese bombers. They had two engines and came in a shallow dive and dropped twenty-one bombs, killing six civilians while eight personnel were injured. Three of our planes were damaged – but repairable. Two of our basha huts were destroyed and a lot of air frames and engine spares were lost. Fortunately, though, the huts were unmanned at the time.

'With the oncoming monsoon, we had to make a quick exit from Assam as it is one of the wettest places on earth. This was the worst journey I have ever had to endure.' It is described in detail by Wing Commander C.G. Jefford in his book *RAF Squadrons*: 'Having seen off their aircraft, the Squadron paraded at Lilehar at 08.45 hrs on 6 June. Entraining at 10.30 hrs, they set off for Chanpur, arriving at 02.00 hrs the next morning. Transferring to a river steamer, they sailed at 11.30 hrs to travel the 70 or so miles upstream to Gaolunds Ghat, arriving there at 01.30 hrs on 8 June. A further train journey, lasting from 01.45 hrs to 11.30 hrs, took them to Calcutta. After a meal in a transit camp and a few hours in the city, the Squadron was back at Howrah Station for 20.15 hrs departure. The train was late and, after sleeping in the station, they finally moved off again at 11.00 hrs on 9 June. For four days the Squadron traversed India from East to West in a series of fits and starts, periods of progress interspersed with pauses to take on water. The Squadron Operations Record Book observes that, over the first 600 miles, they averaged just 9 mph! After thirteen intermediate stops, the ground crew finally reached Kalyan at 18.15 hrs on 13 June.'

Neil's account continued: 'After only a short stay there, we moved to Yelahanka, which is now a suburb of Bangalore. 110 Squadron was known as 110 (Hyderabad) Squadron, after the Maharajah of Hyderabad. When the squadron was formed in 1927, he paid for all the aircraft. While we were in India, he provided us with all our sports gear and, at Christmas 1943, he presented everyone in the squadron with a tankard with our name on one side and the squadron crest on the other. I still have mine. At Yelahanka we handed over our new Vengeance 4s to the Indian Air Force and took delivery of Mosquito 6 fighter-bombers. This meant retraining for pilots and all members of the squadron. For us in the stores, it meant packing up old Vengeance spare parts and receiving spares for our new planes. It also involved us learning the details of the new spares, etc.

'While at Yelahanka I came down with malaria. After recovering at CMH Bangalore, I went up the narrow winding road to Ootacamund to recuperate. It was a lovely place: nice and cool, and I actually saw some snow. Just two weeks after returning to Yelahanka, we packed up once again and took a long train journey to Johari near Cox's Bazar in the Arakan. It was there that I was made up to corporal. Our next move was by Dakota to a place called Kinnmargon, in central Burma near Myingyan. We operated from there until August 1944 when we made our final move, to Hmawbi near Rangoon. It was while there that our commanding officer, Wing Commander Saunders, on patrol over Rangoon saw a sign on the prison roof: "Get your fingers out, Japs gone." Knowing from the language that it couldn't be a trick, he landed at a nearby airfield and walked into Rangoon. The incident is well known as

"One Man Captures Rangoon". I have several newspaper cuttings and it is referred to in quite a lot of books I have read about the war in Burma.

'Knowing that there was an invasion force sailing up the river to Rangoon, the men had taken a sampan to meet them and inform them that the Japs had gone. Although victory over the Japanese was announced on 15 August 1945, shortly after the atom bombs were dropped, a lot of the Japanese kept fighting until the formal document of surrender was signed on 2 September. 110 Squadron had the privilege of dropping the last bomb of the Second World War. It was, of course, long before I joined the squadron that its Blenheim bombers had dropped the very first British bomb of the war. So first and last.

'When we sailed from Rangoon on 11 September 1945, the squadron was making its last move, to RAF Seletar in Singapore. There was nothing really to do on the airfield: we were just waiting for transport to take us home after doing our four years. We did have some very good times there though. We got on well with the local population and found some very good, safe places to eat, with decent food. We were always niggled by the fact single men had to do four years' service and married men only three. We always said that if they had told us this before we went, we could have got married and done only three years. We were asked if we wanted to go home by sea or air. Thinking that it would be quicker by plane, myself and a couple of pals decided we would go by air. BIG MISTAKE. We had to wait sixteen days for a boat to a transit camp in Calcutta! We were then kept there for weeks until our turn finally came up and we flew out, thinking we were on our way to England. BIG MISTAKE. Instead, we flew to Karachi transit camp.

'Finally, on 5 February 1946, we took off from Karachi and landed at Habbaniya in Iraq to refuel and have a meal. Our next stop was a night-time one at Lydda in Palestine, then a very brief stop at El Adam before arriving at Catania in Sicily, where we had a wonderful evening and lovely comfortable beds. The following day, it was another refuelling stop, this time at Marseilles before we arrived home at a frozen Bourn in Lincolnshire in the middle of the night. We were kept hanging about in a huge, freezing hanger; luckily there were some WAAF girls handing out hot cups of tea. Eventually we were given a couple of blankets and accommodation in a corrugated Nissen hut. Everywhere was frozen up – even the toilets. It was just as it was when I left Wattisham to go to India four years earlier. The following day, we were given our railway warrants and sent on leave until our posting orders arrived. They said they would get us as near as possible to our homes. My posting order came through and I was to report to RAF South Witham, which is just outside Grantham. So much for near to home! To get home on weekend leave, I had to catch a train at Grantham for Nottingham, then change trains for Derby, before getting a connection to New Street, Birmingham. While serving at Grantham, I managed to get leave to get married to the girl who had been waiting for me all through my overseas service. Catherine and I were married at St Vincent's, Vauxhall, Birmingham, on 22 April 1946. We had a week's honeymoon at Bournemouth, where it rained the entire time.

Neil Bullock at the laying-up of the Birmingham Branch Standard, St Martin's, Birmingham, 24 October 2016.

'I was finally demobbed on 30 August 1946. Like all ex-servicemen I went to get the job the government had promised us when we were called up. It was very hard because all the jobs seemed to have been taken by immigrants. Although I managed to get a couple of jobs, they were not really suitable for me. I was then fortunate to get a job in the Birmingham office of the Automatic Telephone and Electric Co. They were opening a branch for the installation and maintenance of traffic systems. They soon moved the main factory from Liverpool to Poole in Dorset. During my service, I travelled up and down the country, installing signals all over the Midlands and South Wales, as far south as Plymouth and as far east as Great Yarmouth. I also serviced mine signalling equipment, which entailed me going underground on occasions, and also fire and attack alarm signalling on quite a few RAF stations. I eventually became regional manager of the Midland Depôt. The firm changed its name to Plessey and I was there for thirty-three years before taking voluntary retirement.

'I joined the Birmingham branch of the Burma Star Association on 23 August 1985 [membership number B/4398/85] and had some wonderful times. I have also laid the Birmingham branch wreath at Burma Star Grove at the National Memorial Arboretum in Alrewas. Since 1955 the family has lived at 23 Yenton Grove, Erdington, Birmingham. Unfortunately, my wife died in 2004, but I am very lucky because I have five daughters who take good care of me in my old age: Madeleine, Sue, Karen, Annette and Paula. Looking back, I really enjoyed my time in the service, particularly the discipline when marching and training. We all looked so smart with our clean-shaven faces and short haircuts. All that has now gone, with the exception of the Queen's Colour Squadron, which when I see them, makes me feel so proud.'

1836374 Corporal Eric Davis, Royal Air Force

Eric James Davis, middle son of Charles Davis MM, a gardener, of Pennytros Cottages, Rhiwderin, Monmouthshire, and his wife Edith (née Kite) was born at Rhiwderin on 19 July 1925: 'It was right out in the country: we had no gas, no electricity, no water and no inside toilets – no facilities at all. In order to fetch water, we had to walk 200 yards to a spring at the bottom of the field. We had corrugated sheeting that collected the rainwater for the summer period. We were close to a farm and I was always on the farm. All the family used to come out for haymaking and my job was to collect the bottles of cider. Although I was only 7 or 8, I often used to take a small swig myself. More than fifty years later, the farmer's daughter, Margaret Davis, asked if I had enjoyed the cider – and I thought that nobody had noticed. I didn't find out that I had been found out until I was nearly sixty years of age!'

Until he was 11 and his parents moved to 128 Gaer Park Road, Newport, Eric attended Rhiwderin village school: 'I was rather unfortunate really. At my old school they took the Eleven Plus at eleven, but in the town they took it at ten, so I was too late and was never able to take it.' In July 1939, two months before war broke out, Eric left Gaer School and was taken on as an apprentice by the Co-op, 'delivering groceries on carrier bikes, very often in the blackout'. He soon moved on though, and became an apprentice wheelwright, 'building cartwheels. Everything was done by hand. The stock was made of oak that had been seasoned for six years and we made the spokes before the rims were fitted by the blacksmith in the next village, Bassaleg.

'I wanted to go into the RAF. My elder brother, Oswald John, was a wireless operator in a Halifax, with a Canadian crew. One of them, Smithy, spent his leave with my parents and introduced me to 'whisky chasers'. When they were shot down in October 1943, three of the crew survived and were taken prisoner. After the war, Jack sometimes went to stay with the navigator in Canada. Sadly, Smithy did not survive. There was no ATC before the war, only the Air Defence Cadet Corps, which was only for public school, not for elementary types. I joined the ATC and we did our training at Newport Athletics Club, which is now Newport County Rugby Club. Although I signed up to the RAF at 17½,

> MANY ENTERING THE R A F THROUGH
> GATE No 1 AIR CREW RECEPTION AREA
> AT LORD'S DURING THE SECOND WORLD WAR
> GAVE THEIR LIVES. OUR ENJOYMENT OF
> CRICKET REFLECTS THEIR SACRIFICES

I wasn't called up until I was 18. I was accepted as an air gunner and had to report to the Air Crew Receiving Centre at Lord's cricket ground. They gave me a rail warrant from Newport to Paddington. I had never been more than twenty miles from home before and how I got across London I will never know. We were kitted out with uniform and all the necessary things and had vaccinations and injections and so forth. There were thirty of us in what was called a flight, all taking the same course. We were stuck there for a while so they put us up in luxury flats in St John's Wood. After ten days I got a violent temperature so they sent me to an RAF hospital for a week.

'In the meantime, my flight had been posted – so I was reflighted. The new crowd had lots of experience; they were the greatest crowd of fellows I ever met and they had more money. We only had 14 shillings a week, you know. We went to Bridgnorth in Shropshire but I never did any square-bashing because I was with warrant officers, sergeants and corporals who'd done it all before. One warrant officer had twenty years' experience. One night we had an air raid and someone shouted "Get up! The place is on fire!" We had to see what we could salvage at two o'clock in the morning. It became pretty cold, with no glass in the windows. After doing gunnery training at Pembrey in South Wales, I was sent to an OTU. Unfortunately I failed my aircraft recognition test because they were all Japanese aircraft and I only knew the German ones. Having been a sergeant in the ATC, I was now back to AC2 (aircraftman second class) [AC2s were known either as 'erks' or as AC plonks]. They offered me the option of being an MT [motor transport] driver, a despatch rider or a teleprinter operator. I chose MT and was sent off to Invergordon in Scotland and then to Eastchurch in Kent for driver training. As trainee

AC2 drivers, we started off on private cars for two weeks, before switching to Bedford lorries. There was only one instructor for every five lorries. We used to set off on 24-hour convoys, driving through the blackout. After a final MT course at Blackpool, I was sent on two weeks' embarkation leave.

'Within six months of joining, I was on a ship heading for Burma. We sailed from the Clyde, in the SS *Strathaird*, through the Mediterranean to Bombay. There were 2,000 on a boat built for 500. There were ten long tables in each room, with eight of us round each table. We slept in hammocks and there was no smoking below decks.

1836374 LAC E.J. Davis, Royal Air Force.

I was seasick in the Irish Sea; I was sick quite a lot of the way – I'm not a very good sailor. We spent a fortnight in Bombay before boarding a troop train for the eight-day journey across India to Silchar, in Assam. We were issued with Canadian Chevrolets and Fords – there were no British vehicles. I can still remember the number of my vehicle. They were all old and mine was 1066 – I thought that it had been built then! I was posted to 124 RSU – Repair & Service Unit. Our job was to go out and try and salvage any plane that had crashed, because we were very short of spares, before destroying the rest of it.' One of his colleagues, Frank Colenso, wrote: 'The RSUs were vital, especially early in the war, when the RAF didn't have much in the way of aircraft in the Far East. "Make do and mend" was what kept the squadrons airworthy. We salvaged what we could, and I don't remember ever unpacking any new parts. Our unofficial motto was "You bend 'em, we mend 'em".'

Eric explained: 'We were issued with Sten guns for self-protection. It was a very dangerous job because, apart from the Japanese, we had to watch out for Japanese sympathisers among the Burmese. A few vehicles would go out at a time – you see it depended which type of aircraft had

MT Section, 124 RSU, Burma, 1945.

crashed. In August 1944, I went down to Chittagong for a couple of weeks, before returning to Silchar. The food in Burma was pretty grim: we had dehydrated meat and soya links which looked like sausages but I can't explain what they tasted like. When I arrived in Silchar I weighed fourteen stone; when I left Burma I weighed just seven-and-a-half stone. We slept under canvas, often with a foot of water on the floor. We put our *charpoys* on petrol drums in order to try to stay dry. Towards the end of the year, I went forward for the assault on Akyab Island. In the canteen – there was no NAAFI – the first chap I bumped into had been in the Newport ATC with me.

'After the Japanese evacuation of Akyab, we returned to Imphal. In June 1945, I was driving a jeep south through Central Burma when I saw hundreds of dead Japanese on either side of the road. They had been killed while trying to get east across the country from the Arakan. I stopped for the night and an Indian officer arranged for me to stay with his unit. I was driving a jeep, which wasn't very comfortable to sleep in. I was given a little tent, which I put up, before putting down my bed-roll. An Indian soldier said that he would give me an early morning call. At 6 o'clock he came over, shouting "Chai!", but let out a scream and ran off. I had been sleeping on a nest of snakes – but I was perfectly alright. With so much troop movement taking place, I found myself behind the Japanese lines and was unable to return to base for four weeks.

'When they dropped that lovely atomic bomb I was at Myingyan, fifty miles north-west of Meiktila. I know lots of people say they shouldn't have done it, but it saved a lot of lives. We were heading for Pegu, to prepare for the invasion of Malaya. A medical officer needed a lift through Central Burma to Rangoon. We drew lots and I won. Rangoon was a big city and I didn't know where I was going to stay. Although I was wearing jungle green, I was sent to this place where everyone was wearing barrack dress with white puttees. I moved into a four-bedroom bungalow and all the beds were done up nicely. I was there for three or four weeks and used to go across to the sergeants' mess for meals. I then spent a couple of months in a transit camp. There was nothing to do – we just played pontoon all day long. We were there for Christmas. We were sent out to fetch all the booze for the camp from various depôts and, being transport, a few cases got mislaid!

'On New Year's Day, I left for Singapore in an LCT. All the vehicles were left behind. I was posted to Seletar, and when we arrived we found

Lorain crane, Singapore, 1946.

that the RAF were all on strike. The single people should have gone home after four years and the married ones after three years. There were no ships to bring them home so they went on strike. Only the cookhouse and the transport were working so we could at least use 'liberty trucks' to go into town. One day, an air vice-marshal came to address us. He had just flown in from Borneo where, he explained, "I have been up to my knees in mud." The response was: "We've been up to our necks in mud in Burma and we're now waiting to get home." He didn't appreciate that many of us had been out here for three or four years; he thought that we were onto a good thing in Singapore. I'd only been in Singapore for a day when I was told to take over and manage an American Lorain crane. The roads were so bad in Burma that I'd only ever driven a 5-ton wagon before; all of a sudden, I was driving a crane with a 15-foot jib at the front and a 20-ton crane behind! I did that job for nine months. In total I spent fifteen months in Singapore, finishing up in charge of the drivers, as the Details NCO.

'Before leaving England I had met a girl and we used to write to one another regularly. I addressed her as 'My Sweetheart'. In one of her letters she told me that she had got a new boyfriend, which gave me very bad depression – and you didn't get much help in those days. I was not very happy in Burma. When I knew when I was finally coming home, I sent a telegram to Newport. My train was due in at midnight. My father came down on his motorbike while 'My Sweetheart', who'd now changed her mind, had to get permission to stay out after ten o'clock and came down with her sister. The train was fifteen minutes early, and by the time they arrived my father had already taken me away. We started courting though.'

On 18 December 1948 at Christchurch, Christchurch Road, Newport, Eric married Dilys, daughter of Horace Daniel. They had one daughter, Jennifer. Dilys died on 21 July 2006. Eric continued his story: 'My first job – at 30 shillings a week – was at a bakery. At seven o'clock I started selling bread from a horse and cart. I moved to a factory as a capstan lathe operator, drilling and grinding crankshafts. One day the boss came up to me and told me to unload a lorry so I told him exactly where he could put his job. I really can't thank my wife enough – I had such terrible depression at that time. Then I moved to Land Rover, where I earned twice as much as a wing fitter. I was there for five years but there were so many strikes that in the end I couldn't stand it. I took a correspondence course in selling and spent six months selling encyclopaedias on commission. Why my wife stuck by me, I really don't know. After that I was one of 70 or 80 people who applied for a sales job with Kellogg's. This big Yankee fellow asked me: "What makes you think you can sell Kellogg's?" I replied: "I can sell anything." Although I came close, I didn't get it. The chap who did then decided that he didn't want it after all so I was offered it.

Eric Davis at home in Droitwich.

Although I explained that I didn't want to move north of the Midlands, I worked for Kellogg's for 34 years. I became territory manager for South Warwickshire, Gloucestershire, Worcestershire, South Staffordshire and Herefordshire.'

With the Royal British Legion's 'poppy tours', Eric has twice revisited Burma: 'In 2005 it was just like it was in the war with the military everywhere. We met the lady ambassador [Vicky Bowman], who is married to a Burmese [performance artist Htein Lin]. When I went back in 2013, I met her again. She is absolutely wonderful – it was as if she had known us all our lives. On 11 November 2013, I read the Kohima epitaph at Taukkyan Commonwealth War Graves Commission Cemetery.'

Eric is showing few signs of slowing down: 'Six months ago I treated myself to an extended flight in a Spitfire from Biggin Hill, over the White Cliffs and Beachy Head. All the family came down and they listened to the briefing. The pilot, a former RAF squadron leader, said: "It was a great honour to fly you, Eric, and I would like to offer you a free flight in five years' time." All I have to do is live for another four-and-a-half years!'

14867839 Fusilier Richard Day, Royal Welch Fusiliers

Richard Thomas Day was born on 31 August 1926, second son of Samuel Lewis Day of Arlington Square, Islington ('although they were big houses in Arlington Square, the family only rented two rooms'), and later of Hyde Crescent, Colindale, and his wife Minnie, eldest daughter of William Hoy, brass bedstead maker, of Peabody Buildings, Essex Road, Islington. Private Samuel Day was a regular soldier in the 2nd Battalion, Queen's Own Royal West Kent Regiment. Having disembarked at Basra on 6 February 1915, he remained in Mesopotamia for the duration of the First World War. After leaving the army, he worked as a journeyman painter, and during the Second World War was a member of the ARP (Air Raid Precautions), specializing in rescue and demolition, according to the 1939 Register. Samuel and Minnie had six children: four sons and two daughters. Richard explained: 'I was the only one to go into care. I have been puzzling over that for several years now, but there is no-one left to put one right about what happened.

'I went to four different homes: perhaps Mother was having another baby or Father was out of work, because it was not very plentiful after the war. Someone once dropped a bag of cement on him and broke his leg, so he couldn't work for a while. I first went into a care home when I was very small and my first recollection was sitting in a nursery chair under a glass roof by a verandah. There were six of us sitting round a rectangular table and we were given triangular brown bread sandwiches with the crusts cut off, filled with orange cheese. My last home was in Ramsgate, in a convent run by nuns. They weren't very pleasant; in fact, they could be rather cruel. When I was very young I hardly went to school and couldn't read until I was 8 or 9 because the homes didn't give me any education. Eventually I went to Hyde School in Colindale, which I left at 14 without any qualifications, to become an apprentice maintenance engineer with a firm of dry cleaners. They didn't dry clean the clothes in the shops in those days; instead a 3-ton Bedford lorry used to go round, collect the dry cleaning from the shops and take it back to the factory where the job was done. By the time I was 17, I was driving the Bedford myself; by then the war was on and they didn't worry too much about things like that. I worked with Les Sallibanks, who lived in Neasden, and he taught me how to do the job before he was called up and went to the tank repair workshop in Mill Hill. After that I did the job on my own for a year. When I was in hospital in Colindale with ear problems, I remember that there was a huge explosion in West Hendon, which destroyed about four rows of terraced houses. It was never determined what caused it.

'I joined the King's Royal Rifle Corps as a cadet. Our drill hall was by the corner of Edgware Road and Deansbrook Road, close to Edgware Hospital. We used to go camping at various places and were taught to put up tents and did plenty of drill. We also did rifle training and were once taken to Bisley to have a go at firing a .303. We only met once a week in the evening so we didn't get much time at it, normally just a couple of hours. I was conscripted at 18 and they sent me a rail warrant to go to Scotland. I wondered what I'd look like in a kilt. Three days later they sent me another rail warrant, this time to Shorncliffe in Kent. The barracks had been closed since the start of the war; there was no running water, apart from the cookhouse, and we had to break the ice before we could wash ourselves. There was only one working toilet – and that was across the square in the officers' quarters. On the second day, we were issued with rifles, which had been in store and were absolutely covered in grease. They only gave us one piece of four-by-two each to clean the grease off so some of the lads started to tear up their underpants. I came from a poor home and I certainly wasn't going to tear up my underpants. The food wasn't very good; it was the usual army stuff but quite different from what I was used to.

'The training was hard – with lots of marching and saluting – and it was quite tough on some of the lads. Being in four homes gives you a different attitude to life: when you are passed around from one place to another, you simply learn to cope. Basic training at Shorncliffe lasted six weeks, after which I was sent to Brecon for proper field training. We were based at Cwm Gwdi and used to march up and down the hills in FSMO – Full Service Marching Order – with .303 rifle, 18-inch bayonet, webbing, large pack and, over the top of that lot, we wore a gas cape. There was grass up to our knees so it was difficult to run about, but I suppose that was the idea, to get us used to it. They split us all up and we were taken out at night and dropped off without a map and had to find our own way back to the camp. Although we carried our own breakfast, I once smelled bread being baked for the morning delivery and the baker kindly cooked my breakfast for me. I didn't have any choice about the Royal Welch Fusiliers – that's just where I was posted.

'From a transit camp, I was given another rail warrant and eventually boarded SS *Tabinta*. It was very crowded and extremely stuffy and hot down below. We all slept on stretchers, one above the other, and it was very difficult to get in. Although you weren't allowed to sleep on deck, I found what I thought was a perfect spot and squeezed down between the deckhouse and the life-rafts. I woke up to find water swirling and slopping around and thought that we were sinking. It was the crew washing down the decks, but I daren't move until they had finished because I didn't want to be caught. After arriving at Bombay, I caught a train to Ranchi, where jungle training was going to take place. That was a bit of a farce too. You would be walking along a narrow track and they would pull a chord and a cardboard cut-out with a Japanese face pasted onto it would fly across and we had to aim and pretend to shoot it. We had no ammunition and that was the only jungle training we ever received. We had no training at all about how to live in the jungle.

'We were the relief for the 2nd Division and my party formed a draft for the 2nd Battalion, Royal Welch Fusiliers (2 RWF). Things were changing every day and the officers were a bit remote from us. We were just fitted into 2 RWF where we were needed. By the time I arrived, things were tailing off a bit and we did a lot of clearing up. It was not very pleasant, with bits of bodies, clothing and equipment lying about. We also spent time looking for odd bods who hadn't surrendered and on patrol we sometimes picked up the odd Japanese soldier. When the war ended, we were sent to a transit camp at Nee Soon in Singapore. We all thought we were going home but I was detailed to go to Japan. Initially I went to Kure and then to a requisitioned hotel in Kyoto. I had picked up enough Japanese to make myself understood so that may be why I was chosen to go there. Quite a lot of Japanese could speak English though, because it was their second language. I spent five months in Japan and we all slept, Japanese-style, on the floor. We had Japanese staff to do the washing and the cooking, and because I could speak a little Japanese I got on well with them.

'One of our jobs was to check out buildings that were suitable for commandeering for the occupation forces. I went into this building – without realizing that it was the public baths. The Japanese had all completely stripped off – men and women – and were sitting tightly together, side-by-side, on a ledge, with the water up to their armpits. I didn't know where to put my face really. I felt very embarrassed and made a mental note that this was a public place and was most certainly unsuitable for our purposes! We had one or two little bouts of trouble with the locals who resented us, but the emperor had told them to behave themselves and we treated them well. When it was time to leave, we all went down to Kyoto station to catch a train. One of the girls who had been looking after me put on a kimono, followed us down there and tried to persuade me to come across to another platform because the staff wanted to see me off. I was worried that I might miss my train and be reported AWOL – so I didn't go with her, I'm afraid. When we got back to Nee Soon, we dumped all our kit in empty oil drums and received a completely new issue. By that time, trouble was starting in Malaya. I had a bit of reputation as a driver and I went out on patrol across the causeway, looking for bandits, as they were called then. I arrived back in England at midnight on Boxing Day 1947. We were taken to a depôt but everyone had gone home for Christmas – and we were all given three weeks' leave. I was put on the reserves, and a couple of years later they called me back for a fortnight's training, so I couldn't go to my grandmother's funeral.

'The government decreed that returning servicemen should get their job back for six months. I wasn't being paid very much – just £5 for a 56-hour week – and the job involved going in on Sundays to service the equipment. I asked for a rise; instead they gave me the sack. Then I went to work at the big Frigidaire factory in Colindale; they made cold rooms and not fridges. Not long afterwards, they decided to move the workshops to Scotland, but I declined the offer to join them. My elder brother, Jim, who had been an armourer in the Fleet Air Arm, told me that the

Richard Day, National Memorial Arboretum, 22 August 2021.

motor trade was 'the thing'. So I went to a training centre the other side of Wembley and took a course in coach-trimming. After my training, I worked in a number of different factories: for Armstrong Siddeley, which made luxury cars, and for Thrupp & Maberly, part of the Rootes Group, which made the Hillman Minx and the Humber Super Snipe at the Cricklewood factory on Edgware Road.'

On 9 August 1952 at Burnt Oak register office, Richard married Ivy Louie Larke. They had three daughters: Sally, Jane and Vicky. He returned to Kohima last year: 'I met the elder of the tribe and they gave me a badge of crossed spears with red feathers. I don't know if they made me an elder as well – but I'm certainly old enough!' Richard Day joined the Burma Star Association on 22 June 1991 (membership number D/2155/91). He became very involved with the Association, serving as welfare officer for the St Albans branch and as chairman of the High Wycombe branch: 'I'm the only one left – they are getting a bit thin on the ground now.'

14315501 Lance Corporal Ted Downs, 3rd Carabiniers

Edwin (Ted) Downs was born at Leven, between Beverley and Hornsea in East Yorkshire, on 1 March 1924, elder son of Edwin Downs, a chef at the Grand Hotel in Lowestoft and the Grand Hotel in Scarborough, and his wife May (née Downs). He 'left school at 14 and started work at one of the sand and gravel quarries: there are a lot of them around there.' After being called up at the age of 18, he underwent basic infantry training at the Black Watch Depôt in Perth, followed by special-to-arms training at 156 Training Regiment, Royal Armoured Corps, at Menin Lines, Catterick, before being 'posted to 152nd Regiment, Royal Armoured Corps (152 RAC), one of Hobart's "Funnies" [which had been formed from 11th Battalion, King's (Liverpool) Regiment]. In training we used Matildas, but we were later issued with Churchills. I was the driver. With a 13-million candlepower searchlight on top, they had the codename Canal Defence Lights, or CDL. For training we went to Penrith in Cumberland, where we had lovely classrooms in the stables at Lowther Castle. We did our night exercises along Patterdale so no-one could see us – but they could, of course. We were always hiding away – first at Hawes in Yorkshire and then at Nether Witton in Northumberland – before we had live-firing practice at Linney Head on Castle Martin Ranges in Wales. There was one gun tank for every three CDLs. The CDLs were only used once or twice, at most, during the crossing of the Rhine, I think.'

Before the invasion of Normandy, 152 RAC was disbanded and Ted was posted to the 3rd Carabiniers (Prince of Wales's Dragoon Guards), which had been in Burma since early 1944. He explained: 'I was in one of the first convoys to go through the Mediterranean; before that, all the ships had to go round via the Cape. I joined them at Kalewa in November 1944, by which time the worst – Imphal and Kohima – was over and we were starting to drive the Japs back.' The Carabiniers were equipped with the American M3 Lee medium tank, which had a crew of seven. He explained: 'There are only three of them in the country, one in private hands, one at the Tank Museum at Bovington, and Monty's command tank at Duxford, near Cambridge.' Although Ted was once again a tank driver, 'I wasn't one for very long. Once you lost your tank, that was it – you didn't get another one. We were about twenty miles from Mandalay

Rangoon, June 1945: (back row, left to right) Sykes, Moore and Downs; (front row) Sergeant Bill Higgins and 'Bing' Crosby.

when the engine broke down: we abandoned it, the Japs shelled it, and it was very soon damaged beyond recovery.

'After that, I joined the Scout Group, HQ Squadron. We were equipped with Bren gun carriers and did all kinds of jobs: looking for the Japs around, but never in, the villages and keeping an eye open for roadblocks. The infantry were always ahead, which we all thought was wrong but the powers-that-be thought that they knew better. The 75mm was very useful for blasting Jap bunkers. On one occasion, there was a Jap officer hiding in the undergrowth, who scrambled up onto the tank with his sword and killed the tank commander, Captain Peter Cornaby. The Jap then dropped into the tank and killed the 37mm gunner, Eric Atherton, before the loader, Vernon Jenkins, who was awarded the Military Medal, shot him six times. He still wasn't dead so Jenkins had to give him another six. The sword is now in the Regimental Museum in Edinburgh Castle [where it is one of seven so-called 'star items'].'

On steep ground, the driver's view was so obstructed by the glacis plate that tank commanders had to stand up in open turrets to give instructions over the intercom, which made them particularly vulnerable. On 13 April 1944, during the attack on Nunshigum Ridge, a dominant feature six miles from Headquarters IV Corps at Imphal that rises abruptly some 1,000 feet out of the surrounding paddy fields, seven tank commanders, including two replacements, were shot through the head in quick succession. With all three officers in B Squadron now dead, Squadron Sergeant Major William Craddock took command of the squadron, leading it round the flank and enabling the Dogras to seize the position. When the successor regiment, the Royal Scots Dragoon Guards, is on parade, the squadron sergeant major, by hallowed tradition, commands B Squadron, and the officers march past behind their men. Between April 1944 and May 1945 the Carabiniers lost no fewer than eleven officers killed in action.

14315501 L/Cpl E. Downs, Bangalore, September 1945: 'All my love to my darling Joyce from Ted xxxx.'

Ted explained: 'Nobody used Christian names; everybody had a nickname – mine was 'Downsie' – but they called you other things as well. If you caused a stand-to in the middle of the night by firing your weapon accidentally, you should have heard the names they called you! You had the heat to contend with and you had the Japs to contend with but one of the worst things about Burma was sleep deprivation. The weather was alright till we got to Rangoon and then the monsoon started. I caught pneumonia and went straight into hospital. After evacuation to India in a hospital ship, I was treated at the British Military Hospital, Madras, before going to the Convalescent Depôt in Bangalore, where I was when the war ended. I rejoined the regiment, which was now at Risalpur on the North-West Frontier. We had all new tanks – Shermans and Stuarts – because we were supposed to be going to Malaya but, luckily for us, they dropped the atomic bomb. We used to go through the Khyber Pass, just for something to do I think; we didn't actually shoot at anybody.

'I was made lance corporal but went to see the adjutant because I didn't want the responsibility and I didn't want to leave all the friends I had been with in Burma and join the corporals' mess. I don't suppose that the pay would have made much difference. He told me to sit down, because he thought I was going to sign on; when I told him I wasn't and that I didn't want promotion either, the sergeant major bawled: "Stand Up! Attention!" The adjutant said I must do what I was told and I was appointed as an instructor at the Officers' Training School at Ahmednuggur [where senior members of the Indian National Congress were detained after passing the 'Quit India' resolution' on 8 August 1942 and which is now the home of the Cavalry Tank Museum]. It was like a holiday camp: we only had one parade, when the officers passed out. The Carabiniers was a bullshit regiment. On one parade, the rather elderly colonel said: "Have you fed the horses?" We looked puzzled until the sergeant major explained that he meant: "Have you filled the tanks with fuel?" The colonel really didn't know a petrol tank from a frying pan!'

On 26 September 1947 at St John's, Ashington, Ted was married to Joyce Robson, whom he had met while training at Nether Witton, where

Tidworth Garrison Church, 1993: (left to right) Bernard Bennett, Bob Stoddart and Ted Downs.

she was working as a Land Girl: 'She waited three years for me, until I got back from India. A whole lot of new officers arrived and they weren't very nice. All we wanted to do was get back home and get out of the army. I can't remember any of my friends signing on.'

After the war he worked as a coal miner for more than forty years, going down the pit at North Seaton, Newbiggin and Lynemouth. Ted and Joyce had a son, Stephen, and a daughter, Linda, who also live in Ashington, Northumberland, which is perhaps best known for the footballing Charlton brothers and also the play *The Pitmen Painters*, which was later made into a film. He joined the Burma Star Association in 1989 (membership number D/2116/89) and remembers meeting Richard Hilder at regimental reunions: 'He doesn't look much like an officer – more like a farmer [which he was, of course!] – he's very lanky and gangly.' Although Joyce died twenty-eight years ago, Ted sees his children regularly: in fact, Stephen's partner, Janice, takes him his breakfast and newspaper every morning.

Final Burma Reunion, April 1995: (left to right) Ted Downs, Peter Higginbottom, Ray Chater and Bernard Bennett.

14783968 Lance Corporal Mervyn Ellicott, Queen's Royal Regiment

Mervyn Charles Ellicott was born at North Molton, Devon, on 30 August 1925, only child of Fred Ellicott and his wife Dorothy Laura, eldest daughter of John Ware, trapper and smallholder, of Hole Water, High Bray, South Molton. 51449 Private Fred Ellicott served with the Somerset Light Infantry during the First World War, after which he became a postman, moving with his family from Devon to 66 Hampton Road, Twickenham, Middlesex, in the mid-30s. After attending North Molton Primary School, where 'each teacher had three classes and there were ten of us in each class', Mervyn then went to a school in Hampton, which he left at 14: 'I had a baker's round in Nelson Road, Whitton, but I was only there for a month before I went down with 'flu – just as the war started. When I was better, I did a bit of fire-watching and worked as an errand boy for a small, local electrical firm, a bit of a one-man band. After a year or so our next-door neighbour, Henry, found me a job at a foundry in Hounslow where he worked as a foreman.

'Although I was called up at 18, I was classed as working in a reserved occupation so my call-up was delayed for a year. With D-Day approaching, there were hundreds of vehicles – army troop carriers and jeeps – parked on what is now the start of the M3 but was then a dual carriageway. Just after D-Day, in June 1944, I was sent to the Depôt of the Royal West Kents in Maidstone. I was there until November when we were due to go to Europe after returning from embarkation leave. Just two days before we were due to go on leave, though, it was absolutely pouring with rain and some silly person decided we should go on the assault course. Six of us fell and I hurt my right leg, so we were all sent on leave rather than embarkation leave. When we got back from leave, eight of us, all badged Royal West Kents, joined a platoon from the Queen's Royal Regiment and boarded a troopship, the *Queen of Bermuda* [a British turbo-electric ocean liner that belonged to Furness, Withy & Co and had been requisitioned on 29 August 1939] in Liverpool. We then waited in the bay for three days while the convoy formed up.

'After arriving in Bombay just three weeks later, we were then put on a troop train, and it took another three weeks to get to Shillong [a hill station in north-west India and the capital of the state of Meghalaya]. At Shillong we were all split into training camps: there were six camps altogether and we were moved around them, in the process learning about living in the jungle, having lots of rifle practice and digging trenches. Unfortunately we all got tummy trouble from eating too much fruit. In all, the eight of us from the Royal West Kents spent three months at Shillong, although the Queen's boys went straight on to join the 1st Battalion [1 Queens]. We had to supervise the shooting as others arrived, for example, from the Italian campaign; they were mostly officers or NCOs. At Shillong I did some specialist signals training and learned to use the Morse code. After a train journey, then a river boat on the Brahmaputra, and yet another train journey, I arrived in Rangoon about 48 hours before the news of the first atomic bomb reached us. We all changed from Royal West Kents to the Queen's Royal Regiment on the dockside at Rangoon.

'I remember the poor devils coming back from the railway. On the night of their arrival there was a concert by Gracie Fields at the airport in Rangoon and I was there too [in the first week of October 1945]. Later, I flew from Rangoon to Bangkok: there were three Dakotas but we lost one on the way. We took charge of a prisoner-of-war camp for Japanese [Surrendered Japanese Personnel] and their Indian allies [who served with the Indian National Army] on the outskirts of the city. Among other things, I was responsible for the telephone connections. It was difficult and you could tell they didn't like us by their looks, especially the officers. We only really came into contact with the prisoners at guard-mounting time. They were involved in general tidying-up and were only there until ships were available to take them back to Japan or to India. I was in Bangkok for a couple of months before catching a train to join 1 Queens at Sungei Petani in Malaya [twenty miles north of Bukit Mertajam, immediately opposite the island of Penang].

'I had "acquired" a Japanese push-button radio set in Rangoon: it came with me to Bangkok and also to Malaya. We did quite a lot of local patrolling because there were supposed to be Japanese hiding out after the surrender – but we never found any. Then 1 Queens moved down to Singapore and we were stationed at Selarang Barracks, opposite Changi jail. It wasn't a great job really: we were just providing guards for the headquarters in Singapore. I spent two years in Singapore, and although it was a bit boring and not a very happy time, I did meet a girl, Mia McDougall. The daughter of a New Zealand First World War veteran who worked as a planter, she had been a prisoner of the Japanese, having survived the massacre at Alexandra Hospital in Singapore. I used to go and stay with her mother, who acted as the housekeeper – Mia was a friend and not a girlfriend. When my time was up, I came home. After demob, I was offered a job looking after the old people who lived at Hampton Court Palace, but I only stayed for just over a year because there were too many stairs. After that I got a job working as a delivery driver for an electrical firm before joining ICI, where I worked as a fork-lift truck driver at a warehouse in Sunbury-on-Thames.'

On 3 March 1951 at Hampton Methodist Church, Mervyn Ellicott married Jean Margaret, only daughter of Arthur John Abnett (who was known in the family as 'Little Tim'), of 4 Hill Field Road, Hampton, and his wife Ismay Florence (née Combridge). Arthur Abnett joined the Royal Air Force on 1 July 1918 and was employed on aircraft repair and maintenance. After the war, there was a natural progression and he worked at the De Havilland factory in Weybridge. Mervyn and Jean had two daughters: Janet and Margaret. Unfortunately, they live some distance from their father, who has lived on his own since Jean died six years ago. Mervyn joined the Skegness & District branch of the Burma Star Association on 16 June 1999 (membership number E/1164/99).

3034775 LAC Brian Foster, Royal Air Force

Brian Edgar Foster was born on 14 November 1925, second son of Gaius Foster, an architect with London County Council, and his wife Dora Ethel, eldest daughter of John Henry Gale. During the First World War, Gaius Foster served as a sergeant in the Royal Army Medical Corps because, in Brian's words, 'he wanted to save life, rather than take it'. When he was recommended for a commission, his experience led him to the Royal Engineers, where he helped to lay railway track on the Western Front, before leaving with a 90 per cent disability pension. The family lived in New Maldon in Surrey before moving to 303 Old Shoreham Road, Portslade, after Gaius had retired. Brian explained: 'After a grammar school education, first at Tiffins in Kingston-upon-Thames and then at Hove County School for Boys, I left school at 15 and started work in an accountants' office in Haywards Heath. Our offices fronted on Paddockhall Road with a small garden. Because everyone older than me was being "called up" (for war service) I made rapid progress and was soon, in effect, the managing clerk, though far too young for such seniority. I was nearly 14 when the Second World War started on 3 September 1939 and I immediately joined the ARP service as a messenger. My job was – or would have been, if there had been an air raid – to cycle from one command post to another delivering messages.

'I had no idea how long the war would last – I don't believe I ever gave it a thought – but I knew that if I became involved, I wanted to be in the Royal Air Force. As soon as I turned 16, I joined 172 (Haywards Heath) Squadron, Air Training Corps, to receive preliminary training for what I hoped would be my future in the RAF. On my eighteenth birthday, I received my

ATC Leading Cadet Foster.

call-up papers. Commonly referred to as 'a letter from the King', they informed me that 'My Country Needed Me'. I was to report to a depôt at St John's Wood in London on 19 December 1943, in order to be received into the RAF as an aircrew trainee. Stockleigh Hall, a block of flats in Prince Albert Road, had been requisitioned and my first billet was quite luxurious; however, there were no communal catering facilities for the large number of inhabitants and so each morning we were marched off to breakfast at, of all places, London Zoo! Like every young man of my age, my ambition was to become a Spitfire pilot but, while we were still in the introductory stage, it was made very clear to us that there was no shortage of pilots and we would therefore be trained for other airborne duties, mainly as air gunners.

'This was not at all to my liking, so I sought to re-muster to an alternative ground job and my request was granted. As I was already a trainee accountant, it seemed that the Pay Corps would be most suitable; however, I wanted to contribute more positively towards the war effort and asked if I could be involved in radar, an exciting new discovery which played a hugely significant part in our eventual victory. This request was accepted, subject to my passing the requisite examinations, in physics and mathematics. There was a problem: at school I had been good at maths – which was why I had gone into the accountancy profession – but I had never studied physics and knew very little about the subject. Before sitting the examination, I was told that the pass mark was a modest 40 per cent but that it must be achieved in both papers. When interviewed after the exam, the presiding officer said I had presented them with a difficulty: in physics my score was a miserable 10 per cent but in maths I had achieved 100 per cent, something which had apparently never been achieved before.

'Luckily for me, the view taken by the examining board was that, if I was capable of scoring full marks in one paper, I must be of at least average intelligence and they were prepared to take a chance and enter me for training as a radar mechanic. After a brief interlude at a bomb store at Lords Bridge, Cambridge, waiting for a training course vacancy to become available, I went to Lincoln, where I spent many happy hours in the gardens of the Bishop's Palace, revising and debating. My first billet was in the George Hotel, for which any of my fellow trainees would have died. It was wasted on me because, at that time, I was not a drinker and never frequented pubs, so the landlord did not take to me and asked if I could be moved. For the rest of my time in Lincoln, I lived with a very nice, middle-aged couple on a small estate and was much happier.

'As soon as I passed out, having qualified as a Radar Mechanic (Air), I was told that, with the war in Europe nearing its climax, I would be of more use in the Far East. During my embarkation leave, I saw my first V1 rocket, or 'doodlebug', as it passed over our family home at Burgess Hill in Sussex on its way to London. After a train journey to Glasgow, I boarded the *Tierra del Fuego* for an uneventful journey, although, sleeping in hammocks below the waterline, I was always conscious of the position in which I would find myself if we should happen upon a German U-boat. Of my arrival in India, I wrote home: 'The sea was calm all the way except for a couple of days and I very much enjoyed it but was not sorry to land. You can imagine the excitement as we saw Bombay drawing closer and closer. As we approached the docks we all crowded on deck and sang everything we could think of – the natives seemed rather impressed!'

'When I left the UK, the talk of the war in the Far East was all about the Japanese advance to the very gateway of India and of particularly fierce fighting at Imphal. We were all allocated to various centres and I was horrified to hear that I was being sent to, of all places, Imphal! Of course, the war had by then moved on, the Jap offensive had been defeated and they were now on the threshold of being pushed back to Rangoon and beyond. But I thought I was being thrown to the wolves. Letters home were censored during the war: we had to hand them in unsealed and an officer would read through them to ensure we were not giving away any secrets. It was a requirement that you indicated on the reverse of the envelope – or Air Letter form, which was more popular since we had three a week, free of charge – the language in which they were written. On one occasion, a bored censor had written against my 'Written in English' – 'That's what you think!' I often wonder what became of him.

'A three-day train journey across India was followed by a day or two in Calcutta, where we saw at first-hand the effects of communal strife: there were bodies floating down the Hooghly river, often with vultures feeding on them. We crossed the Brahmaputra by ferry, before a truck ride over precipitous mountain roads to Imphal. I will never forget the majesty of the famous memorial at Kohima, with its renowned inscription:

LAC Brian Foster

When you go home
Tell them of us and say
For your tomorrow
We gave our today

'Recognising the unpredictability of air supply drops earlier in the war, "my" radar – the Rebecca/Eureka system – was developed. A ground transmitter sent signals which were monitored on a small TV screen by the transport aircraft, enabling it to home in on the signal, thus dropping supplies with much greater accuracy. This was of enormous significance in a campaign during which there was constant infiltration behind enemy lines and also the establishment of so-called 'boxes' when under siege by the Japs. On one occasion we were told that Eureka, the ground equipment being operated by a unit operating behind Jap lines at Meiktila, had broken down and needed urgent repairs. I duly flew down in a small aircraft to join this unit, which was deep in the jungle. On landing we were met by a young officer in a jeep, my kit was unloaded in seconds and the plane took off again. When I asked where we were in relation to the Japs, the officer turned a full circle, indicating that they were all around us, and urged me to get moving. We entered the 'box' and I was taken to a tent, which was to be my home for the next few days. Inside I saw what appeared to be four open graves, only to be told that it was necessary to sleep below ground because we would constantly be under attack by Jap snipers and you were only safe if you were below ground level. The 'box' was quite large – perhaps a mile square – and contained a mixture of vegetation: trees, shrubs and paddy fields. Japanese snipers would often infiltrate during the night, establish hidden vantage points and then try to pick off our troops the following morning. It was a suicidal task because once discovered they had no means of escape. Once when I was queuing for breakfast a sniper was found in a tree a few hundred yards away – a flame-thrower made short work of him.

'As the 14th Army advanced south towards Rangoon, we followed, in comparative safety – via Monywa, Meiktila and Pegu – though there was always the chance that we would encounter stray Japanese soldiers. On one occasion there were six of us in a large, canvas-covered lorry, which pulled into a small clearing for the night. Although we all wanted to sleep in the back, it seemed a bit crowded to me, so I said I would sleep in the driver's cab. During the night something slithered in through the open window and I leapt out in alarm, waking every one up because I was convinced that a huge snake had got into the cab. In the morning, we gingerly opened the door, only to find that my 'snake' was just a branch that had fallen from an overhanging tree. I was with 181 Signals Wing (Air Radar), SEAAF, when the war in Europe ended but it meant nothing much to us, except we realised that thousands of families all over the United Kingdom would no longer spend sleepless nights wondering about their loved ones. Our only celebration was a victory parade through Rangoon on 15 June 1945.

'We eventually arrived in Rangoon in May 1945 and, when the prisoners of war had been released and repatriated, we had a few weeks of relaxation before setting off on the next stage of our journey. North of Rangoon is Lake Victoria, now Inya Lake, created by the British towards the end of the nineteenth century in order to provide a water supply for the city. There were luxury holiday homes on the lakeshore and there was a flourishing yacht club. It was a typical British expat colony. When the Japanese captured Rangoon, they commandeered homes and boats, and by the time we arrived all the boats had been sunk by the retreating Japs. Nothing daunted, we set about salvaging and repairing the boats and formed our own flourishing yacht club. Our first boat was called *Eureka* and was followed by *Eureka II* and *Eureka III*. On a much later visit to Rangoon, I looked in on the war criminals tribunal. The president of the court was sitting on a big, gilt 'throne', with an assistant on either side and a huge Union flag behind him. On the left-hand side were the Japanese accused: sixteen of the most vicious-looking thugs I had ever seen. I did not wait for the verdicts, but one was sentenced to death by hanging, four to death by shooting, eight to life imprisonment, and three to twelve years' imprisonment.

'All too soon our happy days came to an end as we prepared for the invasion of Malaya. We sailed towards the end of July 1945 in a huge invasion fleet – collected from Burma, India and Ceylon – and progressed south. On 6 August we heard of a mighty explosion at Hiroshima but it didn't mean much to us. Three days later, another huge explosion shook Nagasaki and it was now obvious that we had a devastating new weapon. What really registered with us, though, was the news of the Japanese surrender. There was no point in our turning back and we continued to Singapore, which we reached in mid-September. There was much excitement and I made a fool of myself by diving for cover when the shooting started, not realising it was fireworks to celebrate the Chinese New Year! Most of us imagined that this was the end of the war for us – but it was not to be. The Dutch East Indies (now Indonesia) had been promised a degree of self-government by the Japanese after they had won the war, and the native Indonesians were not going to be put off by a little detail like Japan not winning the war after all. There was a bloody insurrection and British forces were sent to help the Dutch put it down.

'My first posting was to Jakarta, where I had two of my more bizarre wartime experiences. One was the free issue of money: as part of the rejection of Dutch sovereignty, the Indonesians refused to use the Dutch currency, which was being reintroduced. Since we had captured the Japanese printing presses, it was an easy matter for us to churn out millions of notes and flood the market with them, thus destroying their value. On parade one day, we were told that we would each be receiving a free issue of money. There was only one condition: we must spend it. The plan worked like a dream, and in no time at all the Dutch had resumed control. The second peculiarity was the rearming of some of the Japanese Surrendered Personnel. When the situation looked like getting out of hand, the JSP were persuaded that it was the wish of their emperor that they should assist the British forces. This they accepted without hesitation. A small group was temporarily issued with rifles and small arms and assisted our troops and matters were brought under control again. I had several long conversations with Harry, our interpreter, and found him to be (almost) a normal family man, happy to show me photos of his wife and family back home. After Jakarta, I moved to Medan in Sumatra. The 'powers-that-be' assumed that the Dutch women who had been prisoners of the Japs would be pleased to see British servicemen – so we were all issued with condoms!

'It was in Sumatra that I endured two of the most terrifying experiences of the whole war. On one occasion a group of us was travelling in the back of one of our covered lorries when we came to a level crossing with closed gates. Since no trains were running, it did not occur to the driver to question why the gates might be closed. He soon found out when we came under fire from the signal box. We all scrambled out of the back and took shelter as best we could, behind or beneath the lorry, until the army arrived and took control. Sadly, our driver was killed, having survived the war. The other incident was even more remarkable. A young flying officer was driving three of us in a small car to a radio outpost. As we passed though the market square of a small village, we were stopped by a Scottish soldier, who was evidently lost, miles away from his barracks. He demanded a lift back into town. Our officer said he was sorry but we couldn't help as we were on a duty call, whereupon the soldier cocked his Sten gun and said: "You're not leaving without me." We made to drive off and I am absolutely certain he would have fired if we had. Just at that moment an army truck pulled into the square and excited voices called: "Over here, Jock." He ran off to join his comrades. We assumed he had been up to no good with one of the native women.

'Since the Japanese had destroyed what was there before, my task in Medan was to install navigation equipment at the airstrip so that former prisoners – Dutch women and children – could safely be evacuated by air. Small planes were used to ferry about twenty-four of them at a time to Singapore, where they were transferred either to larger planes or to troopships for the journey home. There was a most rewarding incident when a pilot came into the mess one evening and yelled, "Where's the Radar King?" Assuming that I had made some terrible mistake, I rose nervously to my feet. He came over – to punch me on the nose, I assumed – and his hand came out, only to shake mine. "Very pleased to know you," he said, "I have to thank you for saving my life and, of course, the lives of the whole crew and passengers of the aircraft." It transpired that, having run into terrible weather soon after take-off, he decided to turn back. With visibility down to nil, he would never have found Medan again without the help of our navigation equipment. At this time my section of 181 Wing was the only one of its kind in SEAC and the three of us were reputed to know more about the equipment than any other mechanics in the area. As a result we tended to be kept in reserve for the sticky jobs no-one else could (or would) tackle. Hence most of my work was visiting

3034775 LAC B.E. Foster in Kuala Lumpur, 1946.

aerodromes where some snag had arisen, before putting it right and moving on to the next problem.

'The job complete in Medan, I left for Air Headquarters in Kuala Lumpur early in 1946 and spent the next eighteen months travelling between there, Singapore and Rangoon. Best of all, I had 'mid-tour leave' in August 1946 and was lucky enough to come back to England for four weeks. Worst of all, though, I had to return to Burma. We returned to England in RMS *Samaria* and there was a crew revue, for which I still have the programme. In a letter home I wrote that the best act was 'No. 11 – two boys on two guitars – Jock Hamilton and Bill Mays … Bill Mays was a Merchant Navy chap who could almost 'make the thing talk' he was so good.' Naturally we were all anxious to get home and be demobbed, and I recall that the weather got colder and colder as we neared home and made our way, in my case, to Brize Norton in Oxfordshire. I spent several months there getting used, first of all, to English weather and, secondly, to the discipline expected of peace-time RAF personnel. That was almost the hardest part of the war! Eventually my turn came and I was transferred to RAF Fairford prior to de-mobilisation, kitted out in civilian clothes, given a rail pass and off I went.'

After he had qualified as a chartered accountant, Brian founded his own firm, Brian Foster & Company, based at Wallingford in Oxfordshire. He also served as chairman of Cholsey Parish Council. On 28 September 1957 at the English Martyrs' Church in Reading, he married Carol, daughter of Major Edward John (Teddie) Green DSO, of 5 Monksway, Reading, who was killed at Anzio on 4 February 1944 while serving with the 10th Battalion, Royal Berkshire Regiment, and his wife Dorothy Alfreda, daughter of William Thomas Knight. Brian and Carol have five children: Cathy, Clare, Simon, Benedict and Rosey. 'It pleases me that they are all doing charitable works,' Brian said.

Brian Foster.

315629 Captain Stuart Guild, Royal Artillery

Stuart Alexander Guild, who was born on 25 January 1924, elder son of William J. Guild, WS, of 36 Belmont Gardens, Edinburgh, senior partner of Guild and Guild, WS, and his wife Peggy (née Stuart), was educated at the Edinburgh Academy 1930–39 and then at George Watson's College 1939–42. As a corporal in the Junior Training Corps, he became a member of the Home Guard on his eighteenth birthday and volunteered for the Army on 2 June 1942, enlisting at the Music Hall in George Street on 1 October 1942 and being called up to Bonhill Barracks, Glasgow, for kitting, before taking a six-month engineering course at Queen's University, Belfast. After basic training at the Primary Training Wing at Formby in Lancashire, he then attended pre-OCTU at Wrotham in Kent, where he caught impetigo, before being sent to 123 (RA) OCTU at Catterick. Commissioned into the Royal Artillery on 29 April 1944, slightly later than his peers – because of his earlier illness – he therefore took no part in the Normandy landings.

Instead, after a brief stint with 52 Driver Training Regiment at Whitby, he boarded the former P&O liner SS *Strathnaver* at Gourock: 'There were bunks five-high in the first-class lounge; it wasn't so good for those on the top bunk. There must have been 3,000 of us on board but there were 221 VAD nurses, who were great fun.' Having disembarked at Bombay, Second Lieutenant S.A. Guild was taken to the transit camp in Deolali before being posted as Troop Leader of 'E' (Enterprise) Troop, 37/47 Battery, 27th Field Regiment, Royal Artillery, then based at Maungdaw in the Arakan, on the west coast of Burma. He explained: 'To me it was the most exciting, if one can call it that, time of my life. It was a unique experiment in artillery movement and action suitable to the

Gunner S.A. Guild, Royal Artillery, 1942.

area.' Almost unbelievably, bearing in mind where he was going, he had had scarcely received any jungle training: just a single lecture at Deolali. Fortunately, he kept a personal diary – fleshed out from the Regimental War Diary – entitled *Going Waterborne from Airborne*.

After an 'early Christmas', 'E' Battery drove to Chittagong, where 'we were told that we were to put our guns onto a Z Lighter and fire from it in the various inland *chaungs* to support landings and shore operations. No-one knew what a Z Lighter was. On 7 January 1945, I wrote home with a drawing of myself by Mac [Captain K.W. Macgregor], my troop commander: 'You may not hear from me for a short time but don't worry." Three days later, the soldiers 'went down to the docks where we saw a Z Lighter for the first time. It is a harbour lighter designed for loading and unloading larger ships, transferring cargo to and from the jetty or a loading ramp. It is flatbottomed with a draught of 3–4 feet, with a flat deck about 150 feet long with crew's quarters at the stern below and behind the bridge. Four standard gun platforms were welded onto the deck, the four guns were manhandled aboard and locked onto their platforms while the battery commander's jeep tucked into a corner at the stern of the deck on the starboard side. Ammunition was stacked along the sides along with the men's kit. The craft was commanded by

A party of second lieutenants, Deolali, 1944.

Lieutenant King RNVR. His crew were civilians: Chittagonian Inland Water Transport employees, namely, two serangs, two engineers and three or four others.'

Before embarking on 11 January, Stuart 'went down to the club that evening and swopped my gin tickets for rum ones. I did not fancy gin in those days! Drink was rationed by means of tickets. Each officer got a booklet, which I think lasted a month.' After the occupation of Akyab Island, the Japanese retreated down the coast road, to which the only sea access was through the maze of *chaungs*, for which flat-bottomed boats were essential. In typical style, Lighter *Z-5* was immediately renamed HMS *Enterprise*! Not designed as a sea-going vessel, it was fortunate that 'the Bay of Bengal was calm, the sun was shining and the sky was blue'. Enterprise Troop first saw action on 15 January, when 'we registered dug-in positions at Point 262 later taken, after stiff opposition, by the 3/2 Gurkhas'. There were other tasks though: 'Soon we all got to work filling sandbags, which were to be a protection along the sides against the gunwale.' And a spot of welcome relaxation: 'After the sandbags were filled everyone, less one man per gun and a signaller and ack [artillery assistant], went for a swim.'

The following day, there was excitement of a different variety: 'We expended eighty rounds of gunfire at two targets of dug-in positions, both observed by the Air OP. A newsreel cameraman came aboard and took several shots of the guns firing. I stood beside him as he rested his heavy camera on the rail. In the early morning, the Supremo, Lord Louis Mountbatten, arrived, jumped onto his jeep bonnet and clambered over the rail asking me where our OC was. I said that he had gone forward to the gangplank to meet him. He addressed the men and said that it was an historic occasion and wished us good hunting.'

On 17 January, 'after a swim a rather sudden order came that we were to go ashore. This was not very popular as we were beginning to enjoy the seagoing life'; however, 'the Z Lighter was to be used to bring in some of 8th Field Regiment RA.' The trip from Myebon to Akyab and back did bring some benefits though: 'The mail I brought held a number of letters for me, including a birthday greetings cable, it being close to my birthday. I acknowledged, writing home and saying that I had been doing a lot of bathing lately and could swim on my back. The letter was 'written roasting in the engine room!' I also wrote that I 'occasionally got

Ration D', which is concentrated chocolate. We are living on composite rations and bully, bully, bully & biscuits. Cigarettes and tobacco are in short supply. The lime juice has gone and the rum going. Water is not too plentiful. The cook was quite imaginative with different concoctions of bully beef, mixed with hard tack biscuit. etc.'

On returning to Myebon, there was frantic activity before a convoy set sail on 22 January for a beach landing – and the assault on Kangaw: 'The strenuous exercise must have created the need for a bowel movement, so I went to the stern and sat on the officers' thunderbox, contemplating the following boats and thinking "What a fine way to go to war?" We soon arrived at the beachhead, which must have been the smallest in the world.' It transpired that 'the beachhead was under constant artillery bombardment, not from a number of guns but a few with irritating effect, but quite accurate. It took the commandos two days of desperate hand-to-hand fighting to seize 'Brighton', the feature which dominated the beachhead. The next day I recall sitting on the sloping deck reading a "Dear John" letter from Edith breaking off our engagement, saying that she was a career girl, when a shell fell in the *chaung* setting up a splash about 30 yards away.' There were other threats: 'We had already lost an OP officer to a treeburst in November, so we were very conscious of that. A treeburst is when the shell hits a part of the tree and goes off in the air showering splinters all around. One heard the thump as the shell left the gun then the whoosh and explosion as it arrived. One flattened oneself on hearing the thump since the time of flight was short.'

Meanwhile, the 25-pounders had been manhandled off HMS *Enterprise*: '25 January 1945 – my 21st birthday. What a way to spend it, on a gun position in the middle of a mangrove swamp and paddy field under Japanese shellfire. Yesterday's shelling was at the beachhead, today it was at our gun position. One shell landed about ten yards from the CP. A signaller was slightly wounded and a 22-set put out of action. I was probably about five yards further away from the CP so nothing came my way. By landing in the soft earth, they did not do too much damage. I was given orders to relieve a Medium OP at the north end of Brighton and to support the commandos. We wore cap comforters to be in the same dress as the commandos. We did not take our steel helmets, not thinking that we would be supporting anyone else. I was armed with a Thompson sub-machine gun with 200 rounds of .45 ammunition in ten magazines, which were in my front left pouch; in my right pouch were bags of sugar and tea. My binoculars were inside my blouse and my map folded in my front trouser pocket in the small map-case, which my father had used in WW1. The troop officer was a tall thin blond officer, Lieutenant G.A. Knowland of the Norfolk Regiment.'

Three days later, Stuart 'handed over the OP to Mac and said farewell to him and Knowland, little knowing that it would be the last time I would see either of them'. From an OP on a feature called Milford, 'E' Troop supported 8 Hyderabad in their assault on 'Pinner', which lay 500 yards to their front: 'The advance was along the ridge through the jungle and could be seen progressing until it came to a small hillock at the north end, from which they were unable to dislodge the Japs, and began to retire.' The gunners also faced problems: 'Although we were very careful to conceal ourselves on Milford, the Japs must have realised that the guns were controlled from there and began shelling us from the flank with a 75mm.' The next morning, Stuart, as an FOO, 'attended an orders group given by the Indian colonel of the 2/2 Punjab for the assault on Melrose, another key feature'. Accompanying the company commander forward, he was hit in the back of the neck by a shell splinter. Though not seriously wounded, he was covered in blood and evacuated – via the regimental aid post, canoe, lighter and hospital ship – to Chittagong. Bearing in mind that it was a two-day return journey, it is impressive that he was out of the line for less than a week.

In his absence, the savage fighting continued unabated. In his diary Stuart later noted that '31 January was a sad day for the troop. At 0620hrs the Japs attacked the north end of Brighton and by 1300hrs Mac's OP was reported overrun. "Enterprise" [the troop] was shelling its location. Mac was wounded early on but could not be evacuated due to small-arms fire and was killed, as was Bombardier Sleet. His signaller was wounded and survived, because he lay under the bodies of Mac and Sleet. Lieutenant Knowland of the Commando Troop firing a 2" mortar from the hip also died and was awarded a posthumous VC. The attack was severe but was beaten off. The Japs left behind 347 dead.' The ferocity of the fighting can be gauged by an extract from Knowland's VC citation: 'Such was the inspiration of his magnificent heroism, that, although fourteen out of twenty-four of his platoon became casualties at an early stage, and six of his positions were overrun by the enemy, his men held on through twelve hours of continuous and fierce fighting until reinforcements arrived.'

Lord Mountbatten later described Kangaw as 'the bloodiest battle of the Arakan'.

At this juncture, with the Japanese trying to retreat further east, towards the Thai border, the 14th Army forged ahead and, in Stuart's words, 'we nipped in in front of them, behind their front line'. The outflanking moves included the landings at Ruywa, which was, in reality, just 'a bunch of empty huts, because the villagers had all fled'. From his point of view, Operation Dracula, the airborne and amphibious landings at largely-evacuated Rangoon on 2/3 May 1945, was 'a bit of a disaster'. At the start of a six-hour approach – the longest ever – the LCA hit problems: 'First one engine went, and we went round in odd circles; and then the other engine conked out – and we all transferred to an LCI and eventually walked down the ramp, at the wrong beachhead! Actually, to call it a beach was a misnomer: it was just a muddy bank. The leading companies carried huge, orange golf umbrellas to prevent them being strafed by friendly aircraft, but I never managed to catch up with them. It then took some time to arrange a lift to Rangoon for my party and, on the final run-in to Rangoon docks, the front ramp of the American-manned LCT we were travelling in fell down and water poured in to a depth of 3–4 feet, soaking our 18-set. By the time we walked a few hundred metres inland, it was dusk and I found an empty villa, with a folly with a 360-degree view in the garden. Rather than stay in the house, where we might be jumped by the Japs, we slept there. I said to my bombardier: "Shove the 18-set on the range and give it a bake." It worked fine after that. The following day, we came under heavy small-arms fire and Gunner Wilson-Williams was killed. By the second day, the guns still weren't ashore: it was a most unfortunate assault landing.'

Five days later, on VE-Day, 'the brigadier and his deputy came to a

Lieutenant Stuart Guild, Calcutta, July 1945.

Press visit to Saigon Jail, 1946.

dinner of roast goose and plum pudding. After dinner we had iced rum. We got the ice daily from an Anglo-Indian, whom we knew. I did not stay up to hear the King's Speech as it was at 1.30 am. However, some did and with some trepidation went out onto the balcony and fired a couple of Verey lights over blacked-out Rangoon. After waiting a short time, nothing happened, so they went to bed. That was the total celebration we had. We thought that although we had a long way to go down Malaya to Java etc, with the help of extra troops and some up-to-date equipment, it would still be about a year before the Japs were conquered. Fortunately it was not, and I and many others blessed the atomic bomb, but for which I reckoned I and others might not have survived many more combined assaults. On the last one,

Poster for Poppy Scotland.

my fourth, my signaller was killed, while we were under heavy small-arms fire.'

After the Japanese surrender, Stuart was informed that he was 'going up-country to do bandit work but I was not very keen on that'. Instead he transferred to 114 (Sussex) Field Regiment and was jail quartermaster in Saigon for almost six months, guarding Japanese Surrendered Personnel – as they were called – and also a number of war criminals. Later, as Garrison Regiment in Kuala Lumpur they were also given the unappealing task of guarding, at Kluang, 255 men of 13th (Lancashire) Parachute Battalion accused of mutiny at Muar in Malaya, having refused to obey the CO's orders. All the convictions were later quashed.

Captain Stuart Guild was demobilised on 29 March 1947, studied law at Edinburgh University while serving an apprenticeship with Guild and Guild, and then stayed with the firm for the rest of his working life. After the war, he remained in the TA, became second-in-command of 278 (Lowland) Field Regiment (TA), was promoted to lieutenant colonel, commanded Army Cadet Force Lothians Battalion and received the Territorial Decoration and bar. He joined the Edinburgh branch of the Burma Star Association in 1980 (membership number G/698/80). Although he had known Fiona MacCulloch, daughter of the Indian government's Chief Chemist, since he was seven, they didn't marry until he felt that he could support her, which was five years after the war had ended. Stuart and Fiona had a son and two daughters and she died in 2012.

353446 Major Patrick Hamilton, 18th Royal Garhwal Rifles

by Rita Chakrabarti

My father-in-law, Patrick John Rogers Hamilton, didn't speak much about his time in the army during the Second World War, and when he did, his stories were never about battle. Rather, they were anecdotes, snippets of the life he'd led – often amusing, and often told against himself, which was typical of the wry and modest man that he was. So, when I was asked to make a short film for BBC News about his role in the Burma Campaign, it was difficult to know quite where to start. As a family, we had no overarching narrative. I spent hours with his sons, Paul and Mark, and Mark's wife Susan, in long online exchanges (as we were confined to our homes due to an epidemic), swapping and corroborating stories, and digging out old letters and photographs and mementos. Meanwhile, the three intrepid BBC producers I was working with – Catherine Ellis, Olivia Sopel and Felicity Baker – mapped our family memories onto historical events, and gradually our shadowy understanding of Patrick's past life took shape and burst into colour.

Patrick was born in Scotland, in Alexandria in the Vale of Leven. He was a 23-year-old graduate when the Second World War started. He enlisted in the Gordon Highlanders in Aberdeen, based at the Bridge of Don barracks. While Europe was under siege from Germany, Britain was also looking anxiously at its territories in the east, as Singapore and Burma fell to the Japanese. The great fear was that India was now vulnerable. Patrick was, we were told, thought of as officer material and, after a brief stint with the London Scottish, he was posted to the Indian Army. A keen mountaineer, he nursed a strong hope that he might one day have the chance to trek in the Himalayas. With this in mind, he chose his Indian regiment carefully, calculating that there would be stiff competition to get into the Gurkhas, and opting instead for the Royal Garhwal Rifles, which he joined in 1942. Initially he was stationed at the regimental depôt at Lansdowne, a hill station 150 miles north-east of Delhi, and we have a photograph of him with his fellow officers, seated proudly together in uniform outside the barracks.

It was the start of a lifelong enthusiasm for, and loyalty to, India and also to his regiment. It was here that he prepared for the ensuing campaign in Burma, starting with jungle warfare training. During several weeks' leave in 1943, his gamble paid off, and he went on a climbing expedition in the Garhwal Himalaya, close to the mighty peaks of Nanda Gunti and Trisul. One chilling story I remember him telling was of stumbling across a macabre frozen graveyard, containing a large number of human corpses in various stages of decomposition: travellers who had somehow met their deaths on the mountainside. They were later identified as being part of the Rupkund massacre (which took place around AD 850), but Patrick did not know this at the time. In his curiosity, he reached out to touch one of the faces. Its jaw came off with a crack. The guides he was with took one look and fled in terror and Patrick found himself, as he later recollected, fleeing at speed in their wake.

Patrick served in Burma with the 1st/18th Royal Garhwal Rifles, part of 71st (Indian) Infantry Brigade, from 1943 to 1945. Paul and Mark have no memory of him ever mentioning the horrors he must have lived through there, but we have letters written by him and by his wife-to-be, Jenny, that hint at the huge challenges. In one letter, she wrote to him: 'My darling Patrick, I have been feeling for you tonight, and I am full of sympathy for you. They are putting more and more in the papers about this 14th Army campaign, and I feel nothing can be too good to make up for such a hell.' In turn, Patrick wrote to her about landing at Ramree Island at the start of 1945, as part of the offensive on the southern front of the Burma Campaign. He also wrote about being in Rangoon, we assume as part of Operation Dracula, which led to its recapture. There are few details though – no doubt he wanted to spare her the worst.

After our BBC film was broadcast, we as a family had a huge response, from friends and strangers who

Major P.J.R. Hamilton, 18th Royal Garhwal Rifles.

themselves had fathers and grandfathers who had fought in Burma. The daughter of his CO got in touch with a story which Patrick himself had related to her. In the jungle, Patrick was summoned by his CO, who asked:

"What day is it, Patrick?"
"Thursday, Sir."
"No, what's the date?"
"24th December, Sir."
"So, what is it tomorrow?"
"Christmas Day …?"
"On Christmas Day, we eat turkey. Find me a turkey, Patrick."

So, to his credit, Patrick went out into the jungle and came back with something resembling a turkey, or even two. And they all ate turkey for Christmas!

After the surrender of Japan, it was several months before Patrick returned home. Instead he was sent to help police Sumatra, and worked side-by-side with the defeated Japanese forces to keep the peace. Patrick must have been a fair and considerate officer, because the family is in possession of several gifts given to him by Japanese counterparts. One of great sentimental value is a gold ring, engraved with PJRH (his initials), which he wore as a wedding ring when he had finally arrived home and was married to Jenny. On 22 August 1946, 353446 Major (actg.) P.J.R. Hamilton was mentioned in despatches 'in recognition of gallant and distinguished services in the Far East'.

When he returned to Scotland, Patrick finished his training as a church minister. He worked first in the West Kirk, in the little village of East Kilbride – soon to become a new town – outside Glasgow. In 1958 he joined a new church, the South Parish Church, where he remained until he retired. He was a committed minister, and a fond husband and father. He never forgot his army days, and served as chaplain to the Burma Star Association in Glasgow (membership number H/2258/73). He died on 7 August 2005 and we remember him as a gentle and witty man, who remained reticent about his military life, in which he must have endured such privations and fought with such valour.

GC 63688 Private Joseph Hammond, Gold Coast Regiment

Joseph Ashiteye Hammond was born on 10 May 1925 in Osu-Accra, in what was then the Gold Coast, one of five children of Peter Abraham Hammond, an accountant who worked for the United Africa Company, universally known as UAC. After leaving Osu Presbyterian School, he joined the Army as a driver mechanic on 31 July 1943: 'I was at school when the war broke out. We loved the British very much. Nobody thought we were like slaves and, during the colonial days, life was very good. We had our livings, there was no problem, and we were all happy. I don't want to be a hypocrite because I agree that they did a lot wrong. No human being is perfect and there are mistakes here and there. Mistakes are inevitable and you cannot avoid them. I decided that, after my education was over, I would join the army. I had read a lot about the army and the commanders who were serving in West Africa. General George Giffard was the commander-in-chief of all the West African troops and I personally knew Brigadier Collen Richards, who commanded 2nd (West African) Infantry Brigade. Three of our battalions were in this brigade, which fought in East Africa against the Italians: the 1st, 2nd and 3rd Battalions, Gold Coast Regiment.

'We passed through rigorous training – it was really thorough. I was trained as a mechanic and passed my training with flying colours. I was very determined and worked hard to be successful. After finishing my training at the college headquarters in Ghana, I was posted to a workshop in the western part of the country. I was fortunate to be selected as a driver for the British officers so I learned a lot about the army during those early days. During a tour of the mining areas, there were a couple of technical hitches with my vehicle, which I managed to fix, which pleased my officers. We sailed for Ceylon in May 1944 and later went on to India: my first impression was that it was an extremely hot place. Our initial war training took place five miles from Poona and I was posted to the 3rd Battalion, Gold Coast Regiment, 2nd (West African) Infantry Brigade, part of 82nd (West African) Division. As a mechanic, my principal responsibility was the repair of American jeeps. Of course, as well as specialist training, we had also received basic training in the rudiments of war, so when there were no accessible roads, we became infantrymen.

'There were two West African divisions: the 81st Division and the 82nd Division. The 81st Division completed their training first and arrived in India in August 1943, a year earlier than my division. We took over from the 81st Division and fought ferociously to capture Buthidaung. There was a signal regiment with us and they gathered information on the positions of the Japanese, which would then be passed down from the brigade commander to our battalion commander. I was fearless because I was so young: you don't fear then like you do when you grow up. When you are young, the blood is very hot and you don't care. We fought the Japanese on the banks of the Irrawaddy, which flows all the way to the capital, Rangoon. The Japanese had crossed the river but we pressed them so hard that they started going south – and we followed them. The fighting became so intense when we caught up with them that we often called for support from the divisional artillery, which bombarded the objectives so heavily that the ground shook. Then the RAF would take their turn at bombing the Japanese positions, while we remained in our trenches. It was important to lie low because Japanese snipers were often positioned up trees. If we didn't shoot them first, then they might shoot us.

'We had three days of heavy fighting and it was really hard to urinate when lying low in a trench. Eventually I had to jump out, but you had to think about safety all the time. We were determined to fight and defend the British Empire and the Gold Coast. I am very proud that I took part. We all thought: "If we're not going to defend the British Empire, then who is going to defend it? We have to defend it." If the enemy defeated us, then we would become slaves of the Japanese. We would all rather have died than become slaves of the Japanese – so I feel very proud. We had had excellent training from the British, our spirits were high and we wanted to prove that our troops were better than the Japanese. Sometimes, though, we were so short of food that we had to rely on biscuits and corned beef. For three or four days we had no food at all until a plane dropped food for us by parachute, which worked well. We lost six of our soldiers by the river at Maubin [forty miles west of Rangoon] but war was war. The Japanese mentality was that, when you die in war, you return to Almighty God. If they were captured, then they had disgraced their

Soldiers of the Gold Coast Regiment disembarking at Takoradi after returning home.

family, but when they die in action, they have honoured their family and everyone would respect their family. It was a terrible and hugely different mentality: they were difficult to capture because they preferred to die. It was a case of 'kill or be killed'.

'Our relationship with our officers was strong, and wartime comradeship between the nations excellent: we didn't know 'black' or 'white'. You cannot have enmity with your brother. Anyone who says that there was discrimination is telling lies. We continued fighting until we reached a town called Kindaungyyi, where I realised that my left eye was protruding, so I was flown, with two comrades, from the battlefield to Poona in India. When we arrived there, we were transferred to a huge hospital: there were sick beds as far as the eye could see, full of white, Indian and African soldiers. I was treated by a medical officer called Lieutenant Crockett, who gave me a cup of tea and told me that contaminated blood might have got into my eye. I was going to be sent back to the front line but the war fortunately came to an end.

'In December 1945 we returned home and were the first group to arrive back in the country, in our jungle green battledress. The governor of the Gold Coast, Sir Alan Burns, came and congratulated us. He shook our hands, and when he came to me I looked so young that he first patted my head! I then shook hands with him and I was so happy and proud that the governor was shaking hands with me. When I was discharged from the army in January 1946 [at Arakan Barracks, Takoradi], we all prepared to go into civilian life; however, it was not easy because there were no jobs. They failed with their promise of war pensions so we decided to plead with the governor and presented him with a petition signed by people from across the whole country. Two hundred and ten unarmed veterans [from the Gold Coast Regiment] were marching quietly to Christiansborg Castle to present our petition to the governor [Sir Gerald Creasy]. Ten of us had been selected to present the petition: Sergeant Adjetey was our leader and I was seven feet behind him, in the second line.

'We spoke and spoke but Superintendent Imray wouldn't let us through and he was very unreasonable. Eventually we were forced to scale down from ten people to five but Imray still didn't want us to go. He ordered one of his sergeants to shoot but the man didn't want to do it. He was highly annoyed and grabbed the gun off the sergeant. He first shot Sergeant Adjetey and then two others. Why? We were not armed. All this was going on before my eyes and now I'm the only one left to tell the story of what happened on 28 February 1948. For two weeks, European stores and property were looted, and when the rioting subsided King George VI dispatched colonial officials to set up a commission to see why there had been killings. They realised that Ghana needed a constitution, so we veterans paved the way for Ghana's independence. If the riots hadn't

GC 63688 Private J.A. Hammond, late 3rd Battalion, Gold Coast Regiment.

happened, independence might have been delayed. I honestly feel very proud, but I also feel for my colleagues who died, such as Sergeant Nii Adjetey, Corporal Patrick Attipoe and Private Odartey Lamptey.'

Dining at The Cavalry and Guards Club on 2 November 2021, I found myself seated next to John Norton, who told me that he had served with the Gold Coast Regiment in 1947–48. I naturally told John that I had met Joseph Hammond and he put his own story on paper the following day: 'Just to give you a bit more detail of my involvement, I had volunteered to be seconded from the Ox and Bucks to the 2nd Battalion, Gold Coast Regiment and arrived there in the late summer of 1947. By February 1948, at the age of just twenty, I was second-in-command of a company – though still only a second lieutenant – and with the additional responsibility of being the English officer of the battalion. We had been warned about the march and I was standing by in our lines with, I think, forty men, including experienced NCOs. At some point, I was alerted that there had been trouble and immediately set off at speed for the star of five roads, as I remember, on the approach to the castle. We were confronted with an ugly scene. I suppose the police were still there but clearly something more needed to be done to calm things down and prevent matters from becoming even more ugly. I had been taught 'Aid to the Civil Power' at OCTU including, amazingly, that a hollow square could be the appropriate formation to deal with a riot or similar.

'Summing up the location, combined with the situation, I decided that I should put my training, never so far as I can remember actually practised, into play. I had sufficient men for a small but adequate square – so we formed it. I think I had a loudhailer but can't now remember about a bugler or stretcher bearers but hopefully we had some of the latter. I placed snipers in front and drew a firm line on the ground, announcing there would be action if that line was crossed. I put my men "on guard", with bayonets fixed (actually, they were good old-fashioned swords so that "up 'em they would not like it"). Stones were thrown, but the threat – which I had no intention of carrying out unless things really got out of hand, at which point I would have taken one of my men's rifles (I had been given no ammunition for the Webley in the holster on my belt) and fired a warning shot, in the air, without wounding anyone – worked. Nothing terrible happened and the veterans eventually withdrew. When members of the 2nd Battalion under my command intervened, both the veterans and the military confronting them were from the same RWAFF and I believe that the realisation of that may have helped to produce a calmer atmosphere. I was in Accra all night dealing with the looting and then, in the morning at a roadblock, relieving some female looters in Mammy Wagons of cloth they had found and wrapped around themselves, a delicate operation! If Joseph is still alive, it would be fascinating to be in touch with him as another survivor. The 75th Anniversary is in 2023 and, if I get that far, I hope to offer myself in some way to be involved.'

In 1952, Joseph eventually found a job, as a stores assistant with Gold Coast Machinery Trading, a subsidiary of UAC. During the next three years, he was promoted to stores officer, before taking a job as store manager for the Ambassador Hotel in Accra, which had just been built with government funding in anticipation of Ghana's independence the following year. In 1958 he was appointed as the first transport manager for the Ghana National Construction Company, thus taking full advantage of his army training. Over the next thirteen years, he was involved in many of the country's largest construction projects, including El Wak stadium and the roadworks relating to the main army camp in Accra. Joseph has been married twice: firstly, to Bernice Awo Dormenyo

Joseph Hammond meeting HRH The Duke of Sussex, Field of Remembrance, 7 November 2019.

Joseph Hammond meeting HRH The Duchess of Sussex, Field of Remembrance, 7 November 2019.

Mensah from Anyaku in the Volta region, and then, after her death, to Elizabeth Ayorkor Sabah. There were five children of the first marriage and two of the second.

In 2020 he took inspiration from Captain Sir Tom Moore, a fellow Burma veteran: 'It was marvellous to see what Captain Tom did. I thought that if he could fundraise for people in the UK, then why couldn't I do it for the people of Africa? We planned and I started walking two miles a day to raise funds to help the front-line workers fighting against Covid-19. Everyone is frustrated because it is a deadly disease. Covid-19 is worse than the war – and I was there. At least in Burma we could see the enemy positions and attack them. I wouldn't wish war on anybody but Covid-19 is invisible, which makes the whole thing very difficult and you haven't got much to defend yourself against it. I believe it is more dangerous than war and I saw people dying in large numbers in Ghana, Britain and all round the world. I went to war against all this death so that there can be more money for a vaccine to solve this problem. I would like to see Covid-19 eradicated from the whole of Africa.' For seven consecutive days, Joseph Hammond embarked on a walk along the Osu Oxford Street, in the process raising the astonishing sum of £45,800.

The Royal Commonwealth Ex-Services League (RCEL) supports pre-Independence Commonwealth Veterans 'in their hour of greatest need', with the goal of providing sufficient funding for two nourishing meals a day. The programme is supported by the Foreign, Commonwealth and Development Office. In 2021, Joseph Hammond was receiving £1,020 a year, half in May and half in late October.

2010594 Corporal Peter Heppell, Royal Engineers

Peter Francis Heppell was born on 5 March 1920, elder son of Thomas Daniel Heppell of 4 Victoria Terrace, Finsbury Park, and his wife Nellie, daughter of James William Peters, commercial traveller. 925015 Sergeant Thomas Heppell went to France on 4 October 1915 and served with C Battery, 280th Brigade, Royal Field Artillery, supporting 56th (London) Division on the Western Front. On 1 May 1919 he was awarded the Territorial Force Efficiency Medal. The family later moved to Shepperton, on the River Thames in Surrey, and Peter attended Shepperton Grammar School. By this time, Thomas had become a director of the S.T. Garland advertising agency. Peter explained: 'When I left school, I started work at my father's firm in the studio. I was virtually the office boy, cleaning the place and filing the artwork. It is not a good thing working with your father: he was a director and I was the director's son.

'When war broke out, I attempted to enlist and was advised: "Don't bother to volunteer, lad, you're going to be called up anyway." I was twenty in March 1940, registered in April and was called up in May as a member of the 2nd Chemical Warfare Group, Royal Engineers, stationed at Figsbury Barracks, Winterbourne Gunner in Wiltshire, for basic training, then specialist training in chemical warfare on Exmoor in Devon, billeted in Lynmouth. Our equipment was as used in the First World War. The barrels were perfectly smooth steel tubes, weighing around 180lbs, and carrying them on the moor in winter was hard: our fingers frequently froze to the icy steel. For firing, the barrels were in steel shoes and then rested at an angle on a metal 'M' shape, the angle changed for aiming. Fitness was key: we used to have races on Lynmouth recreation ground, passing barrels and shoes backwards and forwards to one another.

'On returning from a weekend's leave, I found the gutters in Lynmouth's High Street running with bleach and a big clean-up operation under way. There had been a training shoot on the moor and, while the Company should have been issued with training bombs filled with water, they had been given live mustard gas bombs instead. In true Army tradition, the debris from the shoot had to be recovered, resulting in contamination of our transport. An infantry battalion, which had got into difficulties while training on the moor, had lost a Bren gun carrier over the cliffs into the sea, killing the crew. They requested assistance to get off the moor but unfortunately suffered some contamination from sitting in our transport, where small amounts of mustard gas remained. We were not very popular with the infantry! After some time, and with further training – building an army camp, Civil Defence duties, etc – the group was posted to the Far East, arriving in India in 1942. We sailed round the Cape and spent ten days in Durban because our ship needed to have some work done on it. I remember that when we went off on our training marches they used to shower us with oranges. Although we went out to India as a chemical warfare company, the mustard gas started leaking, so we dumped our cylinders in the Indian Ocean and were renamed 67 Field Company, Royal Engineers.

'On arrival in India, we became involved in the civil disturbances taking place at that time, which was not very pleasant. Our platoon was moved to a town close to Poona in central India and we were billeted in a bungalow situated opposite the local prison. Here we mounted a 24-hour ceremonial guard, much to the consternation of the locals, and during the evening patrol we moved on foot through the town with bayonets fixed (and 'one up the spout'), prepared for any trouble that might occur. We were accompanied by the local magistrate who, if the trouble became serious, could declare an 'act of war' and approve opening fire on the crowds – to kill them, not over their heads. The platoon that relieved us on these patrols moved through the town in their transport. The group was later posted to Cox's Bazar [now in Bangladesh] to uprate an RAF landing strip on the Bay of Bengal. It had an immense sandy beach where, when we had finished the day organising local labour working on the strip, we were able to cool off in the nearby sea.

'Two or three of us decided that we didn't want to end the war feeling that we had done nothing, so we volunteered for Special Duties. They told us that it was with the Chindits, which was a bit of a shock – and we suddenly found ourselves doing some pretty strenuous training. When we were at Lynmouth, it became a bit of a joke to find a large empty cardboard box to make our packs look much heavier than they were. As we were climbing Countisbury Hill one day, we were caught out by a kit inspection by the side of the road. When training with the Chindits, though, we used to look out for bricks, rocks and stones to put in our packs because we knew that we would have to carry big loads and just had to get used to it.

'At our base by the Ken River, close to Jhansi, we also did a lot of river crossing training. As part of our equipment, we had folding assault boats: they were flat-bottomed, with canvas sides which collapsed, making them easier to carry. They had 7hp or 30hp outboard motors and, as a Thames-side boy, I found myself in charge of a boat. If you timed things right, you could even get them to plane. We used to do boat drills: "Line ahead! Line abreast! Line astern!" We thoroughly enjoyed ourselves. We also had to get used to the life which we were going to have to lead though. We used to work in pairs, with a 'mucker'. My mucker was Ron Fletcher, who later worked at the Kodak factory in north London. One of us carried the blanket and the other carried the groundsheet and we bedded down together, which the authorities didn't really like. We divided tasks: one would prepare the ground and the cover while the other did the cooking. Although Ron was four years older than me, we spent five months living in one another's pockets. After the war, I once spoke to him on the phone, hoping to persuade him to come to a reunion at the Royal Albert Hall. He didn't come and for years I tried to track

Operation BROADWAY, Burma, 5/6 March 1944 by David Rowland.

him down but never managed to meet up with him. I'm afraid it's a bit late now.

'We flew into "Broadway" on 5 March 1944, my 24th birthday. Our section was divided between two gliders. Each glider was supposed to have a pilot and a co-pilot but we didn't have a co-pilot. Ron occupied the co-pilot's seat, with me in the seat behind him. There was a problem with the towline-releasing catch so he spent most of the flight holding the switch in position so that we weren't cast off. Although the landing surface was uneven, we had skids so it wasn't too bad. The next glider misjudged its approach and hit ours; all I could see was a row of rifles sticking out. Fortunately none of the men was hurt. Our second glider missed the runway and hit the trees. There were no seatbelts, and although two or three at the very back got out, the rest were all killed. Our section commander, Lieutenant Johnny Long, asked me to set fire to the glider. Although it wasn't an order, he said that it was the best we could do for them. I said that I would rather work on the airstrip. I have always regretted that but I have since been back to the cemetery in Rangoon to pay my respects.

'We had had a briefing before we went. My instructions were to organise parties of infantry to prepare the strip for the landing the next

Clearing the airstrip at "Broadway", 6 March 1944: Peter Heppell is on the left with his hands on his hips.

night. There's been a lot of talk about building an airstrip but it was nothing like that really. The ground was baked hard like concrete; the only problem was that teak logs had been laid out for seasoning, before being floated off down the Irrawaddy, and had left very deep furrows in the ground. Most of the gliders lost their undercarriage. We filled the furrows up with earth from round the edge. We had a small bulldozer with a grader attachment, which helped, of course. The following night I saw one of the most amazing things that I had ever seen. We had lit the central strip and there were continual flights of planes, coming in, unloading and taking off again. It was a pretty wide area but only the central strip was prepared for landing.

'I was in 82 Column and, as the leading column to fly in, we provided protection to "Broadway". We sent out lots of patrols and formed the outer defences. Initially, I had a Lee-Enfield .303. You get very attached to your personal arms: it was part of me and I didn't want to part with it. When we got into the jungle, though, someone said: "You don't need that – it's much too heavy." I was issued with an American semi-automatic carbine and they just flung my .303 away. The carbine was a lot lighter though, and it was semi-automatic. When "Broadway" was evacuated, we left with them, and in the hills bumped into a Jap patrol. Half-a-dozen of us became separated and we went on towards Mogaung but finished up at "Blackpool". We were extraneous and didn't really belong to anyone.

'On 23 May, we were dug in on top of a ridge, looking down on the airstrip, when the Japanese attacked across it. We were under heavy mortar fire and, suddenly, there was an almighty explosion and I was thrown back on the bank, with a piece of shrapnel in my left thigh. It's still there. It was a relief that the fragments had missed the three primed grenades in my pocket. I put a field dressing on my leg and hobbled towards the FAP. One of my big fears was getting wounded in the feet or the legs. Looking round, inside the FAP, I realised that my problem was superficial because some people were in a really shocking state. I saw a Dakota make a low pass, dropping supplies, with a chap at the aircraft door. I was gripped by the thought that this wasn't going right. I said to myself: "If this is going bad, I want to be with my mates."

'After the evacuation of "Blackpool", I don't know whether it was the cold or the aftershock, but I was shivering all over. We had very little to eat but made a fire for tea. Some men cut banana leaves and we huddled

Sunderland flying-boat on Indawgyi Lake.

together in the mud under the leaves. They put me in the centre, to try to stop that awful attack of trembling. We took over a village by the edge of Indawgyi Lake. I was in charge of a Burmese house full of sick and wounded, who could not get up and would eventually die there. Evacuation was by Sunderland flying-boats codenamed "Gert" and "Daisy", after a pair of female comedians on the radio [the Walters sisters]. The officer-in-charge and the MO used to come round the various houses to watch us as we walked around. Those with the biggest limp or the largest bandage went on the evacuation list. Naturally there was a temptation to "improve your chances". There were an awful lot of heavily bandaged legs around and I can't say I blame them because morale was very low. I didn't approve because many of those who couldn't get up remained there. I did a lot of boat work, ferrying supplies and people around and keeping things moving. Although my wound wasn't too bad, it was too painful for a long march, which is why I was evacuated. Eventually I boarded a local boat for Mogaung and flew out by Dakota from an American airbase at Shadazup. I couldn't talk about it for a long time. I felt it was of no interest. I was in Burma for five months and saw only one road – and I crossed that on my stomach. It is amazing how quickly one adapts to living rough.

'After a week in hospital, I rejoined the sappers at Faisalabad in northern India. My old unit was in training for a seaborne assault on Rangoon so I finished up by going back to Burma again. We landed at Rangoon docks but the Japs had already evacuated the city and moved east so we missed out on any action. Out of sympathy, I was appointed orderly corporal, which was the worst thing they could have done because I hated office work! I spent my time organising local transport and collecting and distributing rations. We took over a Burmese house on the outskirts of Rangoon and we were quite comfortable, but office work wasn't for me, I'm afraid. Up until then I had always swopped my cigarette ration for chocolate bars; regretfully, on duty on my own in the office one weekend, I started smoking. We got involved with reconstruction work at the University and also at the National City Theatre, where Vera Lynn appeared once, although I neither met nor even saw her. We also did a lot of aid work and I was promoted to the rank of lance sergeant.

2010594 Corporal P.F. Heppell, India, 1944.

'After a couple of months in Rangoon, we sailed to Madras and then travelled on to Bangalore, where the regiment settled back into a normal training routine. When we got to Bangalore we had exceeded our complement of junior NCOs so Ron and I decided voluntarily to drop a rank to avoid being separated: he went to lance sergeant and I became a corporal again. We spent what seemed like a very long time – probably six months – awaiting repatriation and demob. Eventually, along with a lot of other sappers, including Ron, I boarded a Union Castle liner, the *Capetown Castle*, for the trip home through the Mediterranean. That was a bit worrying because we were sailing through a former battle zone and there were German and Italian mines and other armaments lying around on our route, but we were lucky and got through alright. After disembarking at Southampton, I went on a month's leave at my parents' new bungalow in Chertsey on the banks of the Thames, prior to demob.' Throughout the war, Peter wore a ring, 'from a gold watch inherited from my maternal grandfather and made into a signet ring'.

On 9 July 1949 at Christ Church, Clapham, Peter married Dorothy Lucie, daughter of Cecil Victor Jenkinson, who had served as a lance bombardier with A Battery, 280th Brigade, Royal Field Artillery during the First World War, the same unit that Peter's father had served with. Cecil later worked as an advertising manager in Fleet Street and was also the scorer at Essex County Cricket Club. Peter returned to work at Garland's, which was now based at Bexhill in Sussex, for a while, before joining Bowater, the paper and packaging company. He later ran Bowater's graphic design studio, working for the company for more than 25 years, where 'I got my gold watch'. Lucie died in 2001 and she and Peter had three children: Sally, Tom and Mark. Sally explained: 'He was driving till his 100th year and he's looking at me with daggers because he hates that we took the car away.' For his part, Peter said: 'I keep thinking that I must go out to do something when I realise that I can't do it because I haven't got a car.'

Peter Heppell, 77th Brigade Reunion, 2018.

Captain Richard Hilder, 3rd Carabiniers

Richard Waterhouse Hilder was born in York on 3 July 1921, elder son of Major Thomas (Tom) Martin Mountford Hilder, 6th (Inniskilling) Dragoons, of White's Tyrrell Farmhouse, Ingatestone, Essex, and grandson of Lieutenant Colonel Frank Hilder DL JP TD, MP for South-East Essex 1918–23, of Huskards, Ingatestone, Essex. Tom Hilder was commissioned from the Royal Military College Sandhurst on 16 June 1915 and served on the Western Front: at the Somme in 1916, at Cambrai in 1917 and at Amiens in 1918. After leaving Eton in the summer of 1938, Richard explained that he 'wanted to take a commission but they had closed Sandhurst and I decided that it would be a good idea to take Cert B, which would enable me to get a commission in the Territorial Army. I was advised to go into the ranks and get a commission that way.' Although his father had left the army to farm, he was soon called up as a reservist, with the result that Richard and his mother were left to run the 250-acre farm. Although it was a cattle farm, with plenty of grazing, Richard explained that 'we were made to plough it up and grow wheat for the war effort. It was only me and an old boy who had been a sergeant in the 9th Lancers during the Boer War.

Second Lieutenant R.W. Hilder, 5th (Royal Inniskilling) Dragoon Guards, soon after commissioning in early 1942.

'After my father got back from Dunkirk, I joined the Life Guards as a trooper on my nineteenth birthday. We were formed into a composite regiment and were training to go to the Middle East. The regiment was split between Combermere Barracks in Windsor and Knightsbridge Park Barracks. We had square-bashing, riding school, PT, gunnery, all that sort of thing. As long as you were the right height and promised to grow, they would let you in! We mounted King's Guard in khaki and at night we watched out for air raids. We used to do some stretcher-bearing in the afternoon when we had finished training. A bomb once dropped near Combermere Barracks when I was on night stable guard: I remember the shrapnel whistling round and I leapt over the stable door. Our horses were taken away and we became a motor battalion and started to do infantry training. In the autumn of 1941, I went to OCTU at Blackdown outside Aldershot for six months. I was rather puzzled when my name wasn't read out on the passing-out parade: apparently they had lost my exam papers, but they gave me a commission anyway. I was posted to the 5th (Royal Inniskilling) Dragoon Guards, initially in Northampton and later in Norfolk, but was soon sent with a draft of officers to India. We sailed from Gourock in the SS *Louis Pasteur*, a new, fast French liner. Since we were one of the fastest vessels, we sailed on ahead with one or two others and I took turns on what was called 'submarine guard'. We sailed round the Cape and stopped in Durban for several months. I remember the 'Lady in White' singing to us from the cliff-top – it was quite a sight. We had beautiful food, plenty to drink, very cheap – we'd never had it so good. I have very pleasant recollections of the voyage.

'On arrival in India, I went to a transit camp in Bombay. There were riots there at the time: I think it was Muslims against Hindus. We were used for riot control, which was not a very pleasant job. I carried a Colt .45 automatic pistol, which my grandfather had had before me. There were also sordid little interludes like patrolling round the brothels with the military police checking for soldiers. If troops found themselves in those areas of Bombay where they weren't allowed, they very often ended up dead, you see. They were massacred. The whole time we were there we used to be called on as 'Aid to the Civil Power', guarding strategic points like post and telegraph offices. The average Indian was very, very friendly and I have great regard for them, but the Gandhi-wallahs were trouble-makers, pro-Jap and that sort of thing, so you can imagine that they were causing disruption. I was posted to Nera Camp, 40 miles or so from Poona, where I joined a wartime regiment, the 26th Hussars. The regiment was formed from troops from the 14/20th Hussars and drafts of Royal Armoured Corps personnel from England.

'We had very little equipment and no tanks; in fact, precious little at all; we did our training on 14cwt trucks on the Maidan. We were sent on a course at Ahmednuggur Fighting Vehicle School to learn to use Lee tanks before being held in readiness for the invasion of Italy. We didn't go to Italy because we were disbanded and the personnel were sent half to the Carabiniers and half to the Chindits. I went to the Chindits with my troop, joining 14th Brigade, commanded by Brigadier Tom Brodie, on the Ken River near Jhansi. I was told to train my men as infantrymen, which I hadn't much experience of, and my troop – or my platoon – were armoured corps so we had to start from square one. They had always had tanks so the last thing they would do was march anywhere! Now we had no vehicles but everything was done with mules and ponies. We were issued with 100 mules, which the brigadier told me that I must train because he'd looked in my records and found that I had been in the Life Guards, so he thought: 'Just the boy for training mules.' They were totally unbroken and had come from the Argentine: a mule is a very obstinate animal but they are very good when they have been trained. Always talk to them: they accept the human voice.

'Having quite inadvertently won a rifle shooting competition, my platoon was transferred to 16th Brigade and later marched into Burma. I therefore had to form another platoon: there were two platoons in Brigade Headquarters [59 Column]. For training we did a lot of marching, a number of river crossings and plenty of shooting. We all had to swim: if you couldn't swim, you had to learn. From Jhansi we travelled first by train and then by river steamer on the Brahmaputra to Assam.'

On 2 April 1944, after an abortive attempt the previous night due to a huge air pocket, Richard Hilder and his platoon flew into Burma by Dakota: 'We loaded the mules in bamboo crates at the front end while the soldiers all sat in the rear. The landing strip at "Aberdeen" was just a clearing in the jungle. When we landed, I peered out, jumped from the door and dived for cover as a Japanese Zero strafed the strip. It was coming into the monsoon when we arrived and it got very, very muddy. We set off in the direction of Indaw, travelling at no more – but often much less – than two miles an hour, mostly along jungle tracks. The Burmese jungle is quite something and you can't see through the trees. We used to avoid roads because we were behind the lines. The key thing was silence.

'The local Chins were very friendly, very brave and extremely loyal: we used to carry bullion and people were paid, I suppose. The villagers mostly worked for the timber companies and some of the fellows in the Chindits were timber men. There was a terrific number of elephants: they were wonderful for bridge-building and were a great help to us. The K-rations were very meagre to fight a war and to march on. Sometimes we were lucky enough to get some rice from the villages. Our fare was pretty bad. We were supplied by air, supposedly every four days, but we were carrying 80lbs so were very limited. The main discipline was to look after yourself and your friend – everyone worked in pairs. We wore no badges of rank and I was called 'Dick' by the platoon. Platoon headquarters comprised me, my platoon sergeant, two runners and a muleteer and there were four rifle sections each of ten men, so the platoon was 45-strong. We were sometimes loaned out to other regiments if they were short of men: I went to the Leicesters and also to the Black Watch. The enemy were always round us and we lost 50 per cent of our men, mostly through disease. We had Mepacrine pills for malaria but that didn't seem to stop it. I did have malaria for quite a few years afterwards and possibly even a slight touch of it today. With a change of the seasons, I sometimes get a fever but I don't think that any of us were quite the same again. We started with two platoons, together with muleteers, and ended up with one depleted platoon and no mules.

'Our main role was to put blocks on the roads and disrupt communications. We once blew up a railway line, although the Royal Engineers, who were known as commando troops, did most of that. A bullet once hit the top of my water bottle but I wasn't injured. We carried out lots of patrols and a couple of men from the Burma Rifles were often attached to us. We never went into the villages but they would change from uniform into civvies, putting on a longyi, and go in. HQ Platoon often used to take air-drops, sometimes for the whole column. We saw far too many Japanese aircraft: they would sometimes try to shoot up our night laagers, if they could find them. We were behind the lines for six months and ended up being attached to 2nd Black Watch under the overall command of Joe Stilwell, operating up the west side of the Hukawng Valley. 36th Division passed through us and we fought a battle at Labu; although I was out on a flank, I believe that they flew the bagpipes in and played a tune that had been composed specially. The Japanese weren't there long enough to do much damage – we did put the wind up them, you know. We marched to Mogaung and were flown out of Myitkyina to Assam. In Burma we covered about a thousand miles in six months, and carrying 80lbs, that was nasty. When I went in I weighed about twelve stone; when I came out I wasn't much more than seven stone. By the time we had finished, I had a real job to get a dozen men out on a patrol.

'At the military level, the Chindits disrupted three Japanese divisions and took some of the weight off Imphal and Kohima. We dispelled the notion that the Japanese were invincible in the jungle. Until then our soldiers really thought that the Japanese were superhuman. I remember talking to people who felt that way. My time as a Chindit sharpened me. The Chindits gave you confidence – a very strong feeling of self-reliance. I learnt to accept things. If something really lovely is destroyed, I don't mourn it but instead think: 'Well, it's had its day.' The Burmese jungle taught me that material things are just that … things! The Chindit experience left me with one thought: 'You'll never have anything so bloody dreadful in your life again.' Eventually the Chindits were disbanded and we went to Secunderabad, where I briefly fulfilled the role of camp commandant for newly-formed 14th Indian Airlanding Brigade [which was formed from 14th British Infantry Brigade on 1 November 1944].

'Then I was posted as a troop leader to 3rd Carabiniers, who were by then halfway down Burma. I was flown into Meiktila, arriving at B Squadron at reveille early one morning, to be allotted 4 Troop. Soon after joining them, somewhere between Prome and Mount Popa, 4 Troop led an attack on Prome. The Japanese from the Arakan were coming across our front: they were on the run and we kept them going. My leading tank had a bridge blown up just in front of it, we shot nearly all the shells carried by our tank and we were heavily shelled by Japanese artillery, which was fairly exciting. The Indian civilian mess staff came along with us. On a famous occasion, one of them, while answering a call of nature, managed to capture a Japanese and they gave him a medal for it. He was very proud. We went on south, ending up in Rangoon. We didn't get a very good reception from the Burmese: they were not like the tribes in northern Burma. They were bolshie and pro-Jap, although, being in a tank, the times we met civilians were fairly limited. They were the same old tanks which we had trained on in the 26th Hussars in India – old 'Bluebird' and 'Borzoi' I can remember – they had gone all the way down Burma and did a marvellous job. They were absolutely clapped out when we had finished: the wireless sets used to go off the air when it rained and the guns were all coppered up. We pulled our tanks to pieces and they were scrapped.

'We were posted to Ahmednuggur, issued with new tanks and were part of a force that was going to invade the Japanese mainland. Then the atomic bombs were dropped and we went to Rawalpindi. I took a road convoy along the Grand Trunk Road to Rawalpindi – it was a wonderful trip. Almost as soon as I arrived, I was posted back to England and landed near Cambridge on a foggy November day. During a stopover in the Middle East – I can't remember where – I saw three Gurkhas sitting on a bench. They got up, stood to attention and saluted me and I suddenly realised that they all had the VC. That was quite something. They were returning to India after being presented with their VCs by King George VI in London. My last posting was as adjutant of a Polish transit camp at Kingston Bagpuize near Oxford. They had had a bad time and we gathered them together and sent them on their way.

Richard Hilder, photographed by Wendy Aldiss.

'After being demobbed in July 1946, I returned to the family farm: the horses had gone and my father now had tractors. There was clothing rationing and we grew flax, which was processed at a factory in Thetford and made into linen. My father sold White's Tyrrell Farm and I bought Mullets Farm in Stock. Initially it was a dairy farm but this was unprofitable, so I switched to pigs.' On 2 December 1947 at St Peter's, Vere Street, London, Richard married one of my mother's second cousins, June Caroline, elder daughter of Brigadier Rintoul George Edward Carolin, Essex Regiment, and his wife Kathleen, only child of Major William Henry Wreford-Brown, Essex Regiment. Although they had separated many years earlier, she died on 20 February 2013. They had three children: Michael, Nicholas and Jane. At the end of our conversation, Richard Hilder said: 'They were not my favourite years. I've forgotten a lot of it, thank God.'

14524981 Private Idris Jones, Suffolk Regiment

Idris Maldwyn Jones, who was born on 7 August 1924, son of Thomas David Jones and his first wife Blodwen (née Jones), was given his first name by his mother because she could see the Cader Idris in the distance from her bedroom window, while he takes his second name from the Welsh for Montgomeryshire. Until war broke out, Thomas was a shopkeeper and dairyman, with a number of good milk rounds in Bow and Hackney. On the outbreak of the war, Idris's stepmother and her children were evacuated to Wales, where his father later joined them, after selling the shop. With work hard to find, he retrained as a dynamiter in a local quarry, leaving Idris in the care of his sister and her husband in Battersea Park Road. After the early death of his mother, Idris lived with his grandmother and attended a Welsh-speaking school, with the result that he had a language barrier to overcome when he returned to London. He spoke little English when he first attended Monteith Road School in Bow. Leaving school at 14, he found work with Levison & Son, a Danish import/export firm based on Ludgate Hill, and remained in Battersea during the Blitz.

At the age of 18, Idris received a Military Conscription Order and, after a medical examination at Upper Tulse Hill on 30 December 1942, was passed as Grade 1 for military service and ordered to report to Gibraltar Barracks, Bury St Edmunds, on 4 February 1943 to commence basic army training. He explained: 'Towards the end of the training, I was asked where I would like to serve in the army. I chose the Norfolk Regiment but, in the usual way, was posted instead to the Suffolk Regiment. After a series of intelligence tests, I was placed in a specialist platoon for armoured vehicle training in Bren gun carriers – with no knowledge whatsoever of driving at that time. Training to drive and map-read on Bren gun carriers on the quiet wartime roads of Suffolk was a very pleasant introduction to army life though. I passed my Carrier Training Course at 3rd Infantry Training Centre on 19 June 1943. Tactical carrier training at Spilsby and Baumber in Lincolnshire culminated in a final exercise alongside the Green Howards at Fylingdales in North Yorkshire.

'Together with five other army personnel, I was directed to collect a deserter from a police station in London and escort him to Liverpool.

After handing him over to the authorities, we boarded the 19,335-ton Nederland Line *Marnix van Sint Aldegonde* for the voyage to Bombay [there were 2,924 troops, 278 crew and 33 gunners on board]. I was one of those selected for special duties should there be an emergency occurrence during our journey. Having set sail on 23 October 1943, we joined a large convoy [KMF25A] in the North Atlantic and zigzagged our way southward before reaching the Straits of Gibraltar. I understand that this was the second troopship convoy to make its way through the Mediterranean, via the Suez Canal and the Red Sea, to India. Although we kept close to the shores of North Africa, we were attacked at dusk on 6 November 1943 by Dornier 217s of Kampfgeschwader 26 based on Rhodes. The *Marnix van Sint Aldegonde* was torpedoed and immediately started to sink as the torpedo hit amidships opposite the engine room. The lights went out and blue emergency lights came on to light the mess decks.

'There was no panic amongst the passengers – ENSA actors, nurses or troops – as we all sat at our mess deck tables awaiting further instructions. The NCOs encouraged everyone to remain calm. As the evening drew on, orders were given for everyone to make their way to allocated decks before we abandoned the ship. This was where the specialist groups came into action to assist everyone in getting off the ship before they were ferried by small boats to other ships in the convoy. I was very busy doing tasks that needed to be done, under the direction of crew members. Most of the passengers were taken off the ship before midnight while the crew remained on board. Oceangoing tugs and a protective destroyer screen arrived and a tug began to tow the *Marnix van Sint Aldegonde* to an Algerian port. While the working parties rested, the ship continued to sink [under tow she collided with the Grace Line's *Santa Elena*, which had been disabled in the same attack and later sank with the loss of four troops]. Late in the afternoon I was instructed to clamber down the side of the ship and carefully jump into a small boat which was linked to an American destroyer. We were welcomed on board the destroyer and given food. The *Marnix van Sint Aldegonde* upended around 5.30 pm on 7 November 1943.

'We disembarked at the Algerian port of Philippeville and were taken to an army reinforcement camp, where everyone was re-kitted before joining another ship to continue the journey to Bombay. That convoy

[KMF26] was attacked by German aircraft off the coast of Crete although no ship was directly hit. We arrived in Bombay just before Christmas and they then gave us 'survivors' leave' at the transit camp at Deolali. We spent the time by a reservoir, which was very pleasant. The Suffolk Regiment draft travelled by train to Calcutta, which took a few days, before embarking in a ship on the Hooghley River and making our way to Chittagong where we boarded a coastal steamer which took us to Cox's Bazar.'

14524981 Private I.M. Jones, Lahore, 1945: 'My love Maldwyn.'

5th (Indian) Infantry Division (5 Division), with which the 2nd Battalion, The Suffolk Regiment (2 Suffolk) was serving, had captured the small port of Maungdaw on 9 January, shortly before the Japanese launched a diversionary attack, Operation Ha-Go, in the Arakan, to distract attention from U-Go, their invasion of India. Lasting from 5 to 23 February 1944, the fighting in the Arakan is known to posterity either as the 'Battle of the Admin Box' or the 'Battle of Ngakyedauk Pass' and to the soldiery, perhaps inevitably, as 'Okey-doke Pass'. Despite suffering severe casualties, two Allied divisions successfully defended the crucially-important pass. Idris's account continued: 'A large lorry arrived at Cox's Bazar to take the draft to the Admin Company area. As part of 123rd (Indian) Infantry Brigade [123 Brigade], the battalion was then holding one of the front-line positions of 5 Division, which had a divisional flash commonly named 'the flaming arsehole'. On arrival I was interviewed by a senior officer to establish my army trade. I explained that I was a trained Bren gun carrier driver. The officer said that he was sorry but no Bren gun carrier section existed in the battalion. He made an alternative offer of becoming a muleteer. Although I had no real idea what he meant, I obviously understood that it was associated with animals known as mules – and immediately rejected the offer.

'I was directed to D Company, commanded by Major 'Slogger' Leach, and was guided to a section, part of a platoon, and took my place in the front line. Members of the draft were all parcelled out to different parts of the battalion. The area occupied by D Company was criss-crossed by trenches on a sandy hill facing the Japanese front line. 5 Division held the line between Maungdaw and Razabil while the other side of the Mayu Range was the domain of 7th (Indian) Infantry Division. D Company was in a holding position and, although there was no immediate attacking action taking place, patrols constantly probed the Japanese front-line areas. Section positions were sometimes mortared and shelled. Unfortunately, after a while I became ill with malaria and dysentery and was evacuated to hospital at Comilla [14th Army Headquarters, 200 miles east of Calcutta] via an advance casualty clearing station and a series of other medical clearing stations. After doses of quinine and other tablets, the illnesses eventually subsided. After discharge from hospital, I was taken to a reinforcement camp, where I worked in an office for a short time and once saw a Vera Lynn concert.' There was nothing remotely unusual about Idris's experience. According to the official historian of the Royal Army Medical Corps, Lieutenant General Sir Neil Cantlie: 'In the first six months of 1944, the entire South East Asia command lost 40,000 killed and wounded in battle but 282,000 to various tropical diseases, and in October, 14th Army had a malaria rate of 84 per cent.'

Operation U-Go, Fifteenth Japanese Army's advance on Kohima and Imphal, commenced on 6 March 1944, and twelve days later 5 Division was airlifted to Imphal, the first time that such a dramatic tactical manoeuvre had ever been attempted by the British Army. Having recovered his strength, Idris rejoined 2 Suffolk at Imphal: 'Asked once again about my trade, I explained that I was a qualified Bren gun carrier driver. I was told that a Bren gun carrier platoon had been formed, as part of Battalion Headquarters. Along I went to join this new platoon but there was not a Bren gun carrier to be seen. Meanwhile, 2 Suffolk advanced over the many hills that ran alongside the road between Imphal and Kohima, winkling out the Japanese from their positions. We launched bitter attacks on two key features, known as Isaac and James, taking heavy casualties – and failing to capture either position. In the end the Jats took possession of Isaac, after the Japanese retreated. I was a member of a working party led by the battalion chaplain. Sadly we had to bury many of our own men.

'A few days later, while still with battalion headquarters, four of us were carrying a stretcher-bound casualty from the top of one of the hills down to the main road. After passing him to the first aid section, we reclimbed the hill to retrieve some important equipment. Unfortunately, after descending once again, we discovered that the Bailey bridge was impassable. We couldn't get to the road after all and were therefore stuck on the wrong side of the river – without any food. By the following day, though, the flooding had eased and we managed to wade across the bridge and rejoin the battalion. The RSM now ordered me to join a fighting patrol that would outflank the Japanese positions and meet up with the advancing troops of 2nd (British) Division [2 Division]. It was the monsoon season, and after two days of pouring rain but fortunately no Japanese opposition, we finally met the advancing tanks of 2 Division at Milestone 109 on 22 June 1944. The Imphal-Kohima Road was now open.

'As part of an outflanking movement, I was ordered to climb aboard a vehicle and rejoin the battalion, which was now repairing to the start line, the village of Bishenpur on the Tiddim Road. By this time, along with many others I was again suffering from dysentery. While carrying a full load of mortar bombs, I had to fall out of the line of march to relieve myself, by which time battalion headquarters was far out of sight. I therefore thumbed a lift and found myself driving past the still-marching Suffolks. There were consequences though. I was placed on a charge by Sergeant Major Duffy, a well-known regimental character. It was a charge now happily forgotten and, though found guilty, nothing came of it. Many years later I met Sergeant Major Duffy at a Suffolk Regiment reunion and reminded him that he had once put me on a charge. He smiled: "You weren't the only person I charged during my service."

'Our stay in Bishenpur was short and we soon moved forward onto the Tiddim Road, with the prospect of more fighting to come. I had now left battalion headquarters and joined C Company. Operating in section-sized patrols, we harried the retreating Japanese. For some reason I always seemed to be the 'get-away man', trailing a few yards behind the rest of the patrol. The NCOs must have thought that I was fleet of foot! The battalion was ordered to move forward to recapture Manipur Bridge on the Tiddim Road. The rumour mill suggested that the CO complained to the brigade medical officer that his battalion wasn't sufficiently fit to undertake this task. They had been in action for many months and desperately needed a rest. While the main body returned to Imphal, others were given different tasks. It fell to my lot to become a member of the personal escort of Brigadier Geoffrey Evans of 123 Brigade.' Lieutenant General Sir Geoffrey Evans KBE CB DSO** DL was one of the most distinguished senior officers to serve in Burma: he later commanded 5 Division and, together with Antony Brett-James, with whom he had served, wrote *Imphal: A Flower on Lofty Heights* (1962).

The duties weren't onerous: 'It meant touring around in a jeep and on foot looking after the brigadier. A view strongly held by me as a young soldier was that I wouldn't wish to be commissioned because all the young officers were killed almost as soon as they took charge of platoons. After doing my stint as escort, I returned to the battalion at Imphal. The CO then asked if I would like to go on leave to Delhi. This was almost unheard of – and the offer was accepted with much pleasure! With travelling tokens arranged, I had to make my own way to Delhi, using whatever transport was available. This was quite a journey for a young man of just 20 years of age. I used every trick I could: staying at reinforcement camps and travelling by rail to Calcutta, where a traveller could obtain money to help him on his way. On arriving at Delhi Station, I asked the RTO office how to get to the Viceregal Lodge Leave Centre. It wasn't open yet so I made my way instead to the Wavell Club across the road. This Burma veteran then spent some wonderfully restful days at the club before the leave centre opened.

'An entire wing of the Viceregal Lodge had been set aside for personnel on leave from Burma. During my stay there, I met Viscount Wavell and his wife and was shown around the Throne Room and other important places. A ball was held at the governor's residence, where I met General Auchinleck and his wife and spent a wonderful evening dancing the hours away. We were given guided tours of Delhi and attended many marvellous events. Sadly, though, malaria reappeared towards the end of my leave and I had to spend a few days in the garrison hospital, before making my way back to the battalion, which was now at Tamu, preparing to move forward to the Chindwin. I was one of those who now joined the battalion police to work closely with the military police from 14th Army Tactical Headquarters. Our role was to direct and control the movement of troops involved in Operation Capital, which involved crossing the

Irrawaddy at Pakokku and outflanking the Japanese to capture Meiktila. This was an interesting task, as we guided troops and tanks in the right direction. Operation Capital culminated in IV Corps' four-day battle for Meiktila, after which the Japanese finally withdrew.

'After a stint as line of communication troops, I rejoined the battalion, which had crossed the Chindwin and moved forward to Shwebo as a defensive measure. As the days slipped by, there were rumours either that the battalion would move forward towards Mandalay if the task didn't fall to the 19th Division, and 2 Suffolk would be drawn into the attack; or, if Mandalay fell, then 2 Suffolk would be withdrawn from Burma. We were all sceptical about the alternative. The battalion was soon on the move and troops in lorries were singing with gusto the song, *On the Road to Mandalay*; the convoy came to a sudden halt and on the wayside was a large airfield with many Dakotas and other aircraft parked. Orders came fast and furious for everyone to make their way to the aircraft with their kit. It was realised then the rumour was true: that Mandalay had fallen on 19 March 1945 and that we were on the way out after fifteen months of front-line activity. We flew first to Chittagong, where we rested for a while, before returning to Lahore, the battalion's peace-time station.

'Soon after getting back to Napier Barracks, I was approached by the CSM of Admin Company, who asked if I was interested in doing an

British Attached Section (BAS), Lahore, 1945: Idris Jones (back row, left).

Christmas Day 1945: BAS and helpers – Idris Jones (front row, second from left).

office job, with the goal of helping the army railway people to move troops through to Karachi and other places, finding accommodation, etc. After giving the matter little thought, I accepted the offer since it was a welcome alternative to performing camp chores. I therefore joined the British Attached Section (BAS), Lahore Cantonments. While we were separate from the activities of the battalion, we were, however, housed in a large block in Napier Barracks. Although only a small office, we were quite effective. I had a lovely, separate, individual room within the block, with an Indian servant looking after my needs. Eventually I was informed that the time had come for me to return to the United Kingdom, via Deolali and Bombay.

'On arrival, I was directed to South Eastern Area Command Headquarters at Colchester to do yet more office work. After demobilisation in Aldershot in June 1947, I took my accrued service leave and finally left the army in September 1947. Now I could finally marry Menna (Mary Helena) (née Evans), fulfilling a promise I made when returning to my unit before I first went abroad. As the train pulled out of Aberystwyth station, I leant as far out of the window as I could and shouted: "I'll come back and marry you!" We were married in the Methodist Chapel at Penuwch, Cardiganshire, on 26 September 1947. I returned to Battersea, leaving Menna in Wales until I could find work and a place to live. Soon I found a job as a local government officer with the Architect's Department in Battersea Town Hall and my wife joined me in London. In January 1949, though, I joined the newly-formed National Health Service, which was the best thing I ever did. I later became a treasurer with the Family Practitioners' Committee incorporated within the City and East London Health Authority.' In 1990, Idris joined the Burma Star Association, for which he was a membership section volunteer for many years (membership number J/147/90). Menna died on 31 May 2016, after sixty-nine years of marriage; she and Idris had no children. He was absolutely insistent: 'Don't make me out as a hero; I'm just an ordinary sort of bloke making the best of life.'

Idris Jones at the Royal British Legion's Centenary Service, Westminster Abbey, 12 October 2021.

ZBK 13224 Colour Sergeant Maxmos Kettle, King's African Rifles

Maxmos Kettle was born in 1921 in Chiradzulu District of Nyasaland, a former European farming settlement in what is now the Southern Region of Malawi. His father had served with the King's African Rifles (KAR) during the long-running and extremely arduous East African Campaign against the Germans and their Askaris, led by General Paul von Lettow-Vorbeck. Having received a basic education at the local mission school, he started work, at a time when child labour was common, at Namingomba Tea Estate in Thyolo.

At the age of 18, Maxmos volunteered to join the KAR and, following primary training as a rifleman, received driver training, which he greatly enjoyed. When formed in 1902, the six battalions were recruited on a regional basis: from Nyasaland, Kenya, Uganda and British Somaliland. The first two battalions recruited from Nyasaland. During the First World War, the KAR expanded to no fewer than 22 battalions before shrinking back to the original six – divided into the Northern Brigade and the Southern Brigade – by 1939.

Maxmos was posted to the 2nd (Nyasaland) Battalion (2 KAR) and saw active service against the Italians in Italian East Africa – which comprised Abyssinia (now Ethiopia), Italian Eritrea and Italian Somaliland – including a hard-fought battle at Tug Argan in mid-August 1940 as vastly superior Italian forces conducted a skilful withdrawal to the port of Berbera. He then sailed with his battalion from Nairobi to Burma. He explained that he was quite content with military life, even on operations, although he was far from happy with the food. They were provided with rice, whereas he and his fellow soldiers would have greatly preferred their staple diet of *nsima*, or maize porridge. He also observed, not entirely surprisingly, that 'the Japanese were a very formidable enemy, much more so than the Italians'. Meanwhile, 'although I did not have very much to do with the local Burmese, they were generally friendly and welcoming'.

On 16 March 2021, Maxmos explained in a letter to the Royal Commonwealth Ex-Services League (RCEL): 'I am a Second World War veteran, who got wounded during combat in Burma. I was serving under 21st Brigade, 11th (East African) Division. I was shot in the mouth and the bullet came out side to the left of my neck, damaging two teeth in the process. I got treated in India.' Towards the end of 1944, 21 (EA) Brigade – which was commanded by Brigadier John Francis Macnab DSO OBE and comprised battalions from Nyasaland, Uganda and Northern Rhodesia (now Zambia) – pursued the now-retreating Japanese from Imphal, down the Kabaw Valley, in the process helping to establish bridgeheads over the Chindwin. The regimental historian wrote: 'The most outstanding performance within the Division was unquestionably the series of operations carried out on the left flank by Brigadier J.F. Macnab's 21 (EA) Brigade and 5 KAR.' Maxmos said that 'the worst thing about active service was being away from home. We had no long leave, only local R&R.' Since he had become engaged in 1940, shortly before leaving home, he hadn't seen his fiancée for almost six years.

After returning to Nyasaland, he remained with 2 KAR, married his fiancée in 1948 and soon had a son and three daughters. In the autumn of 1953, 2 KAR was posted to Malaya, replacing one of the two KAR battalions already serving there. After two months of intensive training in jungle warfare, they remained on active service during the so-called Malayan Emergency for a further eighteen months. In an Associated Press newsreel, 2 KAR's service in Malaya was described as 'bandit-hunting in the bush', where they proved to be 'expert trackers'. On 3 March 1955, there was a homecoming ceremonial parade in Lusaka, at which Lord Llewellin, Governor General of the Federation of Rhodesia and Nyasaland, took the salute. While serving at home, 1 KAR and 2 KAR rotated between Zomba in Malawi and Lusaka in Northern Rhodesia.

On 31 December 1963, Maxmos was presented with a certificate signed by the prime minister, Sir Roy Welensky KCMG PC JP: 'The Government of the Federation of Rhodesia and Nyasaland acknowledges with deep appreciation the devotion and loyalty of 13224 C/Sgt Maxmos Kettle.' When Malawi and Zambia became independent the following year, the soldiers were given the option of returning to Malawi or joining the Zambian army. Maxmos chose the latter course, serving in the Zambia Regiment until his retirement in 1967. On finally returning home, he found a small plot of land in the valley of the Shire River, the largest in Malawi, instead of settling in the now densely-populated Chiradzulu District. Unfortunately there was no entitlement to a pension from the British government after Independence. In his letter to RCEL, he made a heartfelt plea to 'be considered for assistance to make my life a little bearable. ... Though I was promised to get compensated upon reaching home, nothing came out. I am now too old to do hard manual work, hence a need for assistance to lessen undue hardships. I shall be very grateful if my plea for help is going to be treated positively with the urgency it deserves. It is also my last wish that you arrange with [the] powers that be so that I can be buried as a soldier when I die.'

Representing his long and varied military service, Maxmos Kettle received an impressive number of medals: 1939–45 Star, Africa Star, Burma Star, Defence Medal, War Medal, General Service Medal with clasp 'Malaya' and Long Service and Good Conduct Medal (Rhodesia and Nyasaland). RCEL has arranged for former Colour Sergeant Kettle to receive £612 a year as a welfare grant, half in the spring and half in the autumn. It was suggested by the paying officer that because he lives five miles off the main road, one of his daughters should collect the money for him. To no avail: Maxmos insists on attending payment parade in person!

ZBK 13224 Colour Sergeant Maxmos Kettle in the uniform of the Zambia Regiment, May 2021.

14429428 Sergeant Vic Knibb, Queen's Own Royal West Kent Regiment

Victor Brian (Vic) Knibb was born on 4 January 1925, only child of Stanley Victor Knibb, a clerical officer with the Port of London Authority, of Ashcot, Hampton Court Way, Thames Ditton, and his wife Marion Emma Alice, daughter of William Henry Lee, retail tradesman, of Shedfield, Ashley Road, Thames Ditton. 7450504 Private S.V. Knibb attested for the 25th (City of London) Reserve Cyclist Battalion, The London Regiment, at Fulham House on 24 August 1914; he served on the Western Front for twelve weeks in the summer of 1917 and was awarded the Victory Medal and the British War Medal. Having joined the Home Guard at the age of 16, Vic enlisted on his 18th birthday: 'You got a different number if you were a volunteer. You got a '14 number' against being a draftee.' Joining his local regiment, the East Surreys, he underwent basic training at Number 20 Infantry Training Centre in Shrewsbury.

Early the following year, Vic 'boarded a troopship at Liverpool docks, destination unknown. It wasn't until we reached the Suez Canal that we realised we were heading towards India. On our arrival in Bombay, I saw bananas for the very first time and it wasn't long before I was trading cigarettes for them! We were quickly transported to a transit camp called Deolali. You'll probably recognise the name from the famous phrase 'gone doolally' or 'doolally tap'. People said if you spent too much time there you lost your mind a bit. It was an unpleasant place. Thankfully we were only there for a month before we caught a train to Calcutta.' Posted to Imphal as a reinforcement for the 4th Battalion, Queen's Own Royal West Kent Regiment (4 RWK), which had suffered devastating casualties at the Battle of Kohima, Vic immediately 'won a week of leave in Calcutta at a sports day event. There I stayed in a museum and was hosted by a local British family who kindly took me under their wing. There was a swimming pool at their house, which was quite something. I was used to having to look after myself so it was nice to be taken care of.'

After decisive victories at Imphal and Kohima, the 14th Army began to push through northern Burma towards Mandalay. Vic was in the Mortar Platoon, responsible for carrying the baseplate and the sights: 'Finding food, water and somewhere safe to sleep were the most important things for us. Learning to adapt to the conditions was important. What I learned in the Scouts was very helpful to me. I made fire in the rain, in the monsoon and got something hot to eat. Basic skills: how to keep yourself warm and dry and how to make a bed out of bamboo quite quickly to get ourselves off the ground because otherwise you lay wet on the ground or slept up a tree. From checking water supplies for dead bodies to finding villages that kept geese – they were useful intruder alarms and helped us to get a good night's sleep – we did our best to stay alive. The first contact with the enemy was when we came to a railway line and we sort of bedded down, and then we crossed the railway line. We went and dug a slit trench for protection and in that trench I found a coin, which I put in my pocket and had to the day I left Burma.'

14429428 L/Cpl V.B. Knibb, Calcutta, 1944.

Strictly contrary to army regulations, Vic kept a diary, which survives, despite losing one corner to a Japanese bullet: 'We were woken up about half-past four by the Japanese who attacked us. The diary was in my small pack which I was using as a pillow sleeping on the ground and I got this terrific thump on the back of my head. A bullet went through the diary and took a chunk out of it.' Having defeated the Japanese at the Battle of Meiktila between January and March 1945, 4 RWK, part of 5th (Indian) Infantry Division, 'continued

Vic Knibb's diary, clearly showing the bullet hole.

to fight our way down to Rangoon for the next five months. We'd often divert off the roads into villages to check for any retreating Japanese. It became clear that the main difference between us and them was that they were happy to die. This was disconcerting when they were running at you with grenades in their hands, content with blowing you and themselves up. We wanted to live.

'We had some idea of what was happening outside our bubble. We would get letters from our families but often these were censored. Sometimes my parents would send me a copy of the paper but it would be so out of date by the time I received it, it didn't always help. Many of my fellow soldiers fell by injury or illness. I was one of the fit ones but by the time we reached the south I was covered in sores. I'd been living off half rations for two-and-a-half months. By the time we reached Rangoon, I'd developed jaundice.

'In Rangoon, a corporal came up and called us and said: "An atomic bomb has been dropped on Japan and that should finish it." Well, aren't we lucky; thank goodness for that, we all thought. We had nothing to celebrate with and just wandered about looking for food. A memory that sticks with me is one night while manning the Rangoon docks, I smelt bread. I shouted up to the ship: "Have you got bread up there?" A sailor said: "Of course." I replied: "Give us a loaf." It was one of the finest bits of food I've ever had: a hot, white loaf of fresh bread thrown down from a ship. I hadn't had bread for two-and-a-half years. We didn't have it out there. It was fantastic. When the Japanese arrived to formally surrender Burma, I was selected to act as a guard at the peace talks.' The Japanese delegation flew into Mingaladon airfield, on the outskirts of Rangoon, in two Mitsubishi Ki-57 Topsy transport aircraft, escorted by RAF Spitfires. Vic explained: 'I had to take the sword off

The Burma Star Association AGM, National Memorial Arboretum, 12 May 2018: (left to right) John Giddings (chairman) and Vic Knibb (vice chairman).

the fifth Japanese officer off the plane and pass it to an officer, so I never saw it again. I spent the next few days manning the Conference Room [the Convocation Hall, Rangoon University] and made sure I was well presented. My memory of the conference is limited. I imagine our brains were focusing on getting fed and rested.

'People often ask me if I was relieved at the end of the war. The sense of relief came slowly for us. We were worried about what was going to happen to us. Fighting a war was all some of us knew. I found it difficult. I started labouring but I was 21, had no training and wasn't used to working. It was a difficult time of my life when I came back. The first night I was home, I told my parents what had happened, but after that I never talked about Burma for 30-odd years. You were involved in a different sort of life and it just didn't come up.' In the event, having left school with few qualifications, Vic trained as a carpenter after demobilisation and worked in the building trade for the rest of his life. In 1948 he married Joy Kathleen Hill and they had two sons: Robin and Roy. After Joy died on 15 July 2009, Vic remained in West Molesey, where he kept a large and comfortable cabin cruiser on the Thames. Vic Knibb, a hard-working and committed vice chairman of the Burma Star Association (membership number K/1039/94), died on 25 February 2019, at the age of 94. In tribute, his grandson wrote: 'I've been lucky enough to have had 34 years' worth of amazing memories with you. You may be gone but you'll never be forgotten. You were a legend in my eyes.'

Burma Star wreath at Vic Knibb's funeral, West Molesey, 21 March 2019.

Lance Corporal Wisdom Kudowor, 26th West African Artisan Works Company

Wisdom Kudowor was born on 6 January 1928 at Atiteti in the Volta Region of Ghana. In 1942, having completed his formal education at the EP Senior High School, he decided to fulfil his ambition and enlisted in the army. After training as an artisan at the Army Training School in Kibi, Wisdom was posted to the 26th West African Artisan Works Company, based at Teshie, Accra. He was posted to 82nd (West African) Division, which sailed for Ceylon on 20 May 1944. After acclimatisation and jungle warfare training, the division took part in the third Arakan Campaign, which began in December 1944. During the next six months, before the monsoon broke, they recaptured –

Wisdom Kudowor, 2020.

in conjunction with 81st (West African) Division – mountainous terrain that had been hotly disputed for more than three years.

Following his return to Ghana in August 1946 – after two-and-a-half years in Asia – Lance Corporal Kudowor was demobilised. At that point, he was selected to attend two government-sponsored training schemes – one in Ghana and the other in the United Kingdom – before qualifying as a production engineer. In a recent interview, he made the point that this only happened 'because of the opportunities given to me by the British government'. A combination of Wisdom's wartime experiences, work ethic, training and natural aptitude put him on the path to becoming principal of the Accra Polytechnic and director of the National Official Training Institute, before his retirement in 1984.

On 15 August 2020, Wisdom made a short video, in which he said: 'As we celebrate the 75th Anniversary of VJ-Day at a time when we can't visit them, show you still remember those who fought for peace during the two world wars: share a tribute, share a photograph, share a memory, share your family's history, use the "#ShareYourTribute". Together we will keep their memory alive.'

EC 12735 Lieutenant Ted Luscombe, 19th Hyderabad Regiment

Lawrence Edward (Ted) Luscombe was born on 10 November 1924, eldest son of L 14281 Chief Petty Officer Reginald John Luscombe RN of Ilsham Road, Wellswood, Torquay, and his wife Winifred May, second daughter of Gilbert Henry Edward Lee, bootmaker and dealer, of 7 Wellswood Place, Torquay. Reginald enlisted in the Royal Navy on 10 January 1923, receiving his Long Service & Good Conduct Medal on 31 January 1938, and then served at sea during the Second World War in the cruiser HMS *Kenya* and in the destroyer HMS *Codrington*. After successfully passing his Matric, Ted left Torquay Boys' Grammar School at the age of 16 and enrolled at Kelham Theological College, near Newark in Nottinghamshire. Kelham had been founded by Father Herbert Kelly as part of the Society of Sacred Mission. Ted explained that, having spent two years at Kelham, 'I joined up on my eighteenth birthday and was sent to the Border Regiment as my initial training unit. At Carlisle Castle they identified me as a potential officer and I then went to pre-OCTU at Wrotham in Kent. While I was there a brigadier came round looking for potential officer cadets for the Indian Army and I fell into that trap.

'After sailing out in SS *Mooltan*, I spent six months at the Officers' Training School in Bangalore. It was what was known as a third-class hill station, and a wonderful place to be. I enjoyed my time there. On 19 March 1944, I was granted an Emergency Commission in the Indian Army. There was a limited amount of choice and I was commissioned into the Hyderabad Regiment. My first posting was to the regimental depôt in Agra: they must have thought that I was literate or something and they put me into the A&Q Department. After only a short time at the depôt, though, I was posted to north-east India. Unfortunately, soon after arriving, I contracted malaria and a very bad dose of amoebic dysentery. The whole thing was a blur to me: I was very, very ill and, as part of my recovery programme, I had three months' convalescent leave at Simla. At the end of it all, I was downgraded to Permanent Medical Category 'C' and only received a Burma Star because I crossed the Brahmaputra really. Although an officer in the Hyderabad Regiment, I was posted as adjutant of the Royal Indian Engineers Depôt at Jullundur. It was a huge establishment, accommodating almost 15,000 troops.

'I had had to learn Urdu to join the Indian Army. There were formal lessons at Bangalore but I also employed a *munshi* privately when I was at Agra. At Jullundur I realised that if I also learned to speak Hindi, then I would be paid an extra 100 rupees a month. About £6 I think it was, which certainly helped towards the mess bill. I therefore sat and

Lieutenant L.E. Luscombe, Devonshire Regiment, Jullundur, 1946.

passed the Higher Hindi Exam, which was very useful because Jullundur housed a very mixed group of troops. On VE-Day, which meant nothing to us really, the officers and other ranks played football against one another. We must have been mad: the temperature was 120° in the shade. I got heatstroke and had to be put on a saline drip. On 1 August 1945, I transferred to the Devonshire Regiment with the rank of war substantive lieutenant. I never actually served with the regiment but we had to choose a regiment when we were transferred to the General List so I chose my county regiment. It wasn't till 1946 that the trouble really started and we were employed in what was known as 'Aid to the Civil Power'. Under my command, I had fifty Muslims and fifty Hindus – each with their own VCO or Viceroy Commissioned Officer – and we had to go out and try to keep the peace. We found ourselves in the centre of things, with Muslims trying to move to what was soon to become Pakistan while Hindus moved in the opposite direction and the Sikhs were simply caught in the middle. It was terrible and there was an awful lot of slaughter on both sides.

'On 10 June 1946 at the Garrison Church in Jullundur, I was married to Major Doris Carswell Morgan RAMC. The ceremony was conducted by one of the government chaplains, a priest in the Indian Ecclesiastical Establishment; she was given away by Lieutenant Colonel Peter Tynan, assistant commandant of the Depôt; and my best man was an Australian, Major Arthur Cook, Royal Indian Engineers. She was the daughter of Andrew Morgan, a railway and general carrier with the London North

Eastern Railway, who lived at Barrhead, next-door to the Shanks family, of vitreous china fame. Her first job after qualifying was as the medical officer responsible for caring for the women at Sandhurst. I first met her when she had passed through Jullundur the previous year. Having been station medical officer at both Jutogh [near Shimla] and Dalhousie, she had returned to take up an appointment as 2IC of the Garrison Hospital. When I had a bad relapse of amoebic dysentery, she treated me and most probably saved my life.

10 June 1946: (left to right) Ted Luscombe, Doris Luscombe and Arthur Cook.

'Doris was the only female member of the officers' mess. As vice-president of the mess, I must have been one of the last people to have proposed the toast: "Madam, Gentlemen, the King Emperor." We had a two-week honeymoon at Mussoorie, a hill station in the foothills of the Himalayas – it was a marvellously relaxing time. I then volunteered to stay on another year in India because I liked the country and got on well with the Indians. In July 1947, just a month before Partition, we sailed home together in SS *Mooltan*, the same ship which had brought me to India more than three years earlier. It was a calm trip and a great contrast with the voyage out: this time I had a first-class cabin instead of having to sleep in a hammock below decks. They kept me on strength though, so I received the Indian Independence Medal, together with a commendation awarded by the Governor of the Punjab, Sir Evan Jenkins.

'After I was demobbed, I decided that I really wanted to study law. My brother-in-law, Thomas Morgan, who had been severely wounded while serving with the Seaforth Highlanders in north-west Europe, had returned to St John's College, Cambridge to complete his studies, having already spent a year there. Although I was offered a place at the college, there were so many ex-servicemen in the queue that there was a waiting list of two years. I thought to myself that if I then embarked on a four-year course, I might well be drawing a pension before I got back to work! The family lawyer then said to me: "There's no money in it, boy, accountancy's the future." So I signed up as an apprentice with the firm of Watson & Galbraith in Glasgow [now part of Deloitte Touche Tohmatsu, one of the so-called 'big four' accountancy firms] and was admitted as an Associate of the Institute of Chartered Accountants on 26 March 1952, the day our daughter was born [his daughter, Jean, explained that he chose to attend the ceremony, which only takes place once a year, rather than the birth]. A year later they offered me a partnership, but before I could accept it I spent a year – by arrangement – as a senior audit assistant with Peat Marwick Mitchell, before coming back to a partnership.

'While working for Watson & Galbraith, I did a lot of voluntary work with the church, in the process becoming diocesan treasurer for the Diocese of Glasgow and Galloway. Having recognised that I had a vocation, I gave three years' notice of dissolution of partnership and, studying externally through Edinburgh Theological College, took and passed the General Ordination Exam, while continuing to work at Watson & Galbraith. The Bishop of Glasgow and Galloway had decreed that new ordinands should undertake a one-year postgraduate course, so I attended St Boniface College in Warminster, then part of King's College, London, which was just opposite Lord Weymouth's Grammar School [now Warminster School]. I spent a very happy year taking Sunday Services at St John's, Boreham Road [where, by coincidence, I was baptised on 14 October 1955] and doing a little pastoral work.'

The Most Reverend Ted Luscombe subsequently enjoyed an illustrious career in the Scottish Episcopal Church. Ordained as a deacon in 1963 and as a priest by the Right Reverend Francis Moncreiff, Bishop of Glasgow and Galloway, in May the following year, he served initially as Curate of

The Most Reverend Edward Luscombe LLD PhD, St John's, Forfar, Remembrance Day 2019.

St Margaret's, Glasgow, before being appointed Rector of St Barnabas, Paisley. Between 1971 and 1975 he was Provost of St Paul's Cathedral, Dundee, before being consecrated on 21 June 1975 as the 50th Bishop of Brechin, where he spent fifteen years until his retirement in 1990. In 1985 he was elected as Primus of the Scottish Episcopal Church, holding the most senior appointment in his Church for the next five years. After such a distinguished ecclesiastical career, it is unsurprising that he is the subject of a biography, *Gravitas with a Light Touch* by John S. Peart-Binns, the title suggested by Sir William Gladstone KG, his predecessor as chairman of council at Glenalmond.

Ted retired at the age of 65 to look after Doris, who was six years older and, sadly, was not at all well. She died on 9 December 1992, leaving an only daughter, Jean, a lawyer who sits on the Mental Health Tribunal for Scotland. In his retirement, Ted completed an MPhil and a PhD at the University of Dundee, having already been awarded the honorary degree of Doctor of Laws (LLD) by the same university in 1987 for 'services to the community' – so he did eventually receive a legal qualification after all. On 6 August 1984, Ted Luscombe joined the Burma Star Association as a life member for a fee of £15, serving as an active chaplain to the Dundee branch (membership number L/1703/84). He once took part in a Burma Star Association reunion in the Royal Albert Hall, before standing alongside Viscount Slim and officiating at a service at the Cenotaph the following day. He retained strong military connections, officiating at the re-dedication of the Angus Black Watch Association Standard at St John the Evangelist, Forfar, in 2019. When I said to Jean that her father didn't sound West Country born and bred, she replied: 'Ah no, he made his life in Scotland and never went back to Devon. His 90-year-old brother, John, still lives in Torquay though.' Ted Luscombe died at home on 3 May 2022, at the age of 97.

1820545 Bombardier Neil McInnes, Royal Artillery

Neil Dunn McInnes, eldest son of Neil Robertson McInnes, a blacksmith who served in the Merchant Navy during the First World War, was born on 27 November 1920 in the Oatlands, a sub-district of Glasgow's Gorbals. According to his daughter, Betty: 'The family lived in a 'singalen' (single end, or one-roomed apartment in a tenement building) at 22 Oregon Street. There was no running water, although there was a 'jawbox' (sink) and shared lavatory on each landing.' Having left school at 14, with his schoolmaster's words ringing in his ears – 'His attendance, progress, and conduct were highly satisfactory, and give me every confidence in recommending him to any employer who desires an intelligent, industrious, and trustworthy boy' – Neil started work as a telegraph clerk with the London, Midland and Scottish Railway Company.

After enlisting on 17 July 1941, 1820545 Gunner N.D. McInnes's education continued and he not only received basic military training but also attended specialist driver and vehicle maintenance courses with 53rd Anti-Aircraft Driver Training Regiment, Royal Artillery. On 14 October 1941 he was posted to 'D Troop, 91st Battery, 44th Light Anti-Aircraft Regiment, Royal Artillery (44 LAA) at Penylan Hill, Cardiff. After some months at Blandford Camp in Dorset, 44 LAA embarked, on 26 May 1942, on the two-month voyage to Bombay. Initially posted to Delhi, where the Regimental History records that 'almost everyone had 'Delhi Belly' and life was, generally speaking, pretty poor', Neil was admitted to hospital with his first bout of malaria, less than two months after arriving in India.

1820545 Bombardier N.D. McInnes, Royal Artillery.

Between December 1942 and July 1943, 44 LAA was deployed in the Arakan, where, according to the Regimental History, it 'covered a large area of country extending from

Cox's Bazar and Ramu to the Donbaik Line. At various periods of the campaign, the Jap used his aircraft repeatedly and in fairly considerable numbers notably in raids on Chittagong and on the Brigade areas on the Mayu Peninsula. As a result, the Regiment had plenty of shooting and obtained a number of kills. In particular, five in one morning by 239 Battery near Donbaik and four in one engagement by 91 Battery at Cox's Bazar.' Neil's wartime letters to his Canadian cousin, Lorna, survive. On 21 January 1943 he wrote: 'When the Xmas mail arrived, I got the job of helping to sort it out. For the whole regiment! What a job too! Still, on getting about ten Xmas cards and two parcels, yours and Mum's, I didn't mind in the least. We had quite a guzzle in the tent, eating those marshmallows and sticks of gum; your cheese was very mellow and we had it for tea that night; and those Players cigs, I had to guard them with my life!'

Suffering from malaria once again, he was admitted to 62nd Indian General Hospital in Dacca, East Bengal, on 11 June 1943 and did not rejoin 44 LAA until 25 August that year. He would not appear to have missed very much – and there were unexpected bonuses. According to the Regimental History: 'The year spent in India after Arakan was the most dismal in the Regiment's history. There was no action during this year and training for future operations was greatly restricted by the almost complete lack of practice firing facilities.' During this period, Neil's Battery was deployed to Asansol and Jamshedpur and he attended yet another driving course, writing to Lorna on 21 December 1943: 'I've just arrived back from fourteen days' leave in Darjeeling. ... It was lovely there, up on a hill, and looking down on the other hills. Deep valleys, where it seemed the sun never penetrated, were always in shadow, and away to the north stretched the Himalayas, snow covered and ice bound. Right over the town, the second highest molehill in the world, Kanchenjunga, reared its head in frozen serenity, floating in a sea of clouds, the snow from its top streaming off like smoke, eddying round and round in the sky. ... I met a young miss there and she was, is, I should say, a lovely dancer. Needless to say, with my super-personality-plus (no cracks) I made myself known – did I say well-known? – and monopolized her for the rest of my stay! I'se a-goin back there if I'm spared.' In a letter to *The Daily Telegraph*, Betty wrote: 'My father owned two copies of *Palgrave's Golden Treasury*, one of which only came to light when I was clearing the loft after his death. This was the copy that had sustained him throughout the Burma Campaign, having been given to him by a young woman he had met while on leave in Darjeeling.'

Neil also described the shocking cause and effect of the Bengal famine: 'There's a famine in this land, and there are some very grim sights, heartbreaking to see, yet there's nothing the ordinary soldier like me can do to help these poor people. You see they have a different religion from the one we have, and it forbids them to eat meat and such things that come from animal food; only rice and flour and such things can they eat, so we're stymied. Even money can't buy this precious rice, as it's being hoarded by a black market, and the Government is doing its damnedest to stamp this out. There's a terrific uproar against those people who hoard, and quite rightly, too! They should be shot, as they are the cause of this distress, not the floods.'

Following yet another spell in hospital, Neil rejoined his battery, which deployed to northern Burma via the Indian railhead at Dimapur in late October 1944. The Regimental History notes that 'D Troop had an epic

Bailey bridge over the Chindwin, Kalewa, December 1944.

journey of six days along the most appalling roads before reaching their destination which was only sixty-odd miles from Tamu,' in order to join 11th (East African) Division. On 4 November, 'D Troop had their first action and succeeded in destroying three of a formation of enemy fighters which attacked the supply dropping aircraft and the Medium gun zone. This Troop suffered casualties through two direct hits from A.P. [armour-piercing] bombs registering on a gunpit.' From mid-December, the battery 'remained at Kalewa to cover the Chindwin river crossing where the longest Bailey bridge ever built was constructed and destroyed two enemy fighters of a force which attempted, without any success, to destroy the Bailey pontoon bridge'. In 2004 Neil recalled: 'Hogmanay 1944, Kalewa: 60 years ago (on the Chindwin) at the bridge with [John] Docherty [a childhood friend] at "F" Troop. Had to go back to "D" Troop making my way past 9th Gordon tanks. No challenge and felt so lonely. The way across that Bailey was miles.'

On leave from active service, he once again met up with Nancy (the young woman he had met in 1943) in Darjeeling, writing to Lorna on 9 July 1945: 'I've never told you about a girl, have I? Maybe Aunt Margaret has? At home there is nothing for me now. I had to come to the East to

On leave in Darjeeling, February 1945: (left to right) Neil McInnes, Nancy Wale, John Barraclough and Gwen Bukke.

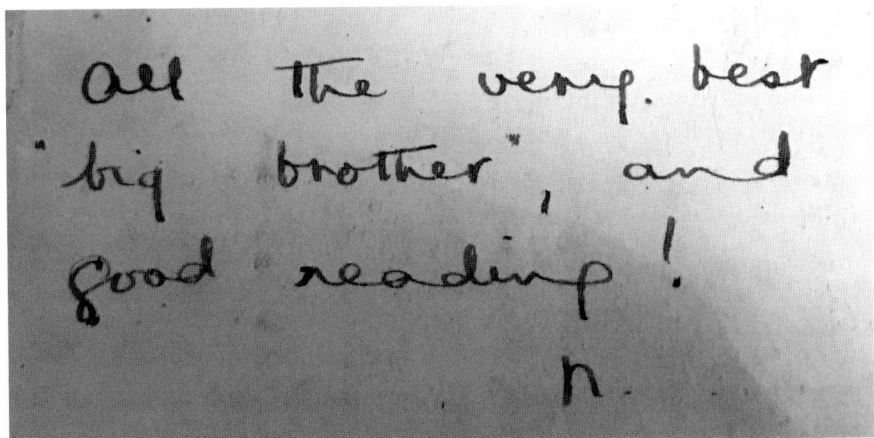

Nancy Wale's presentation inscription in Palgrave's Golden Treasury.

find the girl I want to marry. The trouble is getting her to say "yes". My, but it's a sair fecht – Ha! Ha! Ah well, you'll be given the gen in the next letter – don't split on me, honey bunch – no-one at home knows.' Sadly, as Betty explained: 'For whatever reason, there was no happy ending, although I did establish that the lady in question came to Britain after the war and married an Englishman.'

At Phyu, a hundred miles north of Rangoon, on the iconic road to Mandalay, he wrote about 'the Japanese surrender offer': 'Let me tell you how the first news affected us. It was terrific, cuzz! No-one knew anything of it until it was broadcast late at night on the 10th August. Ye Gods, Lorna, you should have seen us. Everything was quiet and there was hardly a light showing – only a few of us were standing beside the set. Then the news came through and everyone came tumbling over to get the gen – there was one hell of a cheer went up and as if by magic every place was ablaze with light. The boys went daft. Shouting and singing and we broke out some of the rum to celebrate. It was so spontaneous – the relief they showed that the war might be over in a matter of hours. If the Japs had come to our line that night they could have done some damage – nobody cared a damn! Our officer collared two of the boys who were out of their billets and insisted they came to his mess. They appeared next morning and told the tale that he had brought out his liquor and all three sat down and finished the lot – every time a bottle emptied the officer chucked it thro' the window and didn't care a hoot whose head it might land on. They got so drunk together they even started to throw the furniture through the window as well! ... And now we await the result of the surrender offer. The war still goes on in these parts! Please God it will soon be over.'

On 23 October 1945, Neil McInnes boarded SS *Duchess of Richmond*, bound for Liverpool via Calcutta and the Red Sea: 'The war has treated me kindly: I'm all in one piece, by the Grace of God. I wouldn't go through it again.' Of the three years and nine months that he had served overseas, slightly less than half that time was spent in Burma. On 12 April 1946 he was given the war substantive rank of Bombardier (Driver Operator). In response to the observation that Neil should surely have been offered a commission, Betty wrote: 'Highly intelligent, capable, and diligent, but he was from the Gorbals, self-educated, and perhaps lacked confidence at that time. When he was stationed at Stiffkey in Norfolk, waiting to be demobbed, he was given the opportunity of promotion to sergeant and to stay on in the regular army. He wanted to be home.' Demobilised on 11 December 1946, Neil resumed his pre-war career, rising to become a rail traffic controller. On 8 November 1984 he became a life member of the Burma Star Association (membership number Mc/656/84). On 23 September 1949 at the Church of Scotland Church of St Christopher, Pollok, Glasgow, Neil McInnes married Muriel Lawther, daughter of Joseph McClymont. She died on 1 March 1999 and he died on 8 May 2008, leaving Betty, their only child.

14318391 Private Sid Machin, King's (Liverpool) Regiment

Sidney Stanley William (Sid) Machin was born in Tottenham on 6 February 1924, only child of William Howard Clinton Machin, a GPO engineer who had served in the Royal Navy during the First World War, of 68 Chester Road, Walthamstow, and his wife Lilian Maud, daughter of Thomas Underwood. Sid was educated at Sybourn Street Primary School in Leyton, which he left at 14 to start work in the office at the Co-op, explaining: 'It was nothing special and I wasn't there long. I went up to Luton with my mother and took a job with Electrolux, making munitions. I didn't like it so I got a job working for a small firm of insurance brokers in High Holborn. The Blitz was on and I did fire-watching on the roof to put out incendiaries, not that we ever had to but it was a bit hairy at times. I joined the Home Guard when I was 15 and did guard duties at a barrage balloon station at Whipps Cross, next to Epping Forest, although nothing really happened there.

'I volunteered for the Army at 17 but they wouldn't have me so I joined with the first batch of 18-year-olds. They put me into the Royal Berkshires and I did my basic training at Meeanee Barracks in Colchester. Then I went to a base camp in an old holiday camp on the cliff-top at Mundesley, near North Walsham in Norfolk. We did lots of cliff-climbing, exercises and guard duties and I completed a signals course. I boarded the troopship *Empress of Australia* at Liverpool and we sailed through the Mediterranean [Convoy KMF22] to Port Said, where we stopped off and disembarked. We all thought we were going to join the Eighth Army but it was not to be; instead, we boarded the *Winchester Castle* and sailed on to Bombay. When I got to the Base Reinforcement Camp at Deolali, they asked: "What did you do in Civvy Street?" When I said that I had worked in an office, they put me straight into the Orderly Room. I spent my time filling in forms and didn't particularly like the job, but there it was. My mates were all put on a draft. I didn't want to stay there, I wanted to go with my mates, so I joined the 1st Battalion, King's (Liverpool) Regiment [1 Kings] at Jhansi.

'We didn't know when we volunteered that we were going to the Chindits. We did lots of training: mostly long marches with a big pack on your back.' Another Kingsman, Second Lieutenant Crawford Wishart, later wrote: 'For months we trained in the jungles around Jhansi, marching many hundreds of miles with 60lb packs and engaging in Army exercises designed to get us ready for Burma. The Army provided tea, bread, beans, bacon, cigarettes, tobacco and other miscellaneous items. We shot deer and wild peacock for meat.' Sid continued: 'From Jhansi, we went by train to Lalaghat, in Assam. They took us on a single practice run in American gliders [Waco CG-4A], just to see how we got on with flying. We were part of 77th (Indian) Infantry Brigade, commanded by Brigadier Mike Calvert, with the Lancashire Fusiliers, the South Staffs and two battalions of Gurkhas [3rd/6th and 3rd/9th].

14318391 Private S.S.W. Machin, 1 Kings, India, 1943.

'On 5 March 1944 we flew in to a landing zone called "Broadway" as part of Operation Thursday [the second Chindit operation]. We flew at night-time and lost quite a few gliders which dropped off on the way [only 35 out of 61 arrived safely]. When we had sorted ourselves out, we went for a briefing while the engineers started to clear the airstrip. I was in HQ Company, 81 Column, commanded by Lieutenant Colonel Scott, who was known as 'Scotty', not that we called him that.' 1 Kings, which initially comprised 44 officers and 804 other ranks, together with 24 ponies and 117 mules, was relatively evenly divided into two Columns, 81 and 82. Thirty men were killed and twenty-eight wounded during the initial landing. Once the landing strip had been cleared, there were no fewer than 579 C-47 Dakota sorties over the following six nights, with the result that, in the words of the operational commander, Major General Orde Wingate, '18,000 men had been inserted into the enemy's guts'. Walter Scott had been recommended by Wingate for an MC for his command of 8 Column during Operation Longcloth, the previous Chindit operation, which took place between February and May 1943, and was one of his trusted associates.

Sid said: 'We had 22-sets, which weren't much cop; in those jungle conditions, you had a job to get a signal at all. They sent the RAF chaps to do the air-drops so they didn't have much use for us and I joined a rifle platoon. The kit we couldn't carry out on our mules, we handed over to the Chinese. They were a peculiar lot, just like bandits. We couldn't understand them and they just looked that way: very rag, tag and bobtail. As a signaller, I was given a sidearm, a Smith & Wesson .38, and I got an American carbine from somewhere, I can't remember where. We were a floating column, diversionary and not part of the main force. At one point, three of us and a muleteer joined a recce platoon of Gurkhas and we went on two days ahead, sending information back. The officer said: "Do you want to mess in with my men?" So we had some decent meals, which made a change from the K-rations. I don't know what the meat was; they used to have it tied up under their backpacks. We had one or two slight skirmishes but we were lucky and never got involved in any serious fighting. Information was very scarce.'

Between 11 and 25 May 1944, 1 Kings was attached to 111th (Indian) Infantry Brigade and went to another Chindit stronghold, "Blackpool". Crawford Wishart provides a flavour for what happened next: 'They got through the wire on a regular basis, but never in any strength. We had Vickers guns on fixed lines of fire. The perimeter defences were quite strong, but at this point the Japanese were only looking for weak spots. We were supposed to be a floater column, operating outside the perimeter to attack the Japanese before they reached our positions, but all hell was going on at "Blackpool". Soon everyone was needed inside the perimeter.'

A sliver of bamboo went through Sid's foot, which subsequently turned septic. After being carried on an officer's horse for several days, he arrived at Indawgyi Lake but, having missed his Sunderland flying-boat slot, travelled by raft to Kamaing, from where he flew to hospital in Meerut. He said: 'We were in a bit of a state when we came out and they had to fumigate us. I think that it was well done, especially the work of Brigadier Calvert. I remember Major Longley, who used to do a lot of shouting but he wasn't a bad fellow. It was an experience, if nothing else.'

The citation for Colonel Scott's DSO, written by Wingate shortly before he died in an air crash on 24 March and later endorsed by Lieutenant General Bill Slim, emphasised the many challenges faced by Columns 81 and 82 from the outset: 'Colonel Scott commanded this Battalion which carried out the initial glider landings. In doing so his Battalion suffered 120 casualties, of which 60 were killed and wounded and the remainder missing. Immediately before starting from Lalaghat, Colonel Scott was informed that the airfield on which he had expected to land, "Piccadilly", was occupied by the enemy, and he was aware that there must be grave suspicion that the enemy was at "Broadway" as well. Before Colonel Scott left, I told him that I depended on the Kings to ensure that whatever happened "Broadway" was fit for Dakota landings on the following night. His complete cheerfulness and resolution made a deep impression on me. He landed at "Broadway" amid a scene of carnage. A number of gliders through no fault of their own crashed, killing and wounding their occupants. Out of his total force of 750 embarked, only 380 had arrived. Under these circumstances he might well have felt despondent. All on "Broadway", however, testify to the vigour and enthusiasm with which he and the force under his command set to work to prepare the Dakota strip. The strip was completed by the night of D plus 1, and accepted 65 Dakotas that night. Throughout this operation, the 1st Battalion, The King's (Liverpool) Regiment showed the greatest readiness to accept losses and sacrifices in order to make the operation a success. Their cheerfulness in the face of apparent disaster is due in a large measure to the personal example and character of their commanding officer.'

Sid explained: 'I ended up in Meerut, near Delhi, where there was an Army Pay Corps depôt. We had to go into Delhi on IS duties because of the Gandhi problem. We had to guard the railway station and government buildings because there was a lot of rioting going on. We were told not to get involved but to leave it to the Indian Army and they were pretty brutal, to say the least. We lost a lot of casualties in Burma and they were making up the numbers [during Operation Thursday, 1 Kings lost 97 killed, died of wounds or missing, while many others contracted debilitating diseases and were rendered unfit

Private Sid Machin, 1945.

for further active service]. New officers came out and I volunteered to become a batman. He soon went on a course and they had bearers there so he didn't need me. In addition to Operation Python [the repatriation of the service personnel at the end of their overseas tour], there was a leave programme called LILOP. To my surprise, he asked me if I wanted to go home on leave. I flew by Dakota from Karachi to St Mawgan near Newquay, before taking a train from Penzance to London. We must have made four stopovers on the way though.

'I was asked: "Do you want to fly back or do you want to go back by boat?" I said by boat, because it took longer. I sailed in the SS *Orontes* and was travelling independently of any unit so didn't have any guard duties. By the time I got back, my officer had found a new batman, so I went on general duties. Eventually, having come back from India and prior to demob, they sent me back to Regimental Headquarters in Liverpool. Knowing that I lived in the south, I was posted on the staff of an Officers' Training Unit at Maresfield in Sussex. I didn't do a lot, I was just waiting for demob. I was just an odd bod who did guard duties occasionally. I left with the same rank that I joined with – I was never all that ambitious. But it was an experience. I think that it was a great mistake that we ever stopped National Service.'

On Boxing Day 1948, Sid married Gladys Lilian, daughter of Frank Pepper: 'She was a telegraphist, her father worked for the GPO, her two brothers worked for the GPO, my father worked for the GPO, I worked for the GPO and our eldest son used to work for the GPO. We used to keep the Post Office going. I worked there for 42 years and I think they're after me because I've been retired for 32 years and I'm still getting my pension. It's all a bit of a lark!' After more than sixty-eight years of marriage, Gladys died on 17 April 2017. Sid and Gladys had five children: Roderick, Neil, Trevor, Richard and Julie. 'Three of my sons have now retired. I've got quite a few

Sid Machin wearing Chindit blazer badge, Chindit armband, Burma Star Association tie and slouch hat.

Remembrance Day, Horse Guards, 10 November 2019: (left to right) John Hutchin, Peter Heppell and Sid Machin.

grandchildren and a few great grandchildren. I've lost track,' he said. After retirement, they moved from Woodford Green to Highcliffe in Dorset: 'I used to have a couple of caravans and we used to come down this way. We liked it so I retired down here.' Trevor, a police officer who lives less than five miles away, said: 'He's pretty fit for his age. He still drives and I have a flat on the top floor and he always walks up the stairs.' On 16 June 1987, Sid joined the Romford branch of the Burma Star Association (membership number M/3694/87). He was later the welfare officer for the Poole branch, observing sadly: 'We've got so depleted that I'm the only one alive now. We are gradually fading away.' A training facility at Denison Barracks, Hermitage, the home of 77th Brigade, is shortly to be named in Sid's honour.

14532305 Sapper Arthur Massey, Royal Engineers

William Arthur (Arthur) Massey was born in Wrexham on 14 March 1924, eldest son of John Massey of 4, 4th Avenue, Wrexham, Denbighshire, and his wife Jessie, daughter of William Holmes, a colliery engine driver. John, who had served with the Royal Navy during the First World War, worked underground at Glynmally and Llay Hall collieries. After attending Black Lane School in Pentre Broughton, which he left at 14, Arthur 'went straight into working on the surface at Llay Main colliery – I didn't go down, of course'. After a year, he was taken on as an apprentice welder by William Press & Sons of Tottenham Court Road and was based at Marchwiel, two miles south-east of Wrexham. After being called up at Padiham in Lancashire on 4 February 1943, he attended a medical in Blackburn, following which he underwent basic training at the Border Regiment Depôt at Carlisle Castle. Arthur explained: 'They knew that I was a welder so I did an apprentice test in Carlisle before I was selected for the Royal Engineers and sent to Elgin in Scotland for specialist training as a sapper, with follow-up training at Kirby Lonsdale and Halifax in Yorkshire.'

On 15 November 1943, the SS *Ranchi*, a former P&O 'R' class liner requisitioned as a troopship, sailed from the Firth of Clyde. Arthur was one of 3,542 troops sailing to the Middle East: 'We stood on the gangway to observe the two minutes' silence. I was on 'G' Deck; I was alright with the hammocks because my father had been a sailor and I could get in and out of them but some people just couldn't manage it. They tried sleeping on the tables and, after rolling off a couple of times, decided to sleep on deck.' Having met up with the rest of Convoy KMF26, they proceeded through the Mediterranean towards the Suez Canal. The convoy had a harrowing journey. On 26

14532305 Sapper W.A. Massey, Royal Engineers.

November, HMT *Rohna*, which had embarked more than two thousand US troops, was struck by a Henschel Hs 293 wireless-guided glide bomb launched from a Heinkel 177 and sank with the loss of 123 crew and 1,015 troops. The largest loss of life of US troops at sea during the Second World War, the incident was hushed up at the time and not fully acknowledged until 1967, after the passing of the Freedom of Information Act. On 28–29 November, the convoy endured another series of attacks, this time by Heinkel 111 bombers, based on Rhodes: 'The first time I was up on deck and had to take cover; the next day I was down below. We suffered a blast off the bows of the ship on the port side and had to go to Alexandria.' It was a lucky escape.

Arthur had kept a file of newspaper cuttings of *Ranchi* survivors' stories: 'The bomb was heading for a bull's-eye until it struck a hawser of the ship and was deflected away from the lower deck where all the troops were. If it hadn't hit that strand of hawser, it would have ripped out the bottom of the troopship. ... It then went through the matchboard roof of the toilet and through the deck until its nose ended up in a porthole. The force carried away the plate holding the porthole and the whole lot went into the sea. ... A rivet shot up from the deck and killed a soldier. He was

SS *Ranchi* in the Suez Canal.

buried at sea. After the battle, 3,500 people sang *Eternal Father, Strong to Save* and there was hardly a dry eye on board.'

The damage to the *Ranchi* would take almost two months to repair at Alexandria: 'In the meantime,' Arthur explained, 'we were put into a tented camp and started to clear mines which the 8th Army had left behind. The officers served us Christmas dinner, which was a privilege. Eventually we took a train to Port Said, boarded the *City of London*, disembarked at Bombay and spent five weeks at the transit camp at Deolali. That was followed by six weeks of jungle warfare training at Budni, south of Bhopal in Central India. I contracted dysentery and was sent to hospital in Secunderabad. It was almost eight months before I rejoined the Royal Engineers in Karachi.' Shortly after reporting back at Dimapur (the road and railhead for Imphal and Kohima which the Japanese had attempted to capture earlier in the year) Arthur was once again struck down with dysentery, and was evacuated to a hospital in Calcutta. After a much swifter recovery this time, he joined a sapper unit in Chittagong, where 'we helped to unload bridging equipment and stores'. Soon, though, as part of 2nd Division, he was helping to 'build bridges over some of the narrower rivers – not the Irrawaddy, which was too wide – but we worked in such confined spaces. It was also our job to ensure that the roads were kept clear so that supplies could reach the front. I remember that we were moving through the Arakan when we heard the news that they had dropped the atomic bombs.'

At that juncture, 'I was given leave to return home. It took four days: a Dakota to Karachi; then a B-24 Liberator to Habbaniyah in Iraq; to a very basic airstrip surrounded by palm trees at Lydda in Palestine [now Lod in Israel]; to Castel Benito in Libya; and, finally, to Cambridge. My leave was supposed to last a month but because of the weather the return flight was delayed and we all had to sleep on the floor of a hotel in Sloane Square. In the end

Arthur Massey at home in Wrexham.

they cancelled the flight – and we returned by ship. Initially, I rejoined the Sappers in Calcutta, where we had a few skirmishes with the locals, who wanted to know why we were still there when the war had finished. After being flown back to Karachi, we all thought we were at last going home. Instead we landed up at Shaiba in Iraq and had to work on water purification plants for a few months. Lorries then took us to Ismailia – midway between Suez and Port Said – where we waited for a ship to carry us home. I was demobbed in 1947.' On 17 January 1948 at St James's, Rhosddu, Arthur was married to Margaret Gabriel and they soon had four daughters: Marilyn, Christine, Julie and Jacqueline. On 11 May 1995, Arthur joined the Wrexham branch of the Burma Star Association (membership number M/4153/95). Margaret said: 'He has been selling poppies at Sainsbury's in Wrexham for more than thirty-five years and hopes to keep going when the pandemic is over.'

265871 Major Charles Mercer, Nigeria Regiment

Charles Henry Mercer was born on 14 November 1919 at 15 Hollingbury Park Avenue, Brighton, Sussex, son of Vernon Mercer, engineering department storekeeper, of 14 Post Office Road, Crawley, Sussex, and his wife Ada Ellen, daughter of William Henry Mates of High Street, Ifield, Sussex. Charles was educated at Colliers Grammar School in Horsham, Sussex, which he left at the age of 17, having taken his Higher School Certificate. He explained: 'I then spent several years as a trainee manager with Willetts Ltd, being groomed for a management career in the publishing industry: I had to get my hands dirty but that's the way you learn. Sadly, it all came to an end in the autumn of 1939, with the outbreak of war. I decided to volunteer for service in my county regiment, the Royal Sussex Regiment, although in any case I would eventually have been called up. Following three months' basic training at the Regimental Depôt in Roussillon Barracks in Chichester, I was selected for a commission – and officer training. I joined 161 (Royal Military College) OCTU, near Sandhurst, which had by then been closed, but with the legendary regimental sergeant major – RSM Britten – still in post. We lived in blocks and everything had had to be moved round to accommodate the numbers coming through.

'Having received a Regular Army Emergency Commission on 5 March 1943, I was posted to a battalion of the regiment at Haywards Heath, where I gained further experience and training as a platoon commander and attended a number of specialist courses. I had to get used to commanding a platoon: we were given food, a route, and tasks to complete and we used to go off for ten days at a time. With no end to the war in sight, we faced the same dilemma as so

Second Lieutenant C.H. Mercer, Royal Sussex Regiment.

many young people at that time: "Should we marry now – or wait until the war has ended?" I was already engaged to Joan Rice: our families were old friends and we had known each other for many years. In the summer of 1939, Joan completed a three-year course at Croydon School of Art; however, when war broke out, she took a job with Saunders-Roe, a firm of aircraft manufacturers on the Isle of Wight. After a great deal of thought, we were married in Brighton on 29 May 1943. We only had sufficient time for a ten-day wartime 'honeymoon' before, completely out of the blue, I was posted to Nigeria. Although I was a bit surprised, I accepted it as a wartime need. After sailing to Lagos, I made my way to Kaduna, six hundred miles north-east of Lagos, where I joined X Company, 7th Battalion, Nigeria Regiment (7 NR), which was part of 3rd (West African) Infantry Brigade.

'I was given command of 16 Platoon, which comprised thirty young Nigerian soldiers. They were mostly from the north of the country and were of the Moslem faith. Many of them looked extremely fierce, with tribal markings on their faces, formed by cuts made when they were quite young. To begin with, though, I could hardly recognise one from another while we couldn't speak a word of one another's language either. Fortunately within the battalion there were officers who had been district officers before the war so were fluent in Hausa, the language used by all the Nigerian battalions. They gave regular lessons, at intervals during the day and also in the evening. The soldiers were a happy bunch and enjoyed their training. They were a mixture of recruits and a few regular soldiers so they were learning on the spot, just as we were really. To assist me, I had a European platoon sergeant, Sergeant Diamond.

'We trained at Kaduna for six months before sailing from Lagos to Bombay. It was not until arrival in Bombay that we were given the news that we were to join General Wingate and his Chindit Force, which involved a complete reorganisation. Each battalion was split into two independent columns, able either to operate independently or together: one commanded by the CO and the other by the 2IC. It proved to be a flexible and excellent arrangement. We then moved to the Central Provinces, with its vast training area, where we took part in the most severe and sustained period of training that any of us had ever experienced. We lived in the open in all weather conditions, practising ambushes, attacks, river crossings and careful movement, all the while carrying 70lb packs on our backs. The Nigerians met all these challenges with great ability and fortitude.

'There followed a 1,000-mile train journey to Lalaghat in Assam, the take-off point for our entry into Burma. I shall never forget witnessing the Chindit Force take off on 5/6 March 1944. Some 85 gliders and their towing aircraft all lined up on a moonlit night, to land 150 miles behind enemy lines, having flown over a 7,000-foot high mountain range on the way. Sadly, the casualties were high, with some gliders not reaching their destination, while the frail bodies of others collapsed on landing. Nevertheless, the urgent task of building an airstrip to enable troop-carrying aircraft to land with the main body was achieved. It was a magnificent effort. Under the Chindit organisation, 7 NR was divided into two columns: 35 Column, commanded by the CO, Lieutenant Colonel Peter Vaughan, and 29 Column, commanded by the 2IC, Major Charles Carfrae. My platoon formed part of 35 Column. We were briefed as to our role, which was to join Brigadier Calvert and his 77th Brigade in defence of the "White City" block. The importance of this block was that it was strategically placed across a vital Japanese supply route, where the road and railway ran side by side, thus preventing all supplies from reaching their forward troops in that region.

Loading mules into a Dakota: 'The best fun was had by those watching!'

'Although 7 NR advance parties went ahead, it was not until 6 April that the main body landed at "Aberdeen", another stronghold. There were sixty mules per column and we brought all our heavy equipment with us. You can imagine the fun getting the mules into the aircraft – the best fun was had by those watching! Landing soldiers deep behind the Japanese lines for the first time was both mentally and physically demanding. The Nigerians were most impressive: very well disciplined and extremely alert. We were given an RV (rendezvous) outside the block, to which the great Brigadier Calvert came out to welcome us. Our task was to attack the Japanese in their bases and forming-up places around "White City", in particular Mawlu.

'13 April 1944 was a day that no-one in 7 NR would ever forget. A four-platoon company set off, with 16 Platoon leading. From 1100 hrs to 1500 hrs the battle continued, at varying intensities. The noise was terrific. The Nigerians attacked with fixed bayonets, shouting in their native tongues, with deep tribal markings showing on their faces. It must have been a frightening sight for the Japanese'. In the citation for Colonel Vaughan's DSO, the brigade commander wrote that he 'led his Battalion in the attack on Mawlu on 13 April 1944 and at Ywathit on 1 May 1944 and he contrived a large-scale road block south of Mawlu which was maintained for three days and led to the killing of over 40 of the enemy, the destruction of several lorries and the capture of some prisoners (a rarity)'. In turn, Vaughan recommended Major Charles Carfrae for an MC. Charles's story continued: 'We stayed at "White City" until it was evacuated. Six Dakotas took out our heavy equipment and we evacuated "White City" without further losses, which was extraordinary, really.

'We marched off and went further north, attacking various Japanese garrisons on the way. There were also a number of platoon ambushes, some successful, some not. Then came a serious setback with the arrival of the monsoon. Living as we were, entirely in the open, day and night, streamlets and dry ravines quickly became torrents of foaming water – and movement was soon restricted to no more than five miles a day. With irregular air supply, the anti-malaria Mepacrine tablets sometimes failed to arrive, hence there were bouts of malaria. It was a question of "walking it off" or being left behind. There was also the associated problem of dealing with the awful leeches, those slug-like creatures which attach themselves anywhere on the body – and I do mean anywhere! Removal

Chindits from the Nigeria Regiment in Burma.

was only possible by lighted cigarette. It was very unpleasant. The sickness rate had also risen. Peter Vaughan therefore decided to take over a Burmese building in a relatively safe area as a sort of "mini hospital", in which I used to visit some of my Nigerians. It was not a pleasant sight, with delirious and groaning patients illuminated by a flickering hurricane lamp. Under the supervision of the Column's two doctors – the excellent Bob Murray and Neil Leitch – most eventually recovered.

'Later we had several battles and an interesting time at the top of the Kyunsanlai Pass, including successful ambushes. The citation provides more detail: "Lt-Col Vaughan came to the aid of 47 Column, which had just reached the Pass in the nick of time and, after a forced march, the leading platoons of his Column reached the Pass at 0400 hrs. Early next day [he] was responsible for pushing various detachments of Columns as they arrived well down the enemy's side so that the whole position was secure by the time the remainder of 14 Brigade arrived." Subsequently we moved into a defensive location. It was there that Captain Pip Haynes, our Animal Transport Officer, once again asked the CO if he could be given a more frontline activity, being a fully-trained infantry officer. The CO agreed that he should, for a limited period, take over 16 Platoon and I gave him a full briefing. Sadly, on 6 July, on a track well forward of the forward position near Pahok village, he was shot twice by a sniper. Sergeant Perkins of 35 Column gallantly crawled forward and dragged him in. Recently, Pip Haynes's grandson, Lieutenant General Giles Hill, who never met his grandfather, contacted me. He assumes I must be the only person still living who served with his grandfather. We hope to meet when the Covid-19 situation permits.

'Peter Vaughan was wounded in the arm and was replaced as CO by Charles Carfrae while Major Nobby Hall took command of 35 Column. By this time, I was a major, with four platoons under command. Our final battle was at Hill 60, west of Mogaung, where the Japanese were heavily entrenched. 3rd (West African) Brigade attacked it but did not succeed in taking it. We were relieved by 36th British Division and flew out from Myitkyina. That was the end of our fighting war. We rested, reformed and continued training until the war ended. Our only wish then was to return home. Sadly there was no sea or air transport available so we waited some six months at Madras, a very difficult time for all. The great challenge was to look after a battalion of soldiers and keep them busy and happy most of the day.' On 26 April 1945, 265871 Lieutenant C.H. Mercer, Royal Sussex Regiment, attached Nigeria Regiment, was mentioned in despatches 'in recognition of gallant and distinguished services in Burma'.

Charles explained: 'Eventually a ship was found and we sailed back to Nigeria, where the battalion was disbanded. You can imagine the difficulty in saying farewell. We had been together for a very long time and had been through so much. The most important memory of those war years for me is the wonderful comradeship I enjoyed with my fellow Europeans, but particularly with the very splendid Nigerians. The soldiers can see your good parts and bad parts, as we could theirs. There was very little that we didn't know about one another. Sadly, there was no formal parade, so we had our own little private parties. It was so difficult. I had the same orderly throughout the war, Yeli Mundu. He saved my life on a number of occasions and also survived, thank goodness for that.'

When Charles returned to England, he saw his wife, Joan, twin daughter of Charles Alfred James Rice, for the first time in three-and-a-half years. Charles decided to apply for a regular commission and was offered one in his old regiment, the Royal Sussex. In the event, though, 'I went to a meeting at A Branch in London at which it was explained that there would be drastic cutbacks in regiments and corps and it was likely that many would be either amalgamated or disbanded. I therefore decided to go into the Royal Corps of Transport.' He subsequently served a full career in the British Army, rising to the rank of colonel: as well as two tours on the staff at the Ministry of Defence in London, he was twice stationed at Rheindahlen, headquarters of the British Army of the Rhine, and also served in Cyprus as the EOKA Insurgency was drawing to a close in the late 1950s. He explained: 'In the early 1950s, I went back to Nigeria as a staff officer in the Headquarters. The great joy was that I managed to see some of my old soldiers, in particular Sergeant Umoro Numan, who was awarded an MM and was now RSM of the 1st Battalion. He came south to see me and we had a long chat, with my young son sitting on his knee. Unfortunately the West African effort in the war has been poorly presented and was largely disregarded by the official historians.

Colonel Charles Mercer in front of the Chindit Memorial, 10 November 2019.

'After retiring from the army on 10 December 1974, I embarked on a second career, joining Wandsworth Borough Council, where I worked for ten years, as an assistant director.' Joan died on 3 January 1998, leaving one son, Michael, who lives in Australia. Charles lives on his own at Ewhurst in Surrey but still drives regularly to go shopping in the village. His final words, having worked hard to emphasise the Nigerian contribution to the Burma Campaign, were: 'Hopefully you will be patient with what I can only term as "the idiosyncrasies of a very old gentleman".'

PJX 298234 Warrant Officer Roy Miller, Royal Navy

Douglas Roy (known as Roy) Miller was born on 15 December 1923, elder son of George Miller, a constable with the Metropolitan Police, of 19 Pennant Mews, Kensington, and his wife Daisy (née Phillips). Sadly, Daisy died in 1930, at the age of 32, when Roy was six years old and his younger brother, George, just three months old. Two years later, George remarried, to Mary Gwendoline Jenkins, a Nuffield Nurse, who was originally from the Scilly Isles, and they had two sons, Peter and Mac. Roy was educated initially at Bousfield Primary School in Clareville Road, which he described as 'one of the nicest in Kensington', before attending Sloane School in Chelsea. After leaving school, he 'got a job as an office boy with Kensington Council. It wasn't much of a job but it was a start. Then the war started and I wanted to get in it so I joined the Royal Navy as a boy entrant. They used to recruit boys in those days.

'I was only 15 years old when I was sent to HMS *Ganges*, on the Shotley peninsula in Suffolk. There was a big mast which we had to climb – we were called "button boys". We went up the mast to the button on the top: it was a bit of a tremulous trip but you didn't mind when you were young. It was two years before I went to sea in HMS *Indomitable* [an Illustrious-class fleet aircraft carrier] as a seaman 2nd class boy. I remember going to Scapa Flow. After learning the ropes, as it was called, I was posted to HMS *Excellent* on Whale Island in Portsmouth Harbour, where I received training as a seaman gunner. We were close defence ack-ack – or anti-aircraft gunners – using the old pom-poms.

'By this time, I was an ordinary seaman and I was posted to HMS *Bramble*, as a replacement in a temporary post for six months. She was a fleet minesweeper and was a bit more sophisticated than an ordinary minesweeper: she had all the latest equipment. We formed part of the escort on Russian convoys. My main

PJX 298234 Ordinary Seaman D.R. Miller, HMS *Collingwood*, Fareham, 1942.

job was as a "helmsman on the wheel". There were several helmsmen and you did your tricks. We worked in watches: four hours on; four hours off; four hours on; four hours off. It was not very pleasant; in fact it was a bit rough. I still find it difficult to talk about that stuff – they were pretty grim conditions. It was a tough time of my life but we got through it. Frankly, it was one thing after another and we often didn't know where we were, on our arse or our elbow! We used to stop at Murmansk but I didn't go ashore much because we were too whacked when we got there. It wasn't easy, you know. We weren't told half the time where we were going – only the skipper knew. After I left her, she was sunk with all hands by the *Hipper*. I was a bit lucky, wasn't I?'

HMS *Bramble*, a Halcyon-class minesweeper, was a veteran of Russian convoy duty, escorting no fewer than thirteen such convoys between October 1941 and December 1942. While escorting convoy JW61B though, she was sunk on 31 December 1942 at the Battle of the Barents Sea, through the combined efforts of the German heavy cruiser *Hipper* and the destroyer *Friedrich Eckholdt*. Having been detached from the convoy to search for stragglers, she was returning when she encountered the *Hipper* and three escorting destroyers. Although the odds were overwhelming, she successfully distracted part of the German force, thus helping to save the convoy. Commander H.T. Rust DSO – who had only assumed command six weeks earlier – and 120 men went down with the ship. There were no survivors.

Roy continued: 'After HMS *Bramble*, I rejoined HMS *Indomitable* as a seaman: it had to be done and somebody had to do it. We formed part of the escort for Operation Pedestal, one of the Malta convoys. Hell on earth, I'd call it. I was often worried sick and don't let people tell you they weren't scared – we were all scared.' Taking place between 9 and 15 August 1942, Operation Pedestal was one of the most important convoys of the war: comprising 14 merchant ships, including the American tanker *Ohio*, its success was critical to the survival of the beleaguered Mediterranean island. The escort comprised no fewer than 2 battleships, 3 aircraft carriers, 7 cruisers, 32 destroyers and 7 submarines. With a total of 48 aircraft embarked, HMS *Indomitable* was attacked in the late afternoon of 12 August by Ju-87 Stukas, which dived out of the sun, taking advantage of the distraction afforded by torpedo bombers. Two 1,000 kg bombs struck the flight deck, killing 50 and wounding 59

HMS *Indomitable*.

sailors, reducing her speed from 30 to 17 knots and leaving just one carrier operational, following the earlier sinking of HMS *Eagle* by *U-73*. Roy observed: 'The enemy pilots were very good at their job – they weren't amateurs. I don't know how we got out of it you know. My ship went to the United States for repairs while I returned to Portsmouth for more gunnery training. I was promoted to able seaman: it wasn't much of a promotion but it gave me a bit more money.' Just five of the merchantmen eventually reached the George Cross island including, crucially, the *Ohio*, which foundered just as the last of the oil had been safely pumped out.

On 16 July 1943, while supporting Operation Husky, the Allied invasion of Sicily, HMS *Indomitable* was torpedoed by an Italian Savoia-Marchetti SM.79 flown by Captain Carlo Capelli. Roy remembered: 'It was a great bit of flying and he caught us just as we were changing watch. It was around midnight and I was just making my way to the Air Defence Position. There were six of us stationed in the ADP, looking through our glasses in the darkness to spot enemy aircraft, which wasn't at all easy. He put a torpedo into the engine room on our port side. I was halfway up the ladder when the torpedo struck and ended up at the bottom, although I wasn't hurt.' HMS *Indomitable* was once again sent to the United States for repairs, not returning to service until April 1944. She was posted to the British Eastern Fleet in June that year: 'We sailed to Trincomalee in Ceylon and were soon engaged in lots of convoy escort work, at sea for weeks on end, taking care of merchant ships and tankers. We always had oilers because they were always short of fuel out there. Although it was a hard flog, we didn't see much action, to be honest. At that time I received another promotion: you were chosen and I passed the exam and they made me a warrant officer, which is like a senior petty officer.

'We then joined Task Force 57, part of the British Pacific Fleet and quite a formidable force, with half-a-dozen fleet aircraft carriers – *Illustrious*, *Victorious*, *Indomitable*, *Indefatigable*, *Implacable* and *Formidable* – and a large number of cruisers and destroyers. The old battleship *Nelson* was with us for a time. She was slow and vulnerable and the Kamikazes were always after her. We had a briefing from the Americans, who were the first to encounter them. They came on board and explained what we were up against. It was a bit hairy, I can tell you. The six of us on the multiple pom-pom were all kids really, but it was an honour for us to serve. We were a team, with different functions to perform: a senior rating was captain of the gun; there were two gun-layers, left and right, controlling elevation and traverse; while the supply party was responsible for the delivery of ammunition, which came up on racks from the ammunition lockers. Although we were all trained to do any of these jobs, my main role was as a gun-layer, sitting on the right and speaking to the Fire Direction Officer. You were very much controlled and you had to apply fire discipline, otherwise it could all get a bit ragged. It was all coordinated by the FDO and you couldn't open fire until you were told. It was a good weapon and we were good at our job. I lost two of my gun crew, which I don't like to talk about.' HMS *Indomitable* was twice struck by Kamikazes: on 1 April and 4 May 1945.

HMS *Indomitable*'s home station was Sydney, Australia, and she returned there for a refit after the Kamikaze attacks. Roy explained: 'As far as we were concerned, the war just fizzled out. We were the first ship into Hong Kong and our crew were the first ashore, in ship's boats. I remember that a Japanese officer came on board and surrendered. We were issued with .303 rifles, put on our webbing and were sent ashore in parties to assist the military who were taking over everything. We guarded the Post Office and government buildings until the Royal Marines arrived and took over from us. I left HMS *Indomitable* [which embarked on her homeward journey on 3 October 1945] in Sydney and met a lady out there. I was very much in love but I don't want to embarrass anybody! Eventually I got called up to go back to England and I really didn't want to go but I had to say goodbye to her. Sadly, absence didn't make the heart grow fonder and it just filtered away. I sailed back in the cruiser HMS *Devonshire*: I was more or less a passenger so it was quite a relaxing trip.

'Although I was lined up for further promotion, I didn't quite know what to do. I very nearly signed on but decided to come out and give Civvy Street a go. To begin with I didn't make much of a success of it. I returned to my office job in the borough engineer's department at Kensington Borough Council: they had paid me while I was away. After a while I resigned and joined Alfred Bates, a Fleet Street advertising agency.' In March 1957 at Kensington Registry Office, Roy married Betty Eileen, daughter of Charles Nathan Basted, carpet planner, of 2 Rock Avenue, Mortlake, and his wife Ethel Marion, daughter of Private Edward William Galton, Rifle Brigade. Charles Basted served with the Royal Garrison Artillery during the First World War. Roy and Betty lived in Ewell in Surrey and had two daughters: Jennifer and Gillian. He has four granddaughters, and Gill explained: 'Alice Nokes is an actress and doing quite well on TV at the moment while his youngest granddaughter is studying history at Oxford and he's very proud of them all.'

Roy Miller at the Burma Star Association AGM, 21 May 2014.

Roy joined the Epsom branch of the Burma Star Association on 3 November 1994 (membership number M/4119/94). His extensive wartime service, in so many different theatres of war, entitles him to wear the 1939–45 Star, the Atlantic Star, the Arctic Star (authorised as recently as 19 December 2012), the Burma Star with Pacific clasp, the Italy Star and the War Medal 1939–45. In addition to this impressive list of British campaign medals, Roy has received two Russian medals, reflecting his service on the Arctic convoys. His War Medal bears a bronze oak leaf, indicating that he was mentioned in despatches 'for distinguished conduct'. Roy Miller, who was deeply involved with the Freemason community in Surrey, died at home on 10 March 2022.

The National Memorial Arboretum, VJ-Day 2020: (left to right) Rear-Admiral Chris Clayton, Trustee, Burma Star Memorial Fund; Roy Miller; Alice Nokes, Roy's granddaughter.

14532998 Corporal Victor Mock, Devonshire Regiment

Victor John Mock was born on 26 March 1923, second son of Herbert Henry Mock of Lower Sheepsbyre Farm, Chulmleigh, Devon, and his wife Blanch Louise, daughter of James Rice, farmer, of Challacombe, Chulmleigh. Since he was in a reserved occupation, Herbert didn't serve in the First World War. Victor left Chulmleigh Boys' School at the age of 14, explaining that 'that was the end of my university education because I had to go and work on the farm. It was a beef and sheep farm, partly on red soil and partly on clay. Leaning on the garden gate one day, I watched the explosions and flames from the bombing of Exeter; next it was Swansea's turn and then Plymouth's after that. They were bombing all the cities and I thought that can't be right, so, although I was in a reserved occupation, I volunteered to join the Army. I went to Chulmleigh to sign up and they gave me a medical. On 2 February 1943, I was called up and then went to Colchester for six weeks' primary training, before going to North Yorkshire for three months' further training. We were based at the Dugdale's Crathorne Hall estate and used to walk into Stockton of an evening for a drink or go into Yarm for a cup of tea and a bun.

'After embarkation leave, I went to Liverpool and boarded a Dutch liner, *Marnix van Sint Aldegonde*. We sailed on 23 October 1943 – I remember the day because it was my mother's birthday. The ship's captain told us all about the ship we were sailing in and how it had already been attacked twice but was unsinkable. We sailed into the Atlantic and there were lots of problems with seasickness before we entered the Mediterranean. At exactly ten minutes to six on the evening of 6 November we were torpedoed by a German aircraft. Fortunately the *Marnix van Sint Aldegonde* didn't sink until the following afternoon. Our boat station was on the top desk, with the nurses and the medical staff. When they tried to launch the nurses' boat, it tipped at 45 degrees and was wrecked against the side of the ship. So they took our boat instead, leaving us to go into the sea and board rafts, waiting for one of the convoy's ships to come and rescue us.

'Eventually we were taken to Philippeville in North Africa [Algeria]. We had lost everything. I was about to go on duty in the galley and was only left with a pair of trousers and a shirt. They gave us a mug each as well as a single razor between five of us. We tossed a coin for the razor: I won so I got it. Although the mug soon rusted and I had to throw it away, the razor was really something. It came from the British Red Cross and I used it to shave this morning. Before we sailed, my mother had given me a new wallet as a twenty-first birthday present, because she knew that she wouldn't see me on the day. It was ruined in the water, but I liberated a Japanese one – which I still use – in Burma. After ten days or so in Philippeville, we all boarded HMT *Derbyshire* for the voyage through the Suez Canal to Bombay. After docking we all went to the transit camp at Deolali, before dispersing in different directions. A party of us went to Central India for six weeks' jungle training.

'We'd only been there three weeks when news arrived that the Japanese were approaching Assam so we were rushed to Burma and all posted to different regiments. A large group of us – all Devons – were being sent to join the Wiltshire Regiment. We sat together in the front two carriages of the train during the five-day journey to Calcutta, during which we made our tea from water from the engine's boilers. When we got to Calcutta station, we were met by a sergeant from the Devons, who immediately said, "Right, you lot! You're all going back to the Devons." So we discarded our Wiltshire badges and replaced them with Devon badges, which we'd all kept and hidden away. We had nothing against the Wiltshires but we were adamant that we wanted to go back to our regiment and the sergeant guided us back in that direction.

'When we got to Imphal, I was posted initially to Admin Company, commanded by Captain Pope, whose family were legal people from Crediton, just this side of Exeter. When we were needed, though, Admin Company personnel were attached to other companies and I went to B Company. The hills – to which we gave names like Crete, Scraggy and Nippon – were so steep that no transport could get up them and we had to use mules. Although we kept driving the Japs off, they would then drive us back off. Eventually, at great cost, we captured Nippon Hill and spent the day wiring in the position because we knew that they'd come back – and they did, that evening. The next morning, there were 63 dead Japs hanging on the wire, with rice coming out of their stomachs because they'd just had their evening meal. We lost quite a few there too. Then we went on a six-week penetration patrol behind enemy lines. There was water in the *chaungs* which came up to your neck, so you had to hold your rifle over your head with one hand while grabbing onto another member of the patrol with the other. The Japs didn't like anyone behind them so they eventually withdrew and we gradually drifted back to Imphal.

'I was promoted to corporal and joined the Animal Transport Section, responsible for the mules. We took it in turns to do different jobs with the mules and would toss a coin or put a cross on a bit of paper to decide who did what. The person who either made the right call, or chose the crossed bit of paper, took on the job. Ben Newall won the toss instead of me. The mules were loaded with ammunition and supplies but his patrol was ambushed and he was killed [6099499 Private Benjamin George Newall, Devonshire Regiment, was killed in action on 18 March 1945 and is buried in Taukkyan War Cemetery].

'I went right through the war with Francis Latham, who was one of the greatest pals one could ever wish for. If he thought that someone had done the wrong thing, he would always let them know. We first met on the train going to Colchester: he got on further up the line towards Barnstaple and I joined at Eggesford. He had lovely golden hair, which was the envy of all the girls. By the end of the first week though – after three visits to the camp barber – his locks had all gone! B, C and D Companies went on the long patrol, and by the time he got back, Francis, who was in C Company, was not in very good shape. He weighed just nine stone and had every type of malaria you could get, as well as dysentery, so he was sent down the line for medical treatment. I was lucky, and although I had mild dysentery, I kept taking the pills and never caught malaria.

'We turned the Japs round and moved into Central Burma. We were now out of the jungle and all the animal transport was discarded and we were either on foot or mobile. We got to Meiktila and there was a big do there: 500 Japs lost their lives. They flew us back to India from Rangoon and we had six weeks' training for an amphibious landing, although we didn't know at the time that our destination was Malaya. General Wavell, the Viceroy of India, came to inspect us and he walked up and down the lines before addressing us: "Sorry for the delay, you lot, I promise I'll get you back into action as soon as I can. You're experienced jungle fighters and you'll lead the way." Next day, they dropped the atomic bombs and that scuppered that.

'We went to Singapore, across the causeway into Malaya and then on to Kluang. There was an airstrip just up the road and our job was to screen Japanese prisoners before sending them to Singapore and then back home. Our boss was an Australian called Major Earle, who was attached to the Battalion; like me, he was a bit rough round the edges. One day we learned that there was going to be a political protest meeting in the local cinema and were given the task of preventing them from entering the premises. By the time we got there, they were already inside, though, and the place was surrounded by local police. When we went in to get them out, they started to tear up the seats. There were people at the upstairs windows in the houses throwing things at us but a couple of rounds into a windowsill soon put a stop to that and everyone dispersed. Another time we were ordered to escort a prisoner to Kluang Station before he was taken to a jail in Kuala Lumpur, where he was to be executed. There was a bit of a disturbance when the locals tried to grab him. Apparently he had been the local Japanese Provost Sergeant and had given them a hard time during the occupation. When I explained that he was going to be executed, they all calmed down. A truck pulled up, the tail went down and we bundled him in. They then drove away without giving me any paperwork as proof that we had delivered the prisoner. In November 1946, I boarded a boat bound for Southampton and was back home in time for Christmas. After I was demobbed, it was straight back to work on the farm again.'

On 18 April 1949 at St George's, George Nympton, Devon, Victor was married to Elizabeth, only daughter of Frank Radford, smallholder and farm labourer, of Chapel Holding, Little Frenchstone, Queen's Nympton, and his wife Nora (née Bryant). They had one son, Graham, who has succeeded his father at Bircham Farm. After seventy-one years together, Elizabeth died on 23 June 2020. Victor became a member of the North Devon branch of the Burma Star Association on 2 April 1971 (membership number B/1528/71). He explained: 'One evening, I was in the Barnstaple Inn in Burrington playing skittles. Gordon Short was there too. He said to me: "Were you in the Burma Campaign? So was I." We talked about our experiences and I discovered that we were part of the same convoy on the way out. "Why didn't you come back and pick me up when we were sunk?" I said to Gordon.' The last words belong to Victor: 'I don't usually talk about it, but don't forget that I was just one of many who fought in Burma. Many of us never came back and we must never forget them.'

IA 584 Major Drogo Montagu, 2nd Punjab Regiment

John Drogo (Drogo) Montagu was born on 30 May 1916, son of John William Montagu of Wilcot Manor, Pewsey, Wiltshire, and his wife Violet Irene, daughter of James Shuter. Educated at Exeter School and the Royal Military College Sandhurst, he passed out in December 1936 and was commissioned into the Indian Army. After twelve months with the 2nd Battalion, The Border Regiment, in Ferozepore – learning Urdu and passing the mandatory language exams – he was accepted by the 2nd Punjab Regiment and posted to B Company, 2nd Battalion (2/2 Punjab), then stationed at Jullundur. Within a year, he saw active service on the North West Frontier, 'hunting down the Faqir of Ipi on the Sham Plain'. Despite his youth and inexperience, Captain Montagu was put in temporary command of a company in the summer of 1938, before being appointed adjutant. Soon afterwards, the battalion was once again posted to the North West Frontier, this time to Wana, a brigade camp in South Waziristan – where he became fluent in Pashto.

Despite the outbreak of the Second World War, life in India changed little initially, although 2/2 Punjab was steadily cannibalised: 'We lost quite a lot of officers in Peshawar about this time and we lost a lot of troops because we were raising new battalions.' The influx of new blood provided something of an impetus to 26-year-old Drogo Montagu's military career: 'I was a major, had been on and off for quite some time. I mean one went up and down like a yo-yo in the army: major to captain up to major again. I was battle 2IC or 2IC for practically the whole of the war.' The world was changing very fast: 'We had all these thrown at us in Trichinopoly: 3-inch mortars, 2-inch mortars, anti-tank weapons, wireless sets, vehicles, vehicle maintenance garages and workshops. It was a revolution really. We had very little time to train and, of course, the troops were all farmers.'

There was much to be done: 'We were training there for a year almost and getting ready to go to the Middle East when suddenly it was cancelled because of the Japanese coming into the war. Our orders were cancelled immediately and we were told that we were going to Burma and then started another period of training. We moved in March 1943 to Belgaum to do jungle training and we had to waterproof all our vehicles and paint them green and start learning jungle tactics. The great difference was the lack of mobility and the lack of visibility.' As part of 25th Indian Infantry Division, 2/2 Punjab finally 'went from Bangalore by train to Calcutta and then we took a ship from Calcutta down to Akyab. Then we moved up towards Buthidaung where the Japanese were holding the line.' It was a tense situation: 'The leading company was about 20 yards from the Jap position at the top of the hill and several times they tried to attack us in the middle of the night, usually in a rain storm, and we tried to shift them off several times and failed. We were heavily shelled most days in our position with mortars and guns.'

Major Drogo Montagu, 2nd Punjab Regiment.

Of course, the 14th Army had more than the enemy to contend with: 'The conditions in Burma were appalling, mosquitoes by night, flies during the day, the heat, the wet. I was as thin as a rake, I weighed about 10 stone and when we were on any marches or patrols, I'd have to fall out every so often into the bushes and then catch the tail up as it went past me and then get up to the head again. It wasn't easy, but willpower kept you going and one's duty to the regiment kept you going.' A month later, he saw his CO being brought back by stretcher from the front line after being fatally wounded by a grenade – and Drogo duly assumed command of 2/2 Punjab: 'The day after I was made CO, I was summoned to Brigade Headquarters and told that the battalion had to go out on a deep penetration patrol, which frightened the life out of me. It was getting dark so we withdrew and laagered up for the night, wondering whether the Japs would come out and attack us at night. They were very good at that, much better than we were really. But I don't think they were in sufficient strength there and they'd been badly knocked about during the day so they didn't come out. That was my inauguration as CO and I can tell you it shook me to the core.' Over a fourteen-week period, the battalion had lost a quarter of its strength.

A new CO, Lieutenant Colonel (later Lieutenant General) S.P.P. Thorat, one of the first Indians to attend the Royal Military Academy Sandhurst, was appointed when Admiral Lord Louis Mountbatten entrusted the task of intercepting the Japanese withdrawal from Upper Burma, and turning it into a rout, to 51st Infantry Brigade, an all-Indian brigade. At 0700 hrs on 29 January 1945, 2/2 Punjab advanced under heavy fire to complete the task already begun by 8/19 Hyderabad and 16/10 Baluch. Bayonets were fixed and desperate hand-to-hand fighting continued through the night until the Japanese had been vanquished and a hitherto-unknown feature called Melrose, the lynchpin of the Kangaw position, was finally in Allied hands. According to Pradeep Barua: 'The battle only ended when Thorat called in air strikes to smash a Japanese counterattack.' The three battalion commanders – Thorat, Thimayya and Sen – were each awarded the DSO (all three became generals, with Thimayya serving as Chief of the Army Staff 1957–61). At this juncture, 2/2 Punjab was withdrawn to Coimbatore in southern India. 'We had been in Burma for a year and were decimated in numbers,' Drogo explained. Although he was mentioned in despatches on 19 September 1946, his brigade commander, Brigadier Reggie Hutton, wrote privately that he 'hoped you would get something more'.

Officers of the 2nd Battalion, 2nd Punjab Regiment; Major Drogo Montagu is seated third from left in the front row.

While training for a seaborne landing on Morib Beach, south-west of Kuala Lumpur, as part of Operation Zipper, the dropping of the atomic bombs and resulting Japanese surrender intervened – and the landings were unopposed. Drogo witnessed the formal surrender of the Japanese to Mountbatten at the police barracks in Kuala Lumpur, before spending a year in Kuantan, on the east coast of Malaya. In January 1947, he finally left 2/2 Punjab, which 'had been my life for nine or ten years', to 'take over as training major of our Depôt in Meerut'. Little more than six months later, the Partition of India meant that he had to 'split the regiment in half and prepare the despatch of the Muslim element from the depôt to the 14th Punjab in Pakistan and to receive in Sikhs and Dogras to make up the full strength of our battalion'. Two trains were sent to Pakistan and, due to careful planning, 'they arrived with military precision'. Having been promoted to command the Depôt, he was one of the last English COs in the Indian Army. Shankarrao Thorat wrote: 'Drogo Montagu is a first-rate officer and a very fine gentleman. In war he was conspicuous by his leadership, disregard to personal danger, sound judgment and determination. In peace his work was characterised by an organising ability of a very high order. Drogo Montagu is a keen and a good sportsman and takes a genuine interest in the welfare of those he commands. He is an extremely conscientious and a very loyal officer.'

In February 1949, Drogo Montagu resigned his commission, 'packed up and came back'. Initially he took a job with Granada Theatres – but it wasn't for him: 'I couldn't stand the cinema business. I couldn't stand inveigling young people into the cinema on a lovely afternoon. I felt like standing there with a horsewhip and driving them out to get some exercise!' Instead he was offered a job with an engineering company, and within a year was sent as the chairman's representative to a newly-acquired firm based in Brisbane, which was 'the beginning of my industrial career'. Having met her on a 'blind date' in Brisbane, he married Dorothy Boreham, daughter of Charles Edward Chuter, on 24 November 1952. They had three sons and two daughters. In retirement, they lived at the Officer's House in Freshwater on the Isle of Wight. After paying a subscription of £16 (including £1 joining fee), Drogo became a life member of the Isle of Wight branch of the Burma Star Association on 30 October 1991 (membership number M/4017/91). Dorothy died on 28 April 1990 and Drogo died on 18 August 2013.

3608538 Sergeant Vincent Murphy, Border Regiment

John Vincent (known as Vincent) Murphy was born on 28 April 1924, elder son of Edward Murphy of 59 Faraday Road, Northwich, Cheshire, and his wife Martha Ann, second daughter of John Hodgkinson, chemical labourer, of 389 Firth Fields, Davenham, Cheshire. Edward Murphy worked as a labourer for Brunner Mond & Co Ltd, which, in 1926, merged with three other British chemicals companies to form Imperial Chemical Industries (ICI), where his father, John, had also worked. John was born in Belturbet, County Cavan, three miles from the border with Northern Ireland, while his wife, Annie, came from Terenure, in the southern suburbs of Dublin. During the First World War, Edward served with the 7th (Service) Battalion, East Lancashire Regiment, which was raised at Preston in August 1914 – the month that war was declared – and was wounded while serving on the Western Front. The war memorial outside the Winnington Works, which commemorates the 291 Brunner Mond employees who died, out of 2,688 who served, was unveiled on 11 June 1921 by Lieutenant General Sir Belvoir de Lisle; both Roscoe Brunner and Sir Alfred Mond also spoke during the ceremony. Nineteen of those commemorated served with the East Lancashire Regiment. The firm manufactured around half the high explosives used by the British Army during the First World War, at very competitive rates below those at which they had been invited to tender.

Vincent attended St Wilfred's Catholic Primary School in Witton Street, Northwich, before taking a scholarship to Sir John Deane's Grammar School, also in Northwich. He enjoyed a successful school career, playing in the 1st XI cricket and 1st XV rugby teams, joining the Air Training Corps and taking his School Certificate. On leaving school at the age of 16½, he also started work at ICI's Winnington Works, typing shipping manifests for the fleet of barges which took the company's products to Liverpool and, from there, across the world. He explained: 'I was tempted to join the RAF but got so fed up with waiting, because you couldn't join until you were 18, that I volunteered for the Army instead. I was given very little choice. I couldn't join the Cheshire Regiment, the local regiment, or my father's old regiment, the East Lancs, so I joined the Border Regiment instead. I did my initial training at Bitts Park in the centre of Carlisle and then at Durranhill Camp on the edge of Carlisle, where they trained me as a signaller. They offered me an officer's course but I didn't feel that I should be taking command of men at the age of 18. We were then all sent to young soldiers' battalions, known as 70th Battalions, but the Border's young soldiers' battalion had just closed so I was sent to the King's Liverpool young soldiers' battalion instead. It was December 1942 and I caught a train from Middlesbrough to Sevenoaks in Kent. When we arrived, it was glorious sunshine – we don't have days like that in Cheshire – and we marched in full kit to Brasted. Battalion Headquarters was at Westerham and we were a counter-attack battalion in case Biggin Hill was attacked.

'In November 1943, I boarded a troopship, the *Dunnottar Castle*, and we sailed through the Mediterranean, one of the first to do so, instead of going round the Cape. I spent a week or so ashore at Port Tewfik, the entrance to the Suez Canal, until we were transferred to the P&O liner *Mooltan*, which was twice the size, for the voyage to Bombay. I then went to the transit camp at Deolali for more training. One night, we went out on exercise, led by a second lieutenant who used to be a sergeant and had been in the army for years. He got lost and we stayed out all night. My mate got sick and died, which made me really mad. I wrote a letter about it to my parents, which must have been opened, because it was announced in Company Orders that I had been put on a charge for 'causing alarm and despondency'. I was sentenced to seven days' 'jankers'. At the end of my sentence, I was ordered to join the next party to leave for the front. I was posted to the 9th Battalion [9 Border] and made my way by train, boat and truck via Dimapur, Kohima, Imphal and Tiddim to Kennedy Peak, the forward position held by the 17th (Indian) Infantry Division.' The second-highest mountain in Chin State, Kennedy Peak rises almost

3608538 Sergeant Vincent Murphy, Border Regiment, Secunderabad, December 1944.

160 The Final Curtain: Burma 1941–1945

5,000 feet higher than its neighbours, completely dominating the Tiddim Road, a vital artery.

On 6 March 1944, Fifteenth Japanese Army launched Operation U-Go, the assault on the key bases at Kohima and Imphal: 'We were one of the most forward battalions and were regularly on patrol. After getting back from one patrol, we were ordered to get back to Imphal as quickly as we could. We made a good line against the Japanese advance and had to retreat 150 miles back to where I had just come from. After a signaller had been killed, I was posted as a company signaller. When the signals corporal was wounded, I was put in charge.' Evading Japanese attempts to outflank them at Sakwng and Vanglai, 9 Border retained its cohesion and retreated in good order to the Imphal Plain: 'They kept cutting through our lines, which weren't like First World War lines, and were trying to stop us. We had to go round roadblock after roadblock. I have always been pretty active and energetic so I did a lot of extra work like carrying Bren guns because everybody was weak.' Back within the defensive perimeter, the battalion took a full part in actions at Llango

Secunderabad, Christmas 1944: Vincent Murphy (second from right).

near Palel and also at Potsangbam (known to the soldiery as 'pots and pans'), OP Hill and on the Silchar Track near Bishenpur. The cost to 9 Border was very considerable: 7 officers and 81 other ranks were killed and 12 officers and 245 other ranks were wounded. These figures, of course, take no account of those who had fallen sick. At that stage, Vincent hadn't been sick, and so, when the battle for Imphal had been brought to a successful conclusion, he flew back to England on leave.

After he had been back at the front for a few weeks, though, he explained: 'I passed a mirror and couldn't believe it was me – I knew I wasn't well. I was evacuated via a casualty clearing station and a river boat on the Brahmaputra to the base hospital at Trimulgherry on the outskirts of Secunderabad. I was diagnosed with malaria, malnutrition and tropical sprue, which meant that I was getting rid of all the fat in my body. When I arrived at the hospital I weighed just 7st 12lbs. They put me on a diet of 'special foods': minced liver and sour buttermilk. The chap in the next bed didn't like buttermilk so I ate his as well. When I left hospital, I weighed 13st 3lbs. After spending Christmas in hospital, I didn't fly back to rejoin the battalion at Meiktila until just before Easter 1945. 17th Division was ordered to advance south to capture Rangoon but we didn't make it because a bridge across the Pegu river had been blown up by the Japanese. There were Japs to the west of us trying to get eastward.' In *Quartered Safe Out Here,* George MacDonald Fraser, author of the Flashman novels, who was also in 9 Border, described the battle for Pyabwe, the battalion's last major action, including 'the whine and crack of the Jap 75s, … the rattle of our rapid fire as we knelt among the ancient rolling stock, the figures running and falling across our front on the slope, the long painful trudge back from the sniper's nest to the section's final position [and] the faint pfft! of shots fired by some distant Japanese optimist passing high overhead.' Although Vincent 'didn't know him during the war, I talked with him once at the bar during a battalion reunion in Carlisle'.

9 Border was stationed at Waw, west of the Sittang River, scene of Burma Command's disastrous defeat in late February 1942, when news of the Japanese surrender came through. On 1 December 1945, the 9th Battalion amalgamated with the 4th Battalion, with the result that the former now ceased to exist: 'I was now Signal Sergeant but there were two signal sergeants. In Rangoon I had had an interview to attend a

teacher's training course, so they made me Education Sergeant instead. It was very frustrating because nobody really wanted to learn anything and the unit was active all the time chasing up bandits.' In early October 1946, Vincent was flown home from Karachi, before being demobbed the following April.

Long before he had embarked for the Far East, he had met Gladys, daughter of Samuel Robinson, who also worked for ICI, at the Wallerscote Works. They had been in the same class at junior school at Winnington for a couple of years: 'We had a teacher who made us stand on our chairs while she asked us arithmetic questions like "What are seven times seven?". Anyone who got the answer wrong had to sit down – and me and Gladys Robinson B (there were two Gladys Robinsons) were always the last two standing. Her mother and my mother were both members of the British Legion Club. She lied about her age to join up at 16 and worked as a cook for prisoners of war, cycling over every day from home. During my leave from Burma, I exchanged my chocolate and cigarette coupons at her camp and we started to write to one another. Once I had gone through my Army Resettlement Training, we started courting.' Vincent and Gladys were married at St Wilfrid's, Northwich, on 30 November 1949 and they had one son, Timothy (Tim), and two grandchildren. Sadly, Gladys died on 15 April 2009.

VJ-Day 2001, Northwich, Cheshire.

After the war, Vincent returned to ICI as a clerk in the Distribution Department, before moving into the personnel side. Having worked for the Mond Division in Runcorn, he was appointed Assistant Personnel Officer at the Castner-Kellner Works, also in Runcorn, before becoming Personnel Manager at Pilkington-Sullivan Works, Widnes, and, finally, Personnel Manager at the Wallerscote Works. He retired from ICI in 1980, at the relatively young age of 56, as the economic adjustment of the newly-elected Thatcher government prompted significant cost reductions across UK industry. He said: 'I worked for ICI for thirty-nine years and have now been retired for more than forty years.' On 29 June 1969, Vincent joined the Northwich branch of the Burma Star Association (membership number M/1366/69), where he was the secretary for many years. In a typically modest and understated way, he said: 'I don't reckon that I did a great deal; I just did what I was told.' His daughter-in-law, Christine, said: 'He still drives his car and is very independent. He's amazing really.'

Vincent Murphy with a Burma Star Association wreath.

Vincent Murphy after laying the wreath.

14580396 Signaller Dennis Newland, Royal Signals

Dennis Stanley Newland was born on 12 November 1924, younger son of Ernest Arthur Newland of 125 High Street, Berkhamsted, Hertfordshire, and his wife Alice Lily, daughter of Augustus Charles Garrod, porter, of 210 Shirland Road, Paddington. Ernest was the manager of F.W. Fox, an ironmongers in Berkhamsted, 'for which he did the buying as well as the selling'. After attending Park View Road County Council School up to the age of 11, Dennis was awarded a scholarship to attend Berkhamsted School, which was a fee-paying school. Dennis not only described himself as a 'number one chatterbox' but also took the trouble to send me a copy of *What Did You Do In The War, Dad?*, which he wrote and published for family and friends in 2001. He explained: 'Although I achieved five credits in the School Certificate, the equivalent of O-levels, I didn't do well enough for the scholarship to be extended. So I had to leave school at 16, because that was what the original scholarship covered. I did, however, earn an exemption from the London Matriculation, which counted towards the Upper School Certificate, or A-levels. After leaving school, I worked in my father's shop for a few months, while I looked for a job on the railways, but ended up working for the Midland Bank. I worked at the Tring branch, a sub-branch which only employed three staff, and was paid the princely sum of £50 per year. I was the junior clerk but I used to do all sorts of odd things. There were two locks on the safe and there always had to be two people present when it was opened. The branch manager, Mr. Webb – you never called him by his Christian name and I was called Newland – had a car but the petrol ration was so small that he only came over once a week. So, as a 17-year-old, I was responsible for one of the keys to the safe.

'While I was at Berkhamsted School, I was in the School Cadet Corps and rose to the rank of lance corporal. The average school pupil number was around 600. Out of the 125 ex-Berkhamsted School boys killed during the war, 43 of them had been at school while I was there. As the Cadet Corps was a school organisation, I ceased to be a member on leaving school. Youths of my age at that time were expected to be in a Cadet Corps, the Home Guard or the ARP. I chose the ARP and joined the Poison Gas Cleaning Service. On 1 April 1943, after eighteen months with the bank, I was called up and did six weeks' primary training with the Suffolk Regiment in Bury St Edmunds. I did well in primary training as I had done much of it before in the School Cadet Corps. I was interviewed and had to do some practical tests to see if I could do technical things. I could reassemble a bicycle hub, which involved putting in the ball bearings, which most of the others found very difficult. I was probably the best educated in the platoon. In the last week I was given a 'Potential NCO' armband. The hut radio, which was permanently tuned to popular music, ceased to work one day. I quietly mended it, more by luck than skill, but they did not know that. I had arrived! The previously aggressive ones started to ask for help, not only with army matters, but also with their letters. I now knew why they did not write letters; some of them were barely literate.

'Although they were going to send me to the Royal Artillery as a gun position surveyor, I went instead to Catterick to be trained as an Electrician Signals (ES). The title is very misleading in civilian terms. We were trained to repair army radio transmitters and receivers, telephone equipment including small exchanges, and battery chargers. The course lasted three months, until September 1943, after which I got a rating as an A3 Tradesman, which was a very useful qualification. On 9 October, a group of us joined 80th Division, a holding division, at Whalley, a small town between Clitheroe and Blackburn in Lancashire. I did my first guard in the army on 13 October. How I had managed to avoid them for nearly six months I really do not know. Most of us did not have ambitions to become officers; however, we worked hard to help win the war so that we then could become civilians again. You just go where you are sent. Our possible destination started to become apparent when we were issued with khaki tropical kit. We were going somewhere hot. On 13 January 1944 in Liverpool we boarded HMT *Maloja*, a little tub with two triple-expansion steam engines, which worked the Australian route between Tilbury and Sydney. There were thirty signalmen and, as we were the largest draft on board, they made us gunners on the pedestal-mounted Oerlikon 20mm cannons. I was partnered with fellow ES, Freddy Nightingale, on our gun position, built out onto the port side end of the ship's bridge. We had a bit of training but that didn't happen till we got to the Red Sea – and it was a bit late by then. It was now hot and to protect us from the sun we were issued with sun helmets, colloquially called 'Bombay Bowlers'.

'It took a month to reach Bombay and our draft worked a Royal Navy routine: in every three-day period, we were on duty a total of 24 hours. As soon as we disembarked, we boarded a troop train – 3rd Class Indian – for our journey to the Signals Depôt at Mhow: wooden seats; a luggage rack which you could sleep on; and a loo in the corner, a screened-off hole in the floor. As the train passed through the outskirts of Bombay we were struck by the smells, roughly speaking a mixture of sewage and spices. The other thing that amazed us was the cramped conditions in which people had to live and work. The narrow streets contained a large number of very small shops, some selling things we did not recognise. Road transport was a complex mixture of bullock carts with unsprung and unlubricated, squeaking, wooden wheels; a variety of horse-drawn vehicles; bicycles; rickshaws pulled by a man; and a few elderly buses and cars, mainly seen at level crossings.

'Before we went to bed that first night, we were given mosquito nets; it was the first time most of us had slept under one. The forerunners of electric ceiling fans, punkahs, were used to create a draught. These were beams of wood hung like pendulums on two wires from the roof and could be swung to and fro by means of a rope which went through a hole in the wall. This rope was pulled from the outside by an Indian servant, the *punkah wallah*, often lying down with the rope round one of his big toes. Strips of heavy cloth attached to the beams created a draught – or did they just disturb the dust? Our mattresses were hard, but by now we could sleep on anything. The warm Indian nights could be special, particularly when you were on a mobile guard picquet. Walking along with your rifle, with Indian music wafting from a distance, could be strange and a little magical, particularly when there was a distant electrical storm or a light shower of rain.

'Well-educated private soldiers tend to be a bit cynical, particularly if they're technicians. During our six weeks at Mhow we mostly did bullshit things and there was very little technical training, which didn't impress us. We had had some specialist training and wanted to get on and use it. After a long train journey across India, via two or three transit camps, I eventually reached a reinforcement camp at Comilla, now in Bangladesh, and was posted to 14th Army Signals, which was also based at Comilla. Although I was anything but a fighting soldier, 14th Army HQ was organized in a peacetime fashion, with more bullshit and lots of polishing and things like that. We really didn't think that was what we should be doing – we wanted to look after radio sets. On the positive side, they issued us with drill trousers and a monsoon cape. The cape was a very useful garment with straps to hold it in position. It came halfway down my calves and really did keep the rain off. Unfortunately, when I finally came home from Malaya in 1947, I was not permitted to keep it. With all the pointless things we were asked to do, one could only admire the army postal system. Letters followed us round from unit to unit and never seemed to get lost. Mother and I used to number our letters serially and I do not recall one ever getting lost. Those who actually did the fighting really had no concept of what it took to keep them there. I understand that, for every fighting man, the Japanese had just one to back them up, while the British had six and the Americans twenty.

'There must have been around 500 of us but we didn't really have any technical officers. In fact, I think there was only one – and he was also put in charge of the MT. We were running about twenty channels, with a separate transmitter for each one. Of course, it wasn't RT because of the distances and they were sending cypher messages in groups of five letters. The transmitters had to be placed quite a long way from one another to avoid interference, despite the different frequencies. The operators, each with their own receiver, were located five miles away in the Signal Office. You could only use FM at close range and in an uninterrupted straight line, which didn't work in Burma because there are so many hills. Initially I was in a technical maintenance section, although we also did our share of square-bashing, which was a real waste of our training. It was fascinating work and I really enjoyed it: all sorts of things – including a dentist's drill – came in to be mended and we usually managed it.

'I once found out that Noël Coward was giving a concert at the YMCA near Comilla. As I tended to work late, I found that my friends had already left in the truck that was laid on. I scouted round and scrounged a lift, arriving just as the show was about to start and, of course, the building was very full. A helpful military policeman took me round the outside of the building, opened the door and I slipped in as the show started and found a seat at the end of the front row. Front rows were usually reserved for officers, but I think on this occasion they were sitting in the middle. Coward sang many of his songs, including *Mad Dogs and Englishmen*, *The Stately Homes of England* and *London Pride*. A memorable night.

'In November 1944, 14th Army headquarters moved up to Imphal. The journey from Comilla to Imphal with our wireless trucks took a week. We had just received American 399 radio transmitters and I was part of the first team that went up there and we had to do all the wiring ourselves. They were powerful transmitters, by British Army standards, capable of 400 watts RF on the aerial and required a power input of 2 kilowatts to achieve this. Four sets would run off one generator and, because they were American, they ran off 110 volts instead of 240 volts. Each transmitter was contained in a casing approximately a metre wide, one-and-a-half metres high and half a metre deep. At Imphal it was either extremely dusty or very wet so it was difficult to remain on the air. Fault-finding was fascinating because insects could get through the wire of the cages and often shorted out the equipment; a lizard got in on one occasion. The problems became much worse during the monsoon when everything became very wet, or if not wet, then rather damp.

'At Imphal, the transmitting station – or "wireless village", as we called it – was at the end of the airstrip, which wasn't the best place to put it in case an aircraft crashed but someone decided that that was where it should be. 20 November 1944 was the great day when we became operational and took over from Comilla. As well as the links to Delhi and Ceylon, there were transmitters connecting us to the three 14th Army corps – IV, XV and XXXIII – and also ten divisions. There were also links to the Americans in the north, to the Chinese in the east and to Force 136, a unit behind the Japanese lines in Malaya. It was a big operation with about 25 operators on each shift, needing a total of 75 for three-shift working. At first we worked a 14-hour shift every other night plus a morning or evening on alternate days, as we were short of technicians. The petrol generators had to be changed over every eight hours. This required contacting four operators over the telephone, as we had to turn off the four transmitters for several minutes while we made the change. Changeover in the middle of the night was always the most difficult, as it was hard to see what we were doing.

'We were offered places for several people to go to the Indian Electrical & Mechanical Engineers (IEME) establishment at Agra to learn how to repair Type 'X' cypher machines. Type 'X' was the equivalent of the German Enigma machine: they worked in a very similar way and I was told that we had copied the German example. It was a long and complicated journey from Imphal, via Dimapur and Calcutta. As a BOR, I travelled 2nd Class, unlike the troop train. In Calcutta I caught the Delhi train and was met at Agra station by staff car. As the only arrival, I had the vehicle to myself. They do things differently in the IEME! The whole journey took ten days, and by the time I arrived the course had already started. They offered to find something for me to do until the next course started in a fortnight, so I went to the workshop where Italian PoWs from the Middle East were mending things like Avometers [electrical measuring instruments]. They were tradesmen skilled in the repair of electrical instruments and I would be learning from them. I found them easy to get along with and even managed to replace the burned-out coil of an Avometer by myself.

'The course lasted a month, and as well as Type 'X', I also learned about teleprinters. By the time the course had finished, 14th Army HQ had moved to Monywa on the Chindwin, where I rejoined them, having flown in by Dakota. I asked one of the crew, when he went past wearing a parachute, whether there were any parachutes available for us in the event of an emergency. He said that a parachute was of limited use if you fell among the trees we were flying over. You could be left suspended far above the ground and, as the area was sparsely populated, you would probably never be found. With a cheerful smile on his face, he advised me to keep my fingers crossed as there were no parachutes for passengers anyway! When I arrived back at my unit, I was given a booklet entitled *Pocket Guide to Burma*. The 56 pages contained a description of the country with a brief history, together with useful words and phrases. It also contained a list of Do's and Don'ts, including the priceless one: "Treat Burmese women with great respect. They live a much freer life than most eastern women, but their smile doesn't mean they want to go to bed with you."

'I resumed work at the transmitter station and then the monsoon started. It was amazing the amount of paperwork an active service unit was required to handle. I hoped the infantry did not have to do all this as they would have had little time left for chasing Japs. Later we moved to Meiktila, where the army actually organized a VE-Day celebration. Being off duty, two us went into Meiktila for these events. First there was a football match which we did not think was very good. Then General Slim gave an address in which he said he hoped our own victory would not be too long coming. We went back to the main unit for some food and returned for an open-air film show. After this finished, we missed the truck back to the wireless village and thumbed a lift in a jeep, which already contained two doctors and a nursing sister. In those days, army nursing sisters held commissioned rank. There were no female other ranks. Ordinary nursing was done by RAMC male other ranks. A strange system. We were glad when they arrived at their destination and we got off, as the jeep was wandering all over the road. The doctor who was driving was clearly rather drunk. Our second lift was in a staff car, which turned out to be General Slim's own car. His driver told us he was instructed by the general to give lifts to soldiers when the car was running empty. It was now raining and the driver took us back to the wireless village, which was beyond his destination. "Uncle" Bill Slim was highly thought of: he had led the army out of Burma and was now leading it back. Few other generals have done this.

'The roads were mostly a muddy mess and largely unusable, except by tanks, so we drove along the railway lines. Our equipment was so heavy that we had three-axle trucks, which were a little on the large side. There were no trains to worry about because the Japanese had never got that railway working again after it was severely damaged at the start of the war. It was a slow and bumpy ride over the railway sleepers and the 300-mile journey to Rangoon took five days. Like many of our vehicles, the truck in which I was travelling had lost the fluid from its brakes and we had no spare. The foot brakes therefore did not work. Handbrakes are much less efficient than footbrakes, so there was a second person to pull on the handbrake, using both hands when the driver asked. The driver was Wally and the brakes man was an Indian driver. All went well until the truck in front stopped in a hurry. Wally shouted "Brake!", but the Indian's reactions were slow. I think he had fallen asleep. Before he could stop us, we hit the vehicle in front. The lorry behind hit us and the one behind hit that one. I do not think any of the footbrakes worked. Fortunately, American army lorries were substantially-built, with a strong chassis and massive bumpers, so that one lorry could 'shunt' another one if necessary. Little actual damage was done to the vehicles, other than a few more dents. I did wonder, though, what the bump had done to 'my' radio transmitters.

'Since we were a well-organised HQ unit, the decision was almost immediately taken to withdraw us to India to prepare for the invasion of

Malaya. On 2 June 1945 in Rangoon, we therefore boarded MV *Devonshire* for the two-day journey to Madras. A week later, 20 ES joined a convoy for the 450-mile drive to Secunderabad. I was in the back of the leading jeep containing the navigating officer. The rest of the unit went by train. Unfortunately this officer's navigational skills were not good. He did not know the country or the layout of Madras and, very surprisingly, had no map! We got under way at about midday and spent the afternoon trying to find our way out of Madras. The jeep covered 45 miles touring the suburbs, endeavouring to find the road to the north. In the end, the convoy got split up and we all returned to the car park from which we had started. We never heard what, if anything, his superior officers called him, but he was still navigating officer when we set off again next day, this time quite early. Although he still had no map, he had taken the precaution of borrowing a local Indian guide to get us out of Madras onto the road north. I had a fifty-miles-to-the-inch map of India and Burma, purchased in a bookshop in Mhow a few weeks before, soon after I had arrived in India. It seemed to me a useful addition to a signalman's kit. I offered to lend the map to the navigating officer and he seemed pleased to accept. He also appeared as surprised that I should have a map as I was that he did not. He seemed unaware that they were easily bought in local bookshops (I still have the map). He seemed to lack an inquiring mind.

'Everything was focused on preparations for the next phase of the war against Japan. After doing all the preparations, we were sent on three weeks' leave in Ootacamund. Before the war, someone of my rank would never have been allowed to go there. I would have been accommodated at Wellington Barracks, two stops down the line. It was a lovely place and two of us climbed Dobbabetta Peak, at almost 8,000 feet the highest mountain in the Nilgiris, but when we got to the top everything was shrouded in mist. While we were there, though, the Americans dropped the atomic bombs and that changed our lives altogether. We were told that we were urgently needed in Singapore so we went by train to Madras to board the auxiliary troopship *Talma*. She had recently been used by the Indian Army and had been left in the most appalling condition: everything was filthy dirty, the ship was infested with cockroaches and it would take nine days to get to Singapore. So we all mutinied, including the senior NCOs, and refused to embark. Our major came on board, saw the state of the *Talma*, and took a brave decision: he ordered us off so formal disciplinary action was averted. Our grievances were addressed and we duly re-embarked at one o'clock in the morning. Apparently General Slim understood but didn't approve; of course, he had been a private soldier once. By the time we got to Singapore, the requirements had changed and they didn't want us to set up a signal station after all so we were footloose and fancy-free for a fortnight. Then we drove up to Kuala Lumpur. We had to drive ourselves because the decision had been taken not to take Indian soldiers to Singapore. Although I had driven the Berkhamsted shop van unofficially a number of times, I hadn't passed a driving test because I was too young when I joined up.

14580396 Signaller D.S. Newland, Royal Signals, Malaya, 1946.

'Our unit was now renamed Malay Command Signals as, with the end of the war, the 14th Army passed into history. For some reason, we became eligible for a rum ration for the first time in the army. I drank it diluted with orange squash. Had this rum been carried with the Quartermaster's Stores all the way through Burma? Stranger things have happened. My pay at this time, as an 'A' grade army tradesman, was 8s 5d per day, which included 1s Japanese campaign pay and a 12% increase for service in India, Burma or Malaya. This added up to approximately £2 19s per week. Over Christmas we were only working skeleton shifts and I had Boxing Day off as well as Christmas Day. After a quiet morning, several of us went to see one of our number who was in hospital. In the evening we went to the Garrison Theatre to see the comediennes Elsie and Doris Waters doing their *Gert and Daisy* act, which was very popular on the variety stage and the radio at the time. Don't forget there was no television then. These two ladies were sisters of Jack Warner of *Dixon of Dock Green* fame. The show had been advertised on our noticeboard, warning that there would be no reservations and seating would be on the basis of first come, first served. When we got in, after queuing for about an hour, we found that the front twelve rows had been reserved for officers. When they drifted in just before the show started, the officers were cheered, clapped, booed and hissed at. One brigadier smiled very patronisingly when he was clapped, but changed his expression when he was booed. It was Christmas and alcohol had been flowing fairly freely. Fortunately, in spite of this nonsense, the show was very entertaining and lasted some two hours.

'One day, Sergeant Alf Quinlan rushed into our billet and gave me a hug – I thought the sun had got him! But my name had been drawn out of the hat for 'Blighty leave' so, in the summer of 1946, I had six weeks' leave. We were also called upon to carry out electrical work at the local army hospital. It was quite an eye-opener to relatively naïve soldiers like me that one ward had almost as many patients as all the others put together. This was the VD ward. It was apparently not an army offence to contract VD, but it was if you did not seek treatment. Parts of Kuala Lumpur containing brothels were marked 'Out of Bounds to Troops', but this had only a limited effect as the, mainly Chinese, prostitutes toured the streets as passengers in bicycle rickshaws. The passenger travelled in a sidecar, unlike the Indian ones where the passenger seat was behind the driver. Few of our section would have considered taking the risk. Celibacy might have been dull – but it was certainly safe! One of our less bright drivers actually arrived at our billet one night accompanied by a prostitute, with the intention of sharing his bed with her. It took the rest of us several minutes to realise what was happening before we threw them both out. One of the army myths was that our tea was 'laced' with 'bromide' (whatever that was) to dampen down our sexual urges. It obviously had not had any effect on our driver, Cliff.

'My final journey home from Singapore was in the *Queen of Bermuda* in January 1947. I calculate that I travelled 42,000 sea miles during my army service, the equivalent of nearly twice round the world, and spend some eighteen weeks aboard various ships. I got back to the coldest English winter for many years, and we really noticed it, having returned from a tropical country. I then went on a month's disembarkation leave so the army didn't really get much out of me when you think about it. I was posted to Pocklington in Yorkshire: we lived in Nissen huts and there was lots of snow about and no heating because of a shortage of coal. After that I went to Northern Command in York and my demob date came round on June 18th [Waterloo Day].

'As the demob centre was just down the road, we walked there. The actual process involved being medically examined, handing in most of our army equipment, and collecting our demob suits, paperwork and ration cards. We were allowed to keep our canvas kit bags, one uniform, shirts and underwear, a pair of boots and a number of other things. When it was time to depart for the station, we found the commanding officer standing at the gate to shake our hands and wish us farewell. Many were inclined to find this hypocritical and avoided him. This seemed churlish to me, so I shook his hand. After all, I was now a civilian and he was staying there! It was then to the station, where there were more farewells, before we joined our various trains to our homes. Three months' demob leave took me nicely up to September, when it was time to start my university degree course.

'With the help of the Further Education & Training Scheme, I got a place to read physics at Queen Mary's College in the East End of London. After graduating, I got a job with BOC and stayed there for the next thirty years, working my way slowly up the ladder. I started in the Research Department at Morden, working on anaesthetic machines, before moving to the Head Office Sales Department in Bridgewater House, overlooking St James's Park, where I sold large quantities of oxygen to steelworks, on an increased salary. BOC had for a number of years been a monopoly, with customers only having one-year contracts. If the customer did not accept BOC's prices, then they got no gas. Supplying steel works required an oxygen plant to be built next to the steelworks, with long-term – usually ten-year – contracts. Our offices were at the top of the building and had probably once been 'servant's bedrooms'. Subsequently, after several years doing planning work,

Dennis and Enid Newland, Horse Guards, VJ-Day 2015.

my final job was coordinating the production, purchase and distribution of hydrogen.'

On 18 February 1956 at St Francis of Assisi Church, Petts Wood, near Orpington, Dennis Newland married his first cousin, Enid, only child of Albert Edward Newland, his father's half-brother, a journeyman joiner and carpenter, of Chelfield House, 9 Salisbury Avenue, Ramsgate. Albert Newland was one of twenty-seven civilians who lost their lives as a result of a German daylight raid on the town on Saturday 24 August 1940, at the height of the Battle of Britain. Enid was 8 years old at the time. Dennis and Enid had three children: Michael, Stella and Elizabeth. Dennis became a life member of the headquarters branch of the Burma Star Association on 13 December 1999 (membership number N/0981/99) and later served as chairman of the Epsom branch. In his diary on 5 August 1945 he wrote: 'I have now raised my Burma Star ribbon; it must be the glamour boy in me!' Dennis said that he had been 'sent a letter informing me that I might be eligible for compensation for cancer on my head caused by service in the Far East. Although it didn't justify a pension, I received an ex-gratia payment of several thousand pounds.'

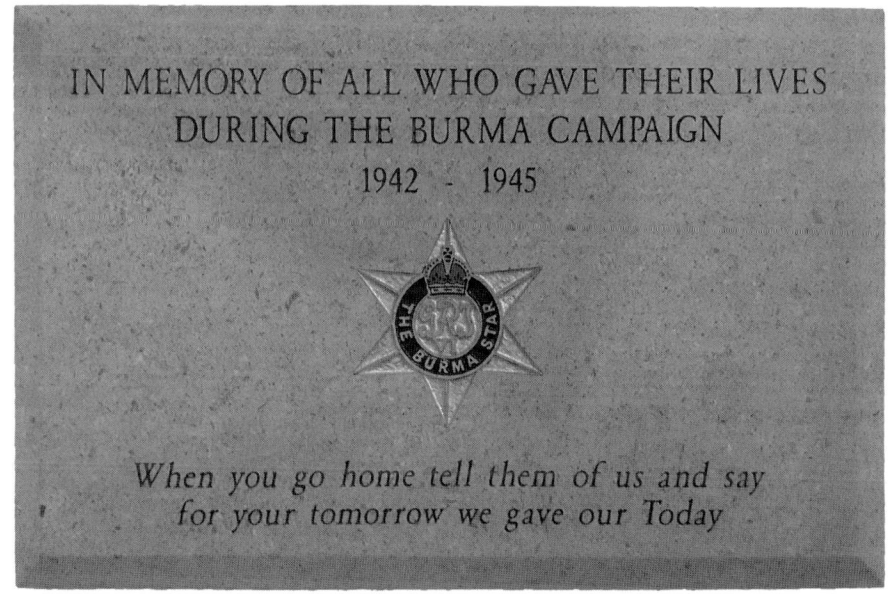

Burma Star Memorial Plaque, St Martin of Tours, Epsom, Surrey.

14408980 Sergeant Ian Niven, Lancashire Fusiliers

Ian Lyneburn Galbraith Niven was born on 23 January 1924, only son of John Carmichael Niven of 6 Craston Road, Manchester, and his wife Mary (Mae), elder daughter of James Edwards, provision dealer, of 67 Ducie Street, Piccadilly, Manchester. Ian, who had left his very expensive hearing aid in the hotel in Barcelona, to where he had been accompanied by his grandson to watch Manchester City play Chelsea in the UEFA Champions League Final the previous week (he lost the hearing in his right ear in Burma), and had misplaced his glasses that morning, explained: 'My father was born on 18 March 1901 at Chorlton-on-Medlock, Manchester, son of a travelling draper from Fife, and joined the Royal Scots as a regular. He was too young to serve on the Western Front but went to Colchester instead. After the war, he came back to Manchester, where he met my mother, who was in charge of a creamery. Although she was Catholic and he was a strict Scottish Presbyterian, she had a very practical approach to religion, saying: "We are all Christians." In the early Twenties, my father went to Ireland to fight the IRA. By then a corporal, he was in an upstairs room of a house with a sergeant and they both had their backs to the wall when an IRA man broke in. He only fired one shot – which killed the sergeant – before deciding that it was best to make his escape and he ran off down the street.

'I was born above a grocer's shop in Plymouth Grove, Manchester. I was the eldest child and my father arranged for a drummer and a piper from the Royal Scots to serenade my mother after she had given birth. I wonder what the neighbours thought. My mother could be stubborn: when my father was posted to India, she refused point blank to go with him. My father later became the orderly room sergeant and re-enlisted in the Intelligence Corps during the Second World War. Although I passed the Eleven Plus and my father wanted me to go to Manchester Grammar School, I wanted to go to a football school. I went to Ducie Avenue Central School [now the Manchester Academy, Moss Lane East], which produced young boys who played football. Football was in my blood: my grandfather had played for Dunfermline while my father was captain and manager of the Royal Scots Football Club. Within a few weeks, we had formed a class team and I was the captain. I later played for – and captained – the school football team.

'At the age of 16, I was about to present myself to Manchester City for a trial, when I realised that within two years I would be called up anyway.' The French signed the armistice on 22 June 1940, just as Ian was leaving school. There is a footballing parallel here, as a London newspaper vendor's sign read: *FRENCH SIGN PEACE TREATY: WE'RE IN THE FINALS.*' Ian continued: 'So I went down to London and passed the exam to become an RAF aircrew. After a weekend in London, I had an interview. "When will you be calling for me?" I asked. "In nine months," came the reply. "The war will be over by then," I said. The interviewer gave me a real ear-bashing but I volunteered to join the Royal Scots the following day. I went to Inverness for my army training and, although I was no good at school, I was top of the shop at Morse code. It was like the school leaving exam all over again, except that this time I came twelfth out of 200 recruits. The top dozen went into signals and I became a battalion signaller. On the ship sailing out to India I was the company runner, which was brilliant because instead of being stuck on the lowest deck I used to go from deck to deck taking messages between the company commander and the CO, and sometimes to the brigadier too. It was a very confusing time and I seemed to change regiment two or three times during the voyage.

'Eventually I was posted to the Lancashire Fusiliers, where I joined a few friends. I particularly remember Louis Rice, son of an Italian ice-cream maker – I have a feeling that he was killed [14380836 Fusilier Louis Rice, son of John Rice, a full-time air-raid warden with Manchester ARP, of 62 Brewery Street, Manchester, and his wife Maria Frances (née Schiavo), died on 13 August 1944, aged 20, and is buried at Madras War Cemetery, Chennai]. I spent six or seven weeks at the transit camp at Deolali. When we got off the trucks they put us in an enormous tent: there were about twenty of us in it. I met a bloke in our tent who played for the Manchester City second team. He said, "We're having a kickabout tomorrow; why don't you join us?" We all had large kitbags and there was enough space for my Manchester City strip, which I had taken with me to India hoping to get a game. I was picked for the team and played three times for Deolali Football Club. I was really enjoying the army, wasn't I? I found that as long as I behaved myself, kept a smile on my face and did the job, that was the way you got on in the army. There's a lot of good sense in it: once you've been trained in the army, it never leaves you.

'We had a parade and they said: "We're going to ask you to volunteer for a new role fighting the Japanese." Although they told us how horrible it was likely to be, the battalion seemed to move forward as one, I remember that, and we nearly all volunteered. We trained hard every day in the jungle in India, which was just like the jungle we actually fought in. There was only one word for it – hell. Lord Louis Mountbatten visited us and said to the CO: "I can't talk to them all; introduce me to your youngest soldier and your oldest veteran." As the youngest soldier, he spoke to me and offered some kind words of encouragement. I remember that he asked me, "Are you fit?" We were told we would be going in for four weeks, that we were going in by air and that they would pick us all up by air. It never happened. We were dropped in and we stayed in. It shouldn't happen to a dog. We left on a Sunday night at midnight and were the second lot into "Broadway", after the King's Regiment. I was in No. 20 Column, commanded by Major Monteith [Major D.J. Monteith, Guides Cavalry, Indian Armoured Corps, who was killed in action on 8 June 1944] and our brigadier was "Mad Mike" Calvert.

'My best mate, Robbie [George Currie Robertson], was a muleteer. He lived at Musselburgh and was involved with upper class dog racing

Allied cemetery in Burma.

in Edinburgh so was very familiar with animals. Our sergeant major was an ex-butcher and once shot one of the mules, butchered it and handed bits round. I wrapped mine in two of the largest leaves that I could find and put it in my pack. Most of the lads immediately cooked and ate their share but their stomachs couldn't cope – and they vomited it all back up again. The sergeant major was unpopular: he used to wander round shouting "Haircut! Haircut! Haircut!" so we used to call him "Haircut". After we moved out of "Broadway", we got involved in a bit of a tussle with the Japanese, it wasn't really a battle. That was my introduction and I think that I fired two shots. We lost a lad from Manchester though: I think his name was Bamford [3535247 Fusilier Robert Eric Bamford was killed in action on 8 June 1944 and was originally buried in Sahmaw Cemetery, near Myitkyina]. We had a ten-minute halt and they threw me a spade and told me to bury him. Luckily two of the lads came to help me. What I did enjoy, though, was blowing up their railway.'

No. 20 Column then marched to "White City", a heavily-defended block on the other side of the railway where they were attacked daily for a period of seven weeks but somehow managed to hold the densely-wired perimeter. After being peppered by grenade fragments and catching dysentery, a heavy mortar round exploded close to his position: 'The blast

14408980 Orderly Room Colour Sergeant Ian Niven (right) with Sergeant Bill Tideswell, Lucknow, 1945.

hit me from the left and I was blown into a trench. Then someone else jumped in and landed with their legs over my shoulders. The back of my neck was wet and I thought he'd been wounded. In fact, he'd pissed himself as he jumped into the trench. I was just happy he wasn't wounded.' In June, the Lancashire Fusiliers were involved in savage hand-to-hand fighting around Pinhmi Bridge, on the approaches to Mogaung: 'When we got into Mogaung it was littered with dead Japanese and I looked around at the devastation. After the battle, I became so ill that I could hardly walk. Having weighed 10 1/2st, I had lost 3st and passed out on the aircraft flying me back to India, where I woke up on a slab in a tented field hospital, with people throwing buckets of ice over me.'

'When we came out, none of us was fit for battle. We could just about stand up. I had terrible dysentery and I spent the next six months in hospital. After discharge, there was only one place where I was fit to serve and that was in the Orderly Room, like my father. As a War Substantive Sergeant, I became the Orderly Room Colour Sergeant. I had now swapped fighting soldiering for administrative soldiering. We were stationed at Lucknow in the United Provinces [now Uttar Pradesh] and, when five young lads arrived from England, they sent them straight to the Orderly Room. I well remember the day when the Japs surrendered. We closed the Orderly Room down and the Adjutant said: "Take yourselves down to the canteen; there are two bottles of beer for each of you." When I joined the Army, I made a vow that I wasn't going to swear and I wasn't going to drink. And I kept it up although I did make an exception on that occasion! They showed us some kindness and did us well that day.

'Almost as soon as I got home, I stupidly got married. The Army sent us here and it sent us there but it didn't send us near any jobs. It took me two years to get a job and I only managed it after sending more than a hundred letters – and I'm not exaggerating. I asked the CO and the Adjutant for testimonials. Eventually, I got a job as a buyer with Richard Johnson & Nephew Ltd., a firm of wire drawers and cable manufacturers.' His son, Ian (there are now four generations by that name in the Niven family), explained: 'After leaving the Army, he used to go round on a bicycle, selling at doors. After more than twenty years with Richard Johnson & Nephew, Dad became a publican. He had the *Fletchers Arms* in Denton, before taking over the *Railway Inn* at Marple Bridge in Stockport and renaming it the *Royal Scot*.' In 1945, Ian married Olive, daughter of Joseph Clare, foreman in an engineering workshop, and they had two children: Ian Stuart and Olivia Margaret Clare. In 1958, he married Dorothy Flynn and, in 1967, he married Marjorie Booth. His son said: 'He was always a bit of a ladies' man.'

Ian is an Honorary President of Manchester City Football Club and, according to the Club's website: 'A lifelong supporter of the Club and part of a proud six-generation City-supporting family, Ian is one of those rare fans who can tell you about the times back in the 1930s from first-hand recollections. Ian joined the Board in February 1972 and remained until 1997. During that time, he oversaw the development of Maine Road and identified the need for City to own their training pitch, leading to the Club buying Platt Fields Park, creating the first academy in the country. Ian was awarded an MBE for his services to the community, particularly his work in Moss Side.' He became a Life Member of the Altringham Branch of the Burma Star Association on 15 June 1987 (Membership Number N/738/87). At the end of the conversation, Ian said, reflectively: 'My philosophy is that I don't want to know what happened yesterday; I want to know what is going to happen tomorrow.' Ian Niven died at home on 5 December 2021, at the age of 97.

Ian Niven, photographed by Wendy Aldiss.

14821064 Private Lawrence Powers, King's Own Scottish Borderers

Lawrence (Lawrie) Powers was born in the village of Rainford, between St Helens and Wigan in Lancashire, on 22 November 1925, third son of John Powers and his wife Elizabeth, daughter of Joseph Mitchinson, a collier, of 10 Douglas Terrace, Wigan. John, who worked below ground at Ravenhead Colliery, was in a reserved occupation so didn't serve in the First World War. Lawrie attended Rainford Church of England Council School, which he left when he turned 14, wryly observing of his education: 'You could always tell the chap who went to the bottom school – but you couldn't tell him much!' After leaving school, he worked at a 330-acre dairy farm in Dairy Farm Road, Rainford, which was owned by Alan Boardman, a member of the Special Constabulary: 'I milked the cows every morning and every evening, twice a day, come rain, hail, ice or snow, before seven o'clock and then again at half-past four. During the day we worked in the fields, doing whatever needed to be done, like cutting hay or corn and planting potatoes. We had two horses – there were no tractors in those days – and they were big fields too. I was paid the princely sum of £1 per week – get your mind round that. We had a few German prisoners of war working on the farm. They are a fine race of people, you know. Give them a piece of wood and they would make a toy for a child. I admired them – smart fellows. One day I had a jam butty – we hadn't much food – and I offered it to a German prisoner. He refused it, saying: "No, you need it more."

'I joined the Air Training Corps in 1941, after which it normally followed that you joined the RAF, so I went for RAF selection at Padgate, near Warrington, about twelve miles away. We had three days of aptitude tests and I was just bordering on air-gunner material. I was interviewed by an officer: "Are you a farmer, Powers?" "No, I'm a farm labourer." "If I were you, I would go back to the farm and eat some more cabbage." I've always been thin, you see, still am. I had a medical and attested for the RAF but Mr Boardman then insisted that he needed me on the farm a little longer, so I joined the RAF Reserve. By the time I was called up, though, they didn't need any more airmen or any more sailors – they just needed soldiers for the impending invasion of Japan. Two of my brothers served but they never went abroad: George, who worked at Fairey Aviation, joined the REME, and Joe joined the Royal Artillery and served in different ack-ack units along the south coast.

'I was called up on 15 August 1944 and spent two nights at St Aidan's Camp, a tented camp near Carlisle. After catching a train to Stranraer, I boarded the *Duke of Roxburgh*, a cattle boat with cattle below and passengers above, bound for Larne in Northern Ireland. We had six weeks of primary training at Ballykinler – square-bashing and polishing your boots so you could see your face reflected in them, you know the sort of thing – before we were all allocated to an army unit. They gave you a preference of sorts. I said that I wouldn't mind joining a Scottish regiment, a Highland regiment, so I was sent to Gordon Barracks at Bridge of Don in Aberdeen. After twelve weeks' infantry training, you were ready for battle. After six weeks, though, when we had marched halfway to Church Parade, we were given the word of command: "Halt!" An officer and a couple of sergeants with clipboards appeared, and as they called out our names, we either marched to the left or to the right. I was in the first group and we were marched back to camp, handed travel warrants and given two weeks' embarkation leave. The others – who were all younger – went on to church and completed their twelve weeks.

'After my leave, I reported to a transit camp at Ayr racecourse. I was badged Highland Light Infantry (HLI), just like David Niven, but he went to Malta. From Ayr we caught a train to Glasgow, where we boarded the SS *Tegelberg* [a Dutch KPM combination liner pressed into wartime service as a troopship]. Sailing in convoy from the Firth of Clyde, we collected more and more ships on the way – from Belfast, Portsmouth and other southern ports – until the convoy had grown into one of the largest ever to sail from the UK during the war. We sailed in January 1945 and it took a month to get to Bombay. I never got off the boat, although some did at Port Said. I went to the new transit camp at Kalyan, forty miles south of Bombay on the main Poona line, before being sent to Comilla for jungle training. There was a big airstrip there and they flew reinforcements in and the wounded out. As a reinforcement, with no questions asked and no bloody argument, the youngest often changed cap badge. I was sort of freelance in a way because there was no HLI battalion in India or Burma. I had a friend on the farm, Tommy Kellett, who transferred from the

King's (Liverpool) to the KOSB so I asked to join the 2nd Battalion [2 KOSB]. I got dysentery twice while at Comilla.

'I was posted from Comilla to Ranchi as a member of a 13-man advance party setting up a tented camp for the remnants of 2 KOSB, who were being withdrawn from Rangoon [after fighting their last battle at Prome in May 1945] but went into hospital again, this time with malaria. I was in Ranchi when they dropped the atomic bombs: I had half a tin of fruit in celebration. The battalion spent a good few weeks resting up in Ranchi. The CO was Lieutenant Colonel Henry Conder, a Norfolk man and the only Englishman to command a Scottish regiment in Burma.

14821064 Private Lawrence Powers, 1946 – photographed by Mela Ram & Sons, The Mall, Peshawar.

News then came through that we were going to embark on a three-day train journey to Peshawar. We had a very good barracks there: Roberts Barracks. I joined the Signal Platoon. With the ATC I had learned Morse code, but we also used semaphore and 48-sets in the Khyber Pass. During the ten months that I spent there, I went on three or four schemes – as they were called – on the Frontier. Each scheme lasted a week or ten days.

'One day the company clerk asked me, "Do you want to go home?" I think it was simply that I was deemed important. What they called 'vital work' was done by electricians, brickies, joiners, carpenters, colliers and farmers. I received a reduced gratuity because I chose to come home, which was only right when some people had been abroad for three or four years. We visited five countries during a 30-hour flight in a converted B-24 Liberator: they just blocked up the bomb bay, put in a couple of planks and there were seven of us on each plank, facing one another. We spent the night at Lydda in Palestine; they showed the film *Two Girls and a Sailor* on a yanked-up sheet. I was demobbed at Strensall Barracks near York. Although there have been many amazing things in my lifetime – like computers and mobile phones – one of the most amazing is that when the war stopped, servicemen were told to report to a barracks where they were given a chalk-striped suit, a Trilby hat, a pair of shoes and a raincoat, all in a cardboard box tied up with a piece of string.'

After being demobbed, Lawrie spent eighteen years as a foreman at Pilkington's television tube manufacturing facility at Ravenhead. After a nephew drowned in an accident off Southport, he took over Richmond, a menswear shop in Wigan, running it for twenty-eight years until his retirement. On 9 February 1955 at St Luke's, Orrell, Lawrie married Jean, daughter of Ernest Meadows of 4 Sandy Lane, Orrell, who worked for the Ministry of Supply.

Lawrie Powers at the final service of the Wigan Branch of the Burma Star Association, 15 August 2020.

They had two sons: Ian and Craig. On 10 October 1974, Lawrie joined the Burma Star Association (membership number P/2294/74). He was secretary of the St Helens branch for nineteen years, attended five reunions in the Royal Albert Hall and almost three times as many in Blackpool, was twice the National Standard Bearer and was very often the Parade Marshal. He also gave lectures at schools about his experiences and frequently visited sick ex-servicemen. For the last forty years, he has read the Kohima Epitaph at the Remembrance Day Service at the Cenotaph in St Helens. Lawrie explained: 'I've nominated six men to take me to my resting place but two of the six have gone by the board so I'm two short!' The last words belong to him: 'For a simple farm labourer, I haven't done badly.'

269213 Captain Maurice Ramsay MC, Royal Norfolk Regiment

Maurice William Ramsay was born in Northumberland on 18 April 1920, elder son of William Ramsay and his wife Kate (née West). As a farmer, William Ramsay was exempt from service during the First World War. In 1929 the family moved south and he took on the tenancy of Church Farm at Woodrising, Norfolk. Maurice explained: 'It was a mixed farm, with cows, sheep and arable. I attended Hamond's Grammar School in Swaffham but left there with virtually no qualifications. Although I passed exams in Geography, History, Mathematics, French, Physics and Chemistry, I failed English so wasn't allowed to matriculate. After leaving school in the summer of 1937, I joined Lloyds Bank and went to work at Wellingborough in Northamptonshire.

Sergeant M.W. Ramsay, Northamptonshire Regiment, Norwich, 1942.

'At Wellingborough I volunteered for the Territorial Army and joined the Northamptonshire Regiment. I started off as an orderly in the office although I also did a certain amount of what was called open-air training. Having become a lance-sergeant, I was called up in April 1939. That June we had a month's call-up and became a searchlight battalion, equipped with Lewis guns. I was trained to operate the standard 90cm searchlight, which could illuminate aircraft flying at up to 25,000 feet, always providing that there was no cloud. A number of those who played for Northampton Saints joined our company and we played quite a bit of rugby in the early days of the war. On 24 August 1939 we received our final call-up and we started off at Stanton near Corby, responsible for ack-ack defence of the steelworks.'

The following month, when the 1939 Register was compiled, Maurice's father was recorded as an Air Raid Warden while his mother had joined the WVS. Maurice continued: 'After eighteen months or so, we were posted to Shardlow, roughly midway between Nottingham and Derby, and were responsible for defending those two cities against air attack. Corby wasn't bombed while we were there and I only remember some glasshouses being struck when we were at Shardlow. I was recommended for a commission and attended pre-OCTU at Wrotham. God! that was an awful place. It was the middle of winter and it rained non-stop, although I did at least manage to get home for Christmas. I was only there for six weeks but that was quite long enough – everything was done at the double.

'Then I was sent to 202 (RASC) OCTU at Southend-on-Sea in Essex. It was quite strenuous in some ways but I didn't do too well on the assault course. It was absolutely pouring with rain and I was marked down for failing to climb the wet log because I was concerned about my manhood! We learned to drive Bedford 3-tonners, which were completely blacked out except for a light under the rear hub axle box. After I was commissioned on 27 March 1943, I wanted to go to an MT company so that I could continue with my driving experience; instead I was sent to a supply depôt at Wellington in Shropshire. We were once called up on an exercise near Tenby in South Wales and I became a despatch rider and was given a Velocette motorcycle. I'm afraid that I don't remember very much about the supply depôt; if it had been interesting work, then I might have remembered more. I remember there was a captain in charge and I was one of his two second lieutenants; the other one was a butcher who cut up the meat before it was distributed around Western Command.

'Eventually, a number of second lieutenants, regarded as surplus to requirements where they were, received orders to report to Gourock on the Firth of Clyde. Although we didn't know where we were going initially, there were some clues when we were given cholera and yellow fever jabs and were put on Mepacrine tablets as soon as we were on board the ship. It was a very unpleasant voyage in a Belgian ship: ninety per cent of us were seasick and the effects stayed with me for a long time. We spent Christmas Day 1943 anchored in the harbour at Gibraltar. After stopping for water at Dakar, we sailed to Freetown, where a lot of us disembarked because our ship was scheduled to go to the Middle

East. I spent a very pleasant six weeks in Freetown, where there was no programme for us and a hand of bananas cost a shilling. We spent most of our afternoons on the beach. There was a decent transit camp so we were properly housed. Eventually another ship took us to Lagos, from where we were taken up-country to Abeokuta [the capital of Ogun State in south-west Nigeria].

'With two friends I was posted to 82nd (West African) Division as a carrier platoon commander. The division comprised three brigades, of which two comprised three battalions of the Gold Coast Regiment and the other one three battalions of the Nigeria Regiment. My brigade, the 2nd (West African) Infantry Brigade, was commanded by Brigadier Weston, who was a very big man. I was posted to the 3rd Battalion, Gold Coast Regiment (3 GCR) and appointed to command the supply platoon. Where necessary, we were responsible for carrying the things that the troops couldn't carry, such as extra supplies of food and ammunition. I only

Lieutenant M.W. Ramsay with two soldiers from the Gold Coast Regiment, Nigeria, 1943.

had a few words of their language, Hausa, so most of the communication was in pidgin English. The soldiers were not sophisticated in any way but once they knew the routine they did things the right way. They behaved remarkably well throughout, carrying their loads and with no problems with discipline. Mind you, I had a very impressive and powerful sergeant major, Mammadu Wongara, who would read them the riot act if he thought it necessary. All of my troops were loyal – without any question – and it made me very happy indeed because if I asked for something to be done, then it was done.

'After six months' training in Nigeria, we boarded the *Queen of Bermuda* in Lagos, for the seven-week voyage to Karachi, through the Suez Canal. On arrival we entrained straightaway for the seven-day journey to Ranchi. It was a desolate place and I don't think that there were any civilians for a few miles around. We were under canvas: the soldiers slept on the ground while the officers had canvas beds. We had a few problems with snakes and scorpions though. After I had lost a man to a krait, we put rough stones around the sides of the tents to deter snakes. The adjutant was so concerned that he got himself a mongoose – I have no idea where he got it from. Our training involved getting used to marching with a full load: small pack containing personal kit, such as razor, towel and soap; large pack, which contained, among other things, a change of clothing; and ammunition in ammunition pouches. The soldiers carried .303s while I carried a Sten gun, to distinguish the officers from the men. We were offered the option of steel helmets or bush hats and we all opted for bush hats. We knew that we were going to hilly country in the Arakan, so we used to go to a couple of hills a short distance away, to practise going up and down. First parade was at eight o'clock but it was so hot in the afternoon that we used to knock off at about two o'clock every day and just lie on our camp beds – or on the ground.

'In late October 1944 we moved up to the front line, marching a hundred miles in just seven days, carrying all our worldly goods, to take over from an Indian regiment on the India/Burma border. We were on restricted rations and I also took a daily salt tablet while we were provided with chlorine tablets for our water bottles. There was one British sergeant per platoon and we were both given ascorbic acid as a Vitamin C supplement. To acclimatise to our new surroundings, we carried out patrols for up to four days at a time. While wading *chaungs*, we came across leeches for the first time: the little devils got onto ankles and lower legs through bootlace holes. They either dropped off of their own accord or were touched with a lighted cigarette so that the bleeding stopped. In early December, we crossed a major river – either by wading or on bamboo walkways – until we were in Burma proper. At that point we were totally dependent on aerial resupply.

'The whole of 82nd (West African) Division was now on the move to assist with the expulsion of the Japs from the Arakan. My platoon was part of 3 GCR, acting mainly as carriers/suppliers of food, ammunition and medical supplies. More important still was to assist with the collection of air drops by establishing and marking dropping zones in the jungle. Although this was difficult, the faithful Dakotas always managed to find us. Food came in 14-man compo packs, which were enough for a week, but it was a limited range: hard biscuits, bully beef, tinned milk, tea, jam and cigarettes. We were moving down the coastal strip of the Arakan, which was inundated with *chaungs*, which were mainly, but not entirely, dried-up river beds. These places were tidal and water became a problem: we often ended up with a salty mix, which was not greatly appreciated, either in tea or in our water bottles. We avoided contamination of the land and, at every location we occupied, a deep trench was dug for all our rubbish and human waste and then filled in when we moved on.

'Our standard practice when setting up camps for a stop of up to five days was to select high ground because it was more easily defensible; however, this made both water collection and air resupply more trying. The latter needed open ground, which was quite rare, so that we could lay out our drop zone markers. With no barbed wire with which to defend our perimeters, we used 'punjis': three- or four-foot sharpened bamboo sticks set in front of our trenches. The Japs regularly taunted us at night, either by calling out in English or by firing randomly, hoping that we would reveal our positions. By mid-February 1945, our forward troops, assisted with air strikes and with the support of a regiment of Indian mountain gunners, had cleared the Japs as far south as Kangaw, some 120 miles from the start line. During this time, we had to endure intermittent shelling, but my platoon was lucky and we were not hit. My opposite number in 2 GCR suffered numerous casualties, including six killed in action. At this juncture the powers-that-be decided that our brigade would be shipped 60 miles south to Ruywa, before moving a dozen miles inland, thus blocking the only escape route by road.

'We started to take casualties but there was no way to evacuate them so they remained within the well-protected brigade area and were treated by our medical team. Two infantry companies managed to block the road, eliminating a Jap gun battery in the process, while we remained in position on Hill 1106, which was covered with bamboo, to cover the escape route. We established a drop zone between 2 GCR and 3 GCR and my platoon started to move forward to collect the supplies while the Dakotas were overhead. Although food and ammunition were dropped by parachute, rice was packed in double hessian bags and mule fodder in large round bales. These were pushed out by 'kickers' and it could be dangerous for those underneath. Since my men were mostly unarmed, we were protected by the HQ Platoon. As we climbed back up Hill 1106, we came under heavy fire. The Japs let our escort go past their position first and then prevented the carriers from getting any further. My men were very spread out and it was impossible to establish the enemy positions. We had no option other than to retreat, in the process abandoning our loads, because we were unable to defend ourselves. Remarkably, we suffered no casualties and we all returned to our base the following day. Two days later we were able to recover our rations virtually intact. The Japs had tried to burn some of our 14-man compo packs but failed.'

On 6 January 1945, it was announced in the *London Gazette* that Lt (T/Capt) M.W. Ramsay had transferred from the RASC to the Royal Norfolk Regiment, retaining his seniority. In the account written at the request of his old school, Maurice modestly fails to mention that he was awarded an immediate Military Cross. The recommendation by Lieutenant Colonel C.F. Tamlyn, commanding 6th (West African) Auxiliary Group, provides more detail: 'Had it not been for Captain Ramsay's coolness and personal disregard for his own safety, together with his quick and accurate appreciation of the situation, his men would almost certainly have failed to carry out their task, and the rations and the Signal Stores vital to the operation would certainly have been captured by the enemy, thus affecting further operations of the Battalion. During these actions, Captain Ramsay dealt with the situation entirely by himself; he being at that time the only European in the Column of one hundred and fifty Africans. Throughout the campaign Captain Ramsay on all occasions showed an exemplary spirit and outstanding leadership. Always cheerful and ready to accept responsibility, he was never daunted by any task given him. The operations described above are typical of this officer's behaviour throughout the campaign, and his conduct inspired confidence in his men with the result that they were prepared to follow him anywhere and undertake hazardous tasks.

'Captain Ramsay was officer commanding a West African Auxiliary Group Platoon which was attached for all purposes to an Infantry Battalion engaged inland from the Ruywa bridgehead. The Battalion position was without rations. On the afternoon of March 7th 1945 rations arrived at the Brigade Harbour about two miles away from the Battalion position on the far side of the valley. Although Captain Ramsay was personally aware that there were enemy in the valley, he led his platoon back to the Brigade ration point and, having collected the Battalion rations, on his return journey the platoon was ambushed. Realising that it was absolutely vital to deliver the rations through to the Battalion, Captain Ramsay executed a skilful withdrawal and took up a defensive position for the night with his platoon a short distance away and remained there until first light. At first light he again set out and managed to reach the Battalion position with practically the whole of the rations. Having accomplished his task and having accounted for all his men, he then retrieved the remaining loads.'

Maurice continued: 'With no immediate way out and with increasing casualties, we were literally boxed in. Meanwhile, the other two brigades were fighting their way south to link up with us and evacuate the wounded. Two events were a source of great anxiety at the time. First, the Japs shelled or mortared Brigade HQ, killing two friends of mine and some African soldiers and injuring the brigade commander, the brigade major and the intelligence officer. As a result, Brigade HQ was co-located with 1 GCR and the defensive perimeter was tightened. Secondly, our dropping zone was restricted and, whether by luck or design, Jap mortaring set it on fire. We therefore had no supplies for four days as a consequence of the danger of exploding ammunition, while there was a serious shortage of water, which became an ongoing problem.

'Towards the end of March 1945, though, 1st Brigade got to within a dozen miles and the sappers managed to hack or dig out a rough track, enabling us to carry the badly wounded casualties out. My platoon was to carry out mainly Europeans, of whom there were thirteen in all. With an allocation of four per stretcher and ten in reserve, that made sixty-two. I led the way along a tortuous route through the jungle, with every sympathy for the casualties, as the Africans carried loads on their heads. We set off at 6 pm in complete darkness and it was twelve hours before we were able to hand them over to the medical teams. We had been boxed in for four weeks and were greatly looking forward to a quiet night. Perhaps sensing that we were bunched up, the Japs had other ideas and we were heavily shelled while 'jitter parties' abounded. With our nerves at full stretch, some of our own troops joined in, leading to some deaths from friendly fire; we lost eight killed and fifty wounded that night. It was a relief to learn that none of my platoon was involved.

'We had hoped for a rest but the brigade was soon given its next objective. We were to relieve 25th (Indian) Infantry Division, which had established a bridgehead behind the Japs at Taungup, 100 miles further south. Setting off on 1 April, the march passed without serious incident and 3 GCR duly took over from 2/7 Rajputs on 13 April. The Japs had now been forced back to their final line of defence: a vehicular track across the Yomas Hills to Prome in central Burma, a hundred miles away. This time we were firmly dug in on the high ground and, although we shared a deep, wide *chaung* with the Japs, we now had the support of 25-pounders, mortars and air strikes. Despite opposition, we made steady progress. By the end of April, we were in control of Taungup and its *chaung*, over which the wooden river bridge remained intact. On 1 May we had the first taste of the coming monsoon. The Japs had now vanished and we were extremely relieved to find numerous bashas to protect us from the weather. We were ordered to stay put during the monsoon, which brought an end to our campaign. My platoon had only suffered one minor casualty: a shell splinter in the back. Plentiful rations came in by sea, there was no shortage of fresh water, clothes could be washed and, at long last, we were able to send mail home. Most importantly, after a 300-mile advance, we had earned an unbroken night's sleep! Throughout the six-month period, the faithful Dakotas had consistently delivered letters from home, together with our monthly alcohol ration: either a bottle of spirits or three bottles of beer.

'When the war ended, my company was tasked with establishing the road from Taungup to Prome and making it jeep-friendly. The road was 100 miles long and I was allocated 50 miles of it. We camped at Milestone 99 and the job lasted six months. From there we went to Bassein in the south-west corner of Burma, mostly to keep the peace in case the natives got restive. All that happened was that my soldiers got VD. When we went to breakfast, we used to ask the MO: "What's the score this morning?" We all had demob numbers and a lot of the officers in our battalion were sent home because their number was up. My date was very close to our troops' scheduled return journey so I volunteered to stay with them and see them safely home. It was a nice comfortable voyage and we were reasonably well fed. Disembarkation at Takoradi was the only time that I touched foot in the Gold Coast. After saying our farewells, I caught the next available ship home.

'After being demobilised in York, I was given three months' disembarkation leave. We were advised to stay on Mepacrine for another month and some of my friends went down with malaria in England. My father had sold out of the farm during the war because my brother had been killed.' 755620 Sergeant Robert Elliott Ramsay, a wireless operator and air gunner with 206 Squadron, Royal Air Force, was killed in an aircraft accident in Northern Ireland on 18 August 1941, aged 20, and is buried in the churchyard of St Nicholas, Woodrising. Maurice's son, Mark, explained: 'My father wasn't told that his brother had died until he got home at the end of the war.' Maurice continued: 'My parents retired to Watton in Norfolk so I unwound there. Lloyds Bank were after me to go back almost straightway so I didn't take all the three months' leave due to me but went back to work after two months. They started me off in

Captain M.W. Ramsay MBE MC, photographed by Wendy Aldiss.

Thetford, which was only a bike ride away from home. The Battle Area was nearby: it was overrun with rabbits and you could get a licence to shoot them. After a year or so, they transferred me to Greenford on the outskirts of London and I had an office romance with Dilys, who worked as a clerk at the branch.'

On 18 May 1949 at Southall in Middlesex, Maurice married Dilys Valmai, daughter of William Evans, a rollerman for Quaker Oats, of 87 Orchard Avenue, Southall, and his wife Doris, daughter of George Holifield, collier, of Pengam, Monmouthshire. Maurice rose steadily through the Lloyds Bank hierarchy: from manager of the branch in Cambridge city centre in the mid-1950s to regional manager and local director for East Anglia by the time he retired at the age of 60. Mark said: 'A few years ago, we had the glorious day of revolution, marking the fact that he had now been paid more by Lloyds Bank in retirement than he had been during thirty-five years working for them!' Having seen an advertisement in the *Cambridge Evening News*, Maurice joined the government's Small Firms' Service as an adviser, for which he was appointed MBE, before working with Lord Young on the DTI's Enterprise Initiative. He became a life member of the Hertfordshire, Cambridgeshire and Essex branch of the Burma Star Association on 4 March 1981 (membership number R/1811/81). Dilys died on 21 January 2007 and Maurice died on 13 February 2022, leaving one son.

EC 3877 Captain John Randle MC, 10th Baluch Regiment

John Pomeroy Randle was born on 17 October 1921, elder son of Gilbert Walter Randle, manager for a firm of pencil manufacturers, of Ardara, North Road, Berkhamsted, and his wife Lucy Norah May, daughter of Joseph Oakley, station master, of Church House, Haston Lane, Hadnall, Shropshire. Although Gilbert joined the Royal Flying Corps on 29 July 1916, at 34 he was deemed too old to fly. Gilbert's younger brother, Private Donald Randle, 1st/21st Battalion, London Regiment (First Surrey Rifles), was killed in action at Givenchy on 25 May 1915. After leaving Berkhamsted School, John passed the entrance exam for the Royal Military College Sandhurst in the summer of 1939, only to find that it closed within weeks for the training of officers for regular commissions and became an OCTU. He therefore applied to the Indian Army and 'after an eight-week very uncomfortable voyage to India, spent six months at a cadet college at Bangalore, before being commissioned in September 1941'.

In the introduction to his candid and revealing book, *Battle Tales from Burma* (Pen & Sword, 2004), John explained: 'Having just celebrated my twentieth birthday, I found myself in command of a company of one hundred and twenty Punjabi Mussulmans, men of that great warrior race of Northern India. Another equally green second lieutenant, Bill Greenwood, was posted as my company officer. I suppose that I might just have made a reasonable section commander; I would have been a pretty raw platoon commander; as a company commander I was quite out of my depth – learning fast, but prone to mistakes of every sort. It speaks volumes for the great spirit and loyalty of the Indian Army, and above all for the trust of the Indian sepoy in his British officers, that he

Captain J.P. Randle, 10th Baluch Regiment, photographed by Bourne and Shepherd, Calcutta, 1945.

was prepared to serve so well and so loyally, against first class opposition and not just tribesmen, under such raw officers.'

His baptism of war could not have been fiercer. Posted to Burma shortly before the Japanese attacked across the Kawkareik Pass on 22 January 1942, John Randle was placed in command of B Company, 7th Battalion, 10th Baluch Regiment (7/10 BR): 'For five days things were fairly quiet – some desultory mortar fire from across the Salween and the occasional dive bombing attack, neither of which were particularly effective. ... On the night of 11/12 February 1942, two battalions of 215 Regiment of the crack 33rd Japanese Division attacked and, after several hours of fighting, overran the battalion. My B Company, consisting of Company HQ, a section of Vickers medium machine guns and 11 Platoon, was required to hold a three-platoon front (10 Platoon had been wiped out the night before and Colonel Jerry Dyer required 12 Platoon to go out on a battalion patrol just before the battle).

'We gave a good account of ourselves and killed a number of Japs, but were eventually overrun. Bill Greenwood and I and two other sepoys from B Company, Pat Dunn (2IC), Siri and George Holden (machine gun officer) and a few VCOs and men (including 12 Platoon) were all able to break out, although it took me two days to get back to British lines. Colonel Jerry Dyer and 288 VCOs and men were killed, and 229, including Bill Cayley, Hugh Mercer (adjutant), 'Toots' Toothill (quartermaster), Jake Jervis and the regimental medical officer were taken prisoner. All our wounded, including Jerry Dyer (but sparing 'Toots'), were butchered by the Japanese, an atrocity which governed the battalion's attitude then and for the rest of the war.' A week later, the Sittang Bridge was blown prematurely, with one hundred members of 7/10 BR still on the wrong side of the river.

The Burma Corps then retreated more than 1,000 miles – over some very challenging terrain – to Imphal in Manipur, which was reached just before the monsoon broke in May: 'Sleep and overcoming it became the predominant factor; all anyone wanted to do was just to sink down wherever one could and go to sleep; even the traditional *fakir*'s bed of nails seemed a delightful prospect. Because it was night I, as the company commander, had the traditional honour, so they said, of being the last man in the company and indeed the very last man of the formed British Army to retreat out of Burma. It was an anxious task and I have to admit to quite often looking back over my shoulder, particularly as, being in bright tropical moonlight, one could see for some distance, always wondering whether we would see the glint of Japanese bayonets and hear the cry of "Banzai". My imagination was over-fanciful: nothing, in fact, happened and we were to learn long afterwards that the Japanese at that particular stage were not following up very hard.

'When we finally reached Ranchi in Eastern India in September 1942 we were in pretty poor shape, physically and mentally. For example, the Pathan Company, whose company commander and all but one of its VCOs were dead or missing (and one that had to be kicked out for cowardice), had had to be disarmed and were almost in a state of moral collapse.' At this juncture, John was appointed adjutant of a battalion that had to be rebuilt, almost from scratch. This took time, a great deal of training and a healthy dose of cultural awareness, particularly concerning 'izzat', the Indian soldier's personal honour. John explained: 'After four months in Ranchi we moved back up the line to Imphal, but after three months there it was realised that, despite our work and enthusiasm, we needed a further period of training outside an operational area. We were then sent for six months to Shillong, an agreeable hill station in Assam in north-east India, albeit very wet indeed in the south-west monsoon.'

There were a number of compensations for the unpredictable weather: 'Shillong had all the usual facilities of an Indian hill station, a club, golf course, hotels, a cinema. It also had the Welsh Mission, which worked wonders among the local pagan hill tribe, the Khasis, teaching them English, western standards of hygiene, and training the beautiful fair-skinned Khasi girls (some of the most nubile girls most of us had ever seen) to be nurses in the first-class hospital there. So beautiful were these girls that some became the mistresses of young bachelor planters in the tea-gardens of Assam. Two such comely girls returned to Shillong when their patrons went to war, were generously paid off and were living each in her own comfortable bungalow. Bill Greenwood, also now a captain, who had been my company officer in the early fighting in Burma, and I reckoned that our chances of surviving the next and fairly imminent encounter with the Japs were not so good and, preferring the pleasures of the flesh to the alternative pleasures of the bottle or bridge, took on one each of these girls as our mistresses. Most days after dinner in the Mess basha, Bill and I set out on our motorbikes for a rewarding evening with our girls.'

At the end of 1943, 7/10 BR rejoined the 17th Indian Division – the 'Black Cats' – in the Chin Hills some 170 miles south of Imphal. The following year, they fought a series of fierce battles against the crack 33rd Japanese Division, known as the 'White Tigers'. Having retreated in contact from Tiddim to Bishenpur, on the edge of the Imphal 'Box', there was a particularly vicious encounter at Red Hill – so-called because of its reddish-brown earth – between 20 and 26 May 1944. John observed: 'There was much to dislike and despise about the way the Japs conducted the war, but no-one who actually fought them on the battlefield could deny their courage and fighting prowess. For a week they had dug in and held that position under constant artillery and mortar fire, with no reinforcements nor resupply of food or ammunition, and no succour for their wounded; they repelled three attacks, well mounted by seasoned battalions and bravely pressed, and inflicted heavy casualties on us.' Concerning 7/10 BR's state, John wrote: 'Of the 640 men of the group who had set out on 20 May only thirty-seven returned who were capable of fighting.' In the late 1990s, the Japanese government was given permission by the Indian government to erect a memorial to 190,000 of their countrymen who had lost their lives in Burma. Red Hill – the furthest point of advance of the Japanese army towards Imphal – was selected as the site for this memorial.

Three months later, 7/10 BR returned to Ranchi once again, for rest and retraining. Following the crossing of the Irrawaddy and the capture – and subsequent siege – of the central Burmese city of Meiktila in March 1945 (during which Naik Fazal Din of 7/10 BR was awarded a posthumous Victoria Cross), 17th Indian Division led the advance southwards. John Randle was awarded a Military Cross for his command of a rifle company during these operations. The citation reads as follows: 'Captain Randle was commanding the company which did the first attack on the enemy bastion on 2 March 1945. It was apparent from later information that this was a fully bunkered position held by over 200 enemy. By very energetic and courageous leadership and by considerable tactical skill, this officer succeeded in reducing two of the enemy strong points and then formed a secure base from which subsequent operations were launched. Throughout the operation, this officer showed a complete disregard for danger and undertook personal recces in the face of enemy fire to pinpoint other centres of resistance. The information thus provided proved most valuable, enabling an effective fire plan to be put into operation, which made the second attack on this bastion a complete success. Captain Randle's work and devotion to duty was outstanding throughout the operation.

'On 30 April 1945 Captain Randle was in command of his company which had been ordered to attack the Pegu Hill feature. His company captured the objective, but its retention was made extremely difficult as the Japanese were securely established on three small hill features in bunkered positions containing MMGs, from which accurate and continuous fire was brought to bear on the captured objective. It was essential to liquidate these bunkers, and Captain Randle put in an attack covered by Battalion Mortars. Immediately the attack got under way, the Japanese opened up with mortars, a 75mm gun and MMGs. The attack had to go through dense undergrowth, where visibility was very restricted. In order to ensure success, Captain Randle personally directed the operations from a completely exposed position and under heavy and continuous enemy fire. Not till the enemy position was overrun and the 75mm gun destroyed did Captain Randle take cover. His cool bearing and calculated leadership, regardless of personal danger, once more achieved a success essential to the effective holding of position on Pegu East.'

By way of contrast, he himself describes an award to a member of the battalion as 'a heart-warming story': 'It was the height of the monsoon, and for that reason and because we had been for several months on half-rations of bully beef and biscuits, almost everyone was suffering from diarrhoea in one form or another, including the platoon of Northamptons. Sweeper Kantu was there sharing the burden of the day. He had sited the officers' mess thunderbox in a dugout, half submerged in water but shielded from any direct Japanese fire. He also dug his own slit trench, which like the rest of them was largely full of water, and also a crawl-trench out through the wire into the jungle. After each use of the thunderbox he had to crawl away along the trench, often under fire, to deposit the contents in a pit that he had dug. Failure to do this would have immeasurably worsened the appalling sanitary conditions and led to even worse bowel diseases. Normally there were only three or four officers in Battalion Headquarters but with the addition of the platoon of Northamptons who had asked and received my authority to use our facilities, Kantu was working virtually round the clock in performing his duties. Day after day this humble little man worked away to make this vital contribution, ceaselessly crawling along the exposed trench, with the added risk of being ambushed when he got beyond the wire. He did so without complaint for about a fortnight, until the intensity of the fighting died down.

'His conduct so amazed the Northamptons that they asked that his work should be recognised. Here was this humble little man, who had started life probably in as lowly a position as any human being on earth, with no benefit of education, yet he was risking his life day after day to do his little bit of duty as he saw it. It is a very remarkable example of the triumph of the human spirit from a most unlikely source and under appalling conditions. Maurice Wright [the CO], having thought deeply about it and having spoken to the brigadier, decided that he would put Kantu in for a "Mention in Despatches". This was duly done, with the citation setting out the circumstances. It was without parallel that anyone should get a "Mention" for "shovelling s..t" but this was agreed by 14th Army commander, that great and understanding soldier Bill Slim, and Kantu was in due course awarded his Mention.'

Denied access to Khasi girls, the Japanese found a different solution: 'In July 1945 my Pathan Company of 7/10 BR was dug in on a redoubt centred on a cockroach-infested rice mill near the village of Kyauktauga on the main Rangoo–Pegu–Tougoo road in Central Burma. … One morning just after we had stood down from the dawn stand-to, I was having a restorative mug of char and shaving when I heard a lot of hearty laughter and Pushtu wisecracking going on outside. I sent my orderly to find out what was going on and he returned shortly afterwards grinning all over his face with the news that one of our patrols had captured some women who the patrol commander was now parading outside for my inspection. Pathan leg-pulling before breakfast did not always put me at my best and I went outside, not perhaps in the best of humour. To my surprise there indeed was the patrol commander, also grinning widely, with six Japanese comfort girls lined up demurely for my inspection. Surprisingly, considering the monsoon conditions and the appalling state under which the Japanese were withdrawing, these girls looked very clean, tidy and cheerful, and not unattractive.

'Each girl was carrying a small cheap cardboard suitcase, which I got them to open; they all contained the same – hundreds of Japanese

Burma 'banana' money notes and a spare pair of knickers. I ordered my company *havildar major* to see that they were given food and drink and then put somewhere in the rice mill under guard. I then sent a signal to Battalion HQ on the lines of "Have captured six tarts. Request disposal instructions." This provoked the response that it was a bit early in the morning for Randle humour. I persisted and in the end got a signal to say that a party of military police would in due course come and collect them. Meanwhile my Pathans were enjoying themselves chatting up the girls, whom I began to suspect might be contemplating offering a bit of business. After all, the oldest profession is an all-embracing one – literally. I was not, therefore, too unhappy when eventually a posse of redcaps did arrive and took the girls away, to the patronising derision that all front-line troops, perhaps unfairly, tended in those days to have for the military police. That evening, over my customary meal with Moghal Baz, he remarked philosophically that it had been a unique day for him. "How so, *Subedar* Sahib?" I asked. "Sahib," he replied, "in all my service I have never seen either women or military police in a front-line position. Today we have had both."'

On 15 August 1945 – VJ-Day – 7/10 BR was little more than sixty miles from where they had been when the Japanese invaded Burma three-and-a-half years earlier. John concluded:

'I suppose the only reason that I survived was because I was adjutant for two years! I was not wounded but was blown up in a minefield at Meiktila (subsequent deafness).' Having transferred to the British Army, he accepted a commission in the Devonshire Regiment, joining the 2nd Battalion in Luneberg in October 1946. His subsequent career is a good example of the range of internal security operations in which the British Army soon became involved: 'Every time I joined a battalion, that battalion went on active service before my

Brigadier J.P. Randle OBE MC ADC, 1975.

tour finished': in Singapore and Malaya during the Emergency; in Kenya during the Mau-Mau rebellion; in Cyprus during the EOKA uprising, and in British Guiana after a coup and the subsequent declaration of a state of emergency in May 1964. During that last tour he commanded the 1st Battalion, The Devonshire and Dorset Regiment, and in recognition of his calm and decisive leadership during unpredictable times, was awarded an OBE the following year. My father succeeded him as commanding officer. John was divisional brigadier, The Prince of Wales's Division, before, most deservedly, being appointed Brigadier Overseas Detachments, which permitted some rather more relaxed travel experiences. In that final role he was also ADC to HM The Queen 1974–76.

John Randle relaxing at home in 2015.

During an active retirement, John was regimental secretary for nine years; president of the Baluch Regiment (UK) Officers' Dinner Club; president, Devon Dumplings Cricket Club 1995–96; and an enthusiastic supporter of the Burma Star Association. A great cricket fan, he kindly proposed me for membership of the MCC in 1999. In 1946 in Berkhamsted, he married Georgina Margaret Kathleen (Peggy) Miskimmin; they had one son, Will, who also served in the Regiment. Peggy died on 15 September 2003 and John remarried in 2010, to Joy Hunt (née Myburgh). John Randle died on 14 December 2020, shortly after his ninety-ninth birthday.

575568 Sergeant George Rice, Royal Air Force

Lionel George (George) Rice was born on 14 October 1923 in Bristol, younger son of 329025 Warrant Officer Charles Lake Rice, Royal Air Force, and his wife Elizabeth (née French). Charles had previously been a driver in the Royal Field Artillery and, as George explained, 'he had been wounded by shrapnel or suffered gas poisoning – they had to put something down on his records – and so he transferred to the Royal Air Force when it was formed on 1 April 1918. Although he was due out in the middle of the Second World War, he stayed in for the duration. He was a blacksmith and coppersmith and served in Ireland during the previous civil disturbance in the 1920s and also serviced aircraft embarked in the aircraft carrier HMS *Argus*. My parents married on 4 October 1919, when my father was 21. They had what was called then a "Married Establishment", which meant that you didn't get a quarter until you were 26. Even then, if you were serving overseas and someone was posted in with a better claim, you sometimes had to get out of your married quarter and find digs. My education was zero, if I may put it that way: I went to at least twelve different schools.

'Before my father was posted to Iraq for a couple of years in 1930, he was stationed at Bircham Newton in Norfolk. After Iraq, he was posted to No. 1 Aircraft Depôt at Drigh Road, five miles outside Karachi, where he was entitled to a married quarter [six years earlier, AC2 T.E. Shaw (aka Lawrence of Arabia) had spent a year in the Engine Repair Shop at Drigh Road]. I attended a very small, two-room school there, taught by some ladies. In 1936 we came back to a married quarter up on the hill at Netheravon in Wiltshire and I went to the village school. That was where we had our first car, a Jowett 7 hp, which really struggled to get up the hill to our quarter. From Netheravon we moved back to Halton, where my elder brother, Leonard, had been born. From conception, we were both destined for the Royal Air Force – we really had no option. Halton Council School was between the barracks and the workshops, and the headmaster, 'Batty' Bates, recognized that there was a real problem with the education of RAF children. We were therefore allowed to study subjects applicable to getting into the RAF: Science, Mathematics, English Composition and General Knowledge. We didn't waste time on subjects like Art!

Sergeant George Rice

'I passed the examination for the RAF Apprentice Scheme, and in January 1939 I was offered a place at the Electrical & Wireless School at RAF Cranwell. My brother had earlier passed for the RAF Apprentice Scheme and joined No. 2 Wing at RAF Halton. I spent a week at Halton getting kitted out, having medicals and all the usual things. It was due to be a three-year training course but, when war broke out, they reordered the training gradually until they got down to my entry, the 39th, which lasted two years. Cranwell was a horrible cold place with an

575568 Aircraft Apprentice L.G. Rice, Cranwell, 1939.

enormous parade ground – remember that we arrived there in February. Unfortunately, I soon went down with spinal meningitis, which put me in the college hospital for a fortnight. I started off as what they called a wireless operator/mechanic and enjoyed the training. While a lot of it was technical and we had to get up to eighteen words per minute in Morse, with most of us going on to achieve twenty-five words per minute, a lot of it was education, because we hadn't had much of it before. My father said: "You'll become a man, my son."

'In January 1941, I left Cranwell and was posted to No. 13 Maintenance Unit at RAF Henlow in Bedfordshire. I was only 17 and not considered a man until I was 17½ so was still considered an apprentice. One day, one of the warrant officers put me on the roster for guard duty. When I told him that I was too young for guard duty, he took me to the cookhouse, ordered a pint of milk and told me that I had to remain in my barrack room after eight-thirty. I started in the radio workshops before transferring to the hangars. Hawker Hurricanes were delivered to the hangars in big, big boxes. They arrived with the engine already mounted in the fuselage. We had to fit the wings, put the propellor on, fit the radios and connect the batteries, before the aircraft were test flown and delivered to their new owners. Some of them were destined for Malta and North Africa. I went

The Rice family serving together in the RAF, 1941: (left to right) Leonard, Charles and George.

on temporary attachment to HMS *Argus* and Hurricanes without either wings or propellers were shipped to Gibraltar. Half were reassembled on HMS *Furious* while the other half were transferred across to HMS *Ark Royal*. I joined HMS *Ark Royal* and her Hurricanes flew to Malta. As far as I can tell, this was the trip before she was sunk [*Ark Royal* was sunk by *U-81* thirty miles east of Gibraltar on 14 November 1941]. Malta later issued a special medal, which was issued to all those who had helped to save the island during the war. I searched for official documentation to prove my involvement but never managed to find any – so I never got my medal!

'We then had to wait several weeks at Gibraltar for someone to take us home. Eventually we came back to Scapa Flow in HMS *Prince of Wales* and I was put down in the signals area with the telegraphists. At the age of 18, I don't think I realised how exciting it was and I certainly didn't think about what would happen if the ship was sunk [HMS *Prince of Wales* was sunk by Japanese aircraft off the east coast of Malaya on 10 December 1941]. In January 1942, I received a posting order and spent rather too many weeks at West Kirby transit camp, a horrible darned place. Eventually we sailed from Liverpool in the QSMV *Dominion*

Monarch. We sailed the long way round, via Cape Town, where we spent a few days and many of us got diarrhoea because the food was too rich. We were faster than the rest of the convoy so sailed on to Bombay alone. I am pretty sure that we were originally destined for South East Asia but Singapore had fallen by then. From Bombay we caught a smaller boat to Karachi and then a lorry – here's a coincidence for you – to Drigh Road [which had just been designated No. 1 (India) Maintenance Unit].

'I was still doing exactly what I had been doing on the aircraft carriers on the Hurricanes while I was posted at Henlow. Early the following year, I was posted to No. 6 Indian Air Force Squadron, which was also equipped with Hurricanes, this time in the photo-reconnaissance role. We were based in the state of Bhopal although we kept moving around. The Indian Air Force (IAF) was formed from coastal defence units and some of the pilots and all the COs – squadron leaders – were Indian. My CO was a Sikh, Squadron Leader Mehar Singh. We had been seconded to the IAF to provide a nucleus of various trades to boost the squadrons as they were formed. While we had a British warrant officer, there were no British officers at all. Although there was still an anti-British feeling throughout India, we got on very well with the rank and file within the squadron. We then moved to Nagpur in the state of Maharashtra. We were in open country, next to No. 2 Prisoner of War Camp, which housed Italian prisoners. I thought that it was amazing to see Italian officers wandering around in uniform with their plumed hats. Although I didn't write home to my mother very often, I must confess, she was certainly most surprised to see my address on the back of the aerogramme – she thought that I was already a PoW.

'From Nagpur, we moved back to Bombay, where another strange thing happened. At Drigh Road we had taken new radios out of the Hurricanes and put back the old ones because they worked with the communications system that they had in India. I was now despatched to Dacca to collect new radio equipment for our Hurricanes because we were now destined for Burma, where they used the new communications system. I was sent off on my own, without an interpreter or anything. I had to sort out the equipment before supervising the loading of the equipment on the trucks and then the loading of the trucks themselves as they were driven onto the train. I can't tell you how many radios I moved from place to place: I was forever changing radios, radio aerials and radio control panels. The old set had a wire aerial; the new one had a radio mast sticking out of the top of the aircraft.

'I stayed with No. 6 Squadron and in early 1943 we went to Cox's Bazar, and from there into the Arakan. We were based at Ratnap, which was in the middle of nowhere as far as I was concerned. It was just paddy fields which had been flattened out: no hangars, no nothing. Our accommodation was in bamboo huts and I wouldn't like to tell you what we called our beds – they were damned hard! There was a British contingent and we did not do much with the Hindus, Moslems and Sikhs outside working hours. We all had our own quarters and separate messing arrangements. There was an RAF squadron just down the road, at a place called Ratnapalong. It was absolutely daft naming the airfield like that but someone must have thought they were being very clever [in fact, the village of Ratnapalong exists and is now in Bangladesh]. We spent six or seven months there, until the monsoon broke. The paddy fields then turned to mud – which is what paddy fields do – so we were withdrawn, via Cox's Bazar and Risalpur, to Kohat on the North-West Frontier. While at Kohat, I was detached to go with the Kochi and Waziristan Scouts to install army radio sets. You wouldn't believe that, with all those Royal Signals chaps floating around, I had to go up there for a couple of months. I used to travel from fort to fort, sitting in the front of a lorry with twenty-five scouts in the back, and another twenty-five in the lorry behind. I thought that it was amazing that I was worth so much. I had to learn as I was going along, as it was all army kit, with which I wasn't familiar. When the job was done, they flew me back to Kohat in a Harvard.

'After spending Christmas 1944 in Kohat, I was posted to Drigh Road and then detached to No. 1 Anti-aircraft Unit at Katni to a target-towing unit. The unit towed targets using Hurricanes and Vultee Vengeances. Confusingly, the CO was Squadron Leader Phillips, who married a nurse from the local hospital, while the adjutant was also called Phillips. I spent almost a year at Katni before I had done my overseas time and received a posting order. I didn't want to come home, to be honest, because I really liked India. I said to the CO: "Can't I just forget about it?" That isn't the way the RAF works though, and I reported to Worli Transit Camp on 25 December 1945. There was no Christmas dinner for me that year. Priority was given to former prisoners of war, the sick and volunteers; as a regular, I was right at the bottom of the list. I must have been at Worli for six weeks and it was terrible because more and more troops were coming in and we had less and less bedspace. There was very little to do although you could see the same film half-a-dozen times if you really wanted to. When we eventually sailed from Bombay, the ship was equipped with

George Rice, Barnstaple, VJ-Day 1995.

little cots which you could let down on the decks in late evening when it was time to go to bed. There was no reception party at Southampton because we were all odds-and-sods although the trusty WVS were there with cups of tea.

'After a week of medical checks, we went on disembarkation leave. As a regular, I only had a week's leave – instead of three weeks, which the others got – and I thought that it was pretty grotty, after four years abroad. Just as I came home, my father left to join the occupation forces in Japan. I went to stay with my mother, who was now living in the village of St Leonards, in the Chilterns between Chesham and Tring. My first posting was to RAF Elsham Wolds in Lincolnshire. I had a wide variety of postings: to South Wales, where my father was stationed at the same time; to No. 16 Maintenance Unit at RAF Stafford; to RAF Gütersloh and RAF Laarbruck in West Germany; and to RAF Woolfox Lodge, north of Stamford next to the A1, where I worked on the Bloodhound surface-to-air missile. At Laarbruck I worked with the CPN4, an American ground-controlled, pulse navigation radar, which was only used once while I was there, to bring a Hastings down safely.

'I was commissioned in 1959 and received a branch commission, rather than a general purpose commission, into the Signals Branch. Between 1964 and 1966 I was in charge of the ground radar servicing unit at RAF Khormaksar in Aden. It was lovely in the winter – just the right temperature – and I had a little Fiat so we could move round a little bit: to Steamer Point and to the beach at Tarshine, just below the Officers' Club. My last posting was at SHAPE in Belgium, at the NATO Programming Centre (NPC). NPC was a special unit which wrote computer programs for NATO air forces. I was a junior technical author, writing descriptions for the diagrams. NPC was multi-national but no-one seemed to understand what the Italians had written! I used to have a bit of trouble with senior officers; apparently I wasn't terribly diplomatic. I only know that now because I requested a copy of my records. I applied for Premature Voluntary Release – or PVR – in April 1976, after thirty-seven years in the RAF.'

George received seven medals during that time: 1939–45 Star, Africa Star, Burma Star, Defence Medal, War Medal, General Service Medal with clasps for Radfan and South Arabia and the Long Service and Good Conduct Medal. Although it came earlier and he said that he wasn't expecting it, the Africa Star was compensation for not receiving the Malta medal.

On 6 September 1947 at St Leonards, George was married to Margaret, only daughter of Jack Eggleton of 8 Chiltern Cottages, Buckland Common, and his wife Lilly Emma (née Terry). Jack served as an ARP warden in Amersham during the Second World War. George and Margaret had two children: Brian and Jennifer. He became a life member of the North Devon branch of the Burma Star Association on 3 March 1988 (membership number R/2158/88). At Barnstaple on VJ-Day 75 in 2020, George read the Kohima Epitaph, without notes (which he wouldn't have been able to read very easily anyway).

George Rice at home, VJ-Day, 2020.

109503 Captain John Riggs, Bedfordshire and Hertfordshire Regiment

John Sydney Riggs was born on 1 March 1920, son of Sydney Chilton Riggs, who was awarded his Master's Certificate for 'Foreign-Going Steamships Only' on 17 September 1917, and his wife Kathleen Dorothy, fourth daughter of William James Ansell Shadrake, a wine merchant's clerk, of 4 Clova Road, Forest Gate, West Ham. Four years later, John, his mother and younger sister, Kay, embarked for China, where they were to join Sydney, who was working in the Treaty Port of Hankow, now part of Wuhan, which has since become famous for all the wrong reasons. A couple of years after that, when Sydney's job moved to Shanghai, John was despatched back to England, initially to St Paul's Cathedral Choir School and subsequently to Magdalen College School, Oxford. After leaving school in December 1937, he was offered a job with the Hong Kong and Shanghai Banking Corporation (HSBC), on condition that he first gained experience with a firm of City accountants.

With war threatening, John volunteered for the army and was accepted by the Artists' Rifles. Within eighteen months, the regiment had been redesignated 163 OCTU and was accommodated in the *Daily Sketch* Holiday Camp for Children near Dymchurch, Kent. In December 1939, 109503 Second Lieutenant J.S. Riggs was commissioned into the Bedfordshire and Hertfordshire Regiment and posted to the 1st Battalion (1 BHR), then based in Palestine. Having spent a few weeks in Ramallah, John was appointed to command 1 BHR's signal platoon. After a period on the Greek island of Lemnos, during which John explored 'the hilly goat tracks on my motorcycle', and a campaign against the Vichy French

Private J.S. Riggs, The Artists' Rifles, 1939.

in Syria, where 'the intensity of the conflict was remarkable', 1 BHR sailed to Tobruk on 21 October 1941 to relieve elements of a hard-pressed, besieged garrison. John explained: 'My signallers' job was to maintain the telephone network. About 24 men were barely enough for this ongoing task.' That Christmas, after the siege had ended, was 'noteworthy: plum pudding made with bread and fried potatoes. Unfortunately the cooks had failed to soak the dehydrated potatoes beforehand.'

After the siege of Tobruk, John was briefly an instructor at an OCTU in Cairo, before rejoining 1 BHR, which had accompanied 70th Division to India four months earlier, at around the same time that his father was imprisoned by the Kempeitai, the Japanese military police, in Shanghai. John wrote about the problems in India: 'The unrest sometimes involved disruption to the main railway routes: Bombay – Delhi – Calcutta (about 3,000 miles), which interrupted supplies for our forces facing the Japanese on the eastern frontier. This could not be tolerated. Our continuous training had to be interrupted while we were sent to ensure the railway was kept open and functioning. The battalion was given a stretch of railway to guard about 300 miles to the west of Calcutta while others had other stretches up and down the line.

'It was not an unwelcome move to undertake a new task many miles north of Ranchi; however, the journey in Indian Army transport could be hazardous. The newly-recruited Indian drivers were not expert in handling very large lorries. Twenty to thirty of our soldiers in the back on wooden benches cursed and swore on bumpy country roads while the officers up front were scared to death by the drivers' inability to control the vehicles and their lack of any road sense. In the event we were lucky, but others went off the road and down the hillside. By this time I was a captain and second-in-command of B Company, so I could no longer take one of my signals motorcycles and avoid these hazardous lorry rides. When we reached the railway, the Battalion HQ picked the largest and most comfortable-looking railway station and spread the rest of us up and down the line to occupy the lesser stations and halts.'

There were compensations though: 'In the 1920s and 1930s all small boys dreamt about being able to drive one of the latest great steam locomotives – from London, the *Royal Scot* to Glasgow, the *Flying Scotsman* to Edinburgh, the *Cornish Riviera* to Penzance and other expresses. I had made a point of cultivating the Anglo-Indian drivers and, if I was allowed, riding in the cabs of their great steam engines. They were the patricians of the railway, in charge of handling the trains from Bombay to Delhi to Calcutta and back. Always dressed in spotless white overalls, they had underlings to stoke the engines, take on water and fuel *en route*, polish the brass work, etc. At last, 'Captain Sahib' was invited to drive one of these engines. Small boyhood dreams had not entirely faded at the age of 22. Under instruction, I was shown how to pull the levers to open up the valves and pistons to start the very heavy train moving.'

Following a year of internal security duties, 1 BHR was posted to Bangalore, more than 1,200 miles further south, when it was 'realised that it was not a good idea to leave some 3,500 or more experienced front-line troops to rot away for much longer'. Within days, 70th Division was 'reorganised for a Long-Range Penetration incursion into Burma … in short we were to be reformed into separate, self-contained columns in a Special Force to be planted hundreds of miles deep into Burma to cause trouble and mayhem in the rear areas of the Japanese army engaged with our units on the Indian border.' There then followed six months of intensive training, which took place in an area one hundred miles south of Jhansi. Operation Thursday, known to history as the second Chindit raid, involved almost five times as many Allied soldiers as its predecessor, Operation Longcloth. John Riggs commanded the recce platoon of 16 Column: 'My platoon would have numbered up to 40 men, comprising the Karens [from the hill tribes on the Thai border], three rifle sections from the battalion, each under a sergeant or corporal, and signallers and mule leaders. We were more lightly armed than the rest of the Column, enabling us to move faster and farther.'

Although Operation Thursday commenced on 5 March 1944, 16 Column did not fly into the stronghold called "Aberdeen" until 31 March: 'My plane-load included three mules and half my recce platoon. It was my first-ever flight, as it would have been for all the others on board, including the mules. They were held in makeshift bamboo stalls, close behind the backs of the pilots and crew. There was no bulkhead behind the cockpit: it had been removed, along with the doors and other fittings, to maximise space. We sat on our packs on the steel floor of the aircraft and viewed the jungle cover of the Chin Hills through a gaping doorway in the side of the plane, which felt rather too close for comfort, especially when we met turbulence as we flew eastwards.

16 Column, The Chindits: (left to right) Captain Lee Turner RE; Major John Barrow (Commander); Captain John Riggs.

'We had orders to shoot and kill the mules if they kicked away their stalls and broke loose. Luckily our mules were docile as their leaders stood by their heads and gave them some fodder. The mules had to be coaxed out of the planes at "Aberdeen". They had lost their sense of balance during the flight and had to be walked round for some time before they stopped staggering about as if drunk and recovered their usual steadiness and sure-footed gait. It became very cold compared with the temperature at ground level as we climbed to about 12,000 feet to clear the hills. All this added to the strangeness of this first flight, coupled with the remote possibility of interception by the Japanese Air Force – we had no fighter cover and would have been sitting ducks. At last we became aware of our descent and bumped along the rough airstrip at "Aberdeen". One of our platoons on another flight had a bad landing and many were injured, and some were flown to hospital. No seats … so no seatbelts.

'The hills throughout this northern area of Burma were extensively covered in uncut teak forests, through much of which the going was not difficult. Where the teak had been cut and abandoned there would be secondary growth which could be dense: bamboo, thorn, creeper and every kind of low level scrub, which could become a major obstruction and through which a path had to be cut. The cutting had to be near to the ground so that remaining stumps, particularly bamboo leaving a sharp edge, would not cut the mules' flanks. It was a very arduous task and the cutters had to be relieved very frequently. Progress of the column was very slow in the most dense and difficult secondary growth, so here was another task for the recce platoon: to find, if possible, an easier way through, by using elephant tracks, for example.'

Three battalions – all divided into columns – then embarked on a 30-mile approach march towards Indaw, a major road and rail hub: '16 Column set off first, to be followed by 61 Column the next day: Riggs and his recce platoon leading the battalion into action! The tracks across our southward route were frequent and showed signs of recent use. In line with our training, we approached with caution and sent small groups up and down the track while the platoon crossed. Even just thirty men and the mules took a worryingly long time to clear the track and erase their footprints so that we would not be followed. The frequency of this track drill meant that our progress was too slow, and the column would be catching up. A quicker but potentially more hazardous crossing was adopted. We marched up the track for a few hundred yards, turned north, away from our southward route, and then walked backwards into the jungle leaving our footprints pointing in the wrong direction. After a few yards we resumed our southwards course.'

Discipline was essential: 'After watering the mules we moved off into the jungle and brewed up. Scarcely had we moved away than fourteen enemy trucks came by loaded with troops, possibly looking for us. This was a tempting situation for us to lay an ambush, but our orders were to approach Indaw undetected. … The Bedfords' rifle platoons moved up towards Indaw and carried out aggressive patrols against the outlying villages. They travelled light with three days' rations. They discovered and destroyed extensive enemy fuel dumps dispersed around the villages, many of which they set alight, but they were too extensive to be completely destroyed. Consequently one column's RAF officer was flown out in a light aircraft and guided in a flight of US Air Force bombers to drop incendiary bombs – with success. Other patrols reconnoitred with our Royal Engineers the branch railway line that ran eastwards from Indaw to Katha on the Irrawaddy.'

After Major General Orde Wingate had been killed in an air crash on 24 March, he was succeeded by an American general, 'Vinegar Joe' Stilwell, who, in John's opinion, 'was a rabid Anglophobe and had no idea how to use our Chindit columns effectively. Our trials and tribulations and casualties were multiplied from then on by his misuse and by the monsoon rains. Stilwell's one and only objective was to capture Myitkyina without the direct participation of the hated "Limeys". Nevertheless, he decided that all these Chindit brigades should move from their present positions closer to his operations in the north. All nine columns – the Brigade HQ formed one column – set off northwards as quickly as possible on their own separate routes. The Black Watch moved east of the railway. We were sent to the west of Indaw and too close to it for comfort. Only a short way down the line from Indaw, two enemy troop trains were held up due to the brigade's demolitions. The trains were thought to contain about 2,500 troops between them. A nearby station was bombed as one of our columns protected the crossing while the other columns crossed, and one of our platoons had to drive off an enemy patrol. An officer and three others were wounded. The column covering the brigade crossing blew up the railway line before leaving.'

Mawlu was attacked and the position held for three days while preparations were made for the evacuation of the "White City" stronghold: 'Soon after dark on 9 May the Dakotas started arriving. It was a bright clear night. All the airstrip landing lights were lit and the planes' navigation and headlights were on. From my tree-covered ridge across the paddy, I had a grandstand view of this amazing operation. It was like a peacetime airport on a fine summer's night. The Dakotas came and went most of the night taking away all heavy guns and other equipment, while the garrison of "White City" laid extensive booby traps in preparation for moving out. The other interesting aspect of this unique evacuation is the complete lack of any reaction from the Japanese. Presumably they would not have known whether "White City" was being dismantled or reinforced with more men and equipment. The lack of enemy response was tribute to the good work of the Bedfords at Mawlu.'

Two days later, 14th Brigade embarked on their approach march to the Kyunsanlai Pass at the southern end of Indawgyi Lake: 'For the first day or two it was very hot but then the monsoon broke. Several days of torrential rain and the steep country slowed our progress at times to one mile a day up and down the slopes of 2,000 to 4,000 feet. For every slope we had to cut steps and manhandle mule loads and even the mules themselves. Parties had to make long descents with water bottles and *charguls* to hump water back up for mules and men. Rain thunders down onto broad leaves. It's so loud we have to shout to be heard. During lulls, one can hear it approaching across the hills, like a roaring cataract increasing in volume. During much of this long painful northward march the recce platoons moved either with their columns or only a few hundred yards ahead of them. Night bivouacs were spent within the columns, often on steep slopes. Resting at 45 degrees with one's feet against a tree was no problem: we were exhausted and wet through.

'One member of my platoon, a big man, developed a high fever which I assumed was malaria or scrub typhus. All officers carried syringes and phials of quinine. Intravenous quinine sorted out even a bad case of malaria very quickly. This was the only time I administered intravenous quinine. I was anxious to remain mobile because there may have been Japanese in the area. There was no time to hang around. The results of the quinine shot were quite amazing. The man was up on his feet within twenty minutes. He could march, although his pack went on a mule. I was relieved because I had never been so close to leaving someone behind.' After leading a patrol north of Indawgyi Lake, 'to make contact if possible with the Chinese and Americans', John reported to the column's MO, 'hoping he could do something about the sore on my back which was becoming increasingly painful'. Diagnosed with 'an outsize abscess, much too large for him to try to clean it out', John was evacuated – despite his desperate pleadings – in a Sunderland flying-boat.

At the end of November 1944, John embarked in SS *Almanzora*, in charge of a draft of 100 soldiers, for the voyage from Bombay to Glasgow. After a brief spell at the Infantry NCOs' School at Warrington, which soon merged into the newly-established School of Infantry in Warminster, he was demobilised in August 1946. That June, he married Marjorie Arabella, elder daughter of George Albert Neale of 25 Kingsbridge Road, Parkstone, Dorset, who had died just six months earlier. John and Marjorie had three children: Rosie, Barbie and David. The job with HSBC didn't work out, with the bank's doctor insisting that he couldn't return to the Far East because of his malaria. In response, John 'explained that everyone had had malaria, including the bank staff interned by the

Japanese'. Nevertheless, the Riggs family spent sixteen years in the Far East, initially in Singapore and subsequently at Yokohama in Japan, where he worked for Jardine Matheson: 'We were surprised and had a pleasant stay in Japan. I had expected to find it difficult, but I didn't.' Back in England, John rose to become chief accountant for the Royal British Legion, representing his employers on the Burma Star Association's National Council from 1978. It was a source of enormous pride to John and his family that he

John Riggs, Horse Guards, VJ-Day, 2015.

had a leading role during the VJ-Day 70th anniversary commemorations on Horse Guards on 15 August 2015. John was vice president of the Association (membership number R/1613/77) at the age of 100, when it was merged into the Burma Star Memorial Fund on 15 August 2020. John Riggs died on 8 December 2021, at the age of 101.

Gunner Stanley Seymour, Royal Artillery

Stanley George William Seymour was born in Portsmouth on 14 October 1919, younger son of Alexander Seymour, a skilled labourer in HM Dockyard, of 23 Owen Street, Portsmouth, and his wife Elsie (née Kenney). Educated at Francis Avenue School and later at Portsmouth Junior Technical College, Stanley started work as a tailor's salesman with Montague Burton in North End at the age of 17. Having enlisted in the 6th Battalion (Duke of Connaught's Own), Hampshire Regiment (6 Hamps) the previous year, he was called up on 23 August 1939, eleven days before war was declared. Within a matter of weeks, 6 Hamps was redesignated 59th Anti-Tank Regiment, Royal Artillery. In Stanley's none-too-encouraging words, this 'involved firing 2-pound shells at tanks which was [sic] said to bounce off.' Having 'already been through quite a lot before the war, my mates Charlie, Alex and I had our first promotion soon after call-up to train (help to) the militia (call-up of 18s & over) after courses at Salisbury Plain in Wiltshire.' The prospect of rapid progress through the ranks was soon scotched, however: 'I carried the can for a light showing from a guard room out in the country somewhere, being in charge of it, so that put paid to any ambition I had.'

All was not lost though, and Stanley's talents were soon recognised: 'I was used by instructors to show "this is how it is done" so I eventually got away, finishing up at Clarewood Camp, Durban, South Africa, from where, after a very short stay, I found myself at the School of Royal Artillery, India.' This transfer presented an opportunity and Stanley soon 'joined a regular unit, 8th Field Regiment, Royal Artillery (8 Field), as a Battery Surveyor'. The regiment was equipped with the Ordnance QF (quick-firing)

Gunner S.G.W. Seymour, Royal Artillery.

25-pounder, perhaps the most iconic British artillery weapon of the Second World War, which remained in service with the regular army until the 1960s and with some training units until the 1980s. With reference to the complexity of his own wartime role, Stanley cynically observed that 'now it's all done by touching buttons – no brain work at all'! 8 Field joined 25th (Indian) Infantry Division (25 Division) on 11 November 1943, was posted to the Arakan on 21 March 1944 and remained in Burma until 28 May 1945, when it was withdrawn for Operation Zipper, the assault on Malaya and Singapore. In a letter to his daughter, Hilary, Stanley described the role of a battery surveyor: 'Position of 24 guns and enemy positions had to be worked out and plotted on a special board from which the distance between was ascertained and wired through to a pivot gun (No. 1) who positioned the other 23. It's a hundred times more complicated than I can say. The eight of us were never that far from enemy positions as we had to direct the firing, but as I told you I think, we often had the Gurkhas with us in open work – couldn't do two jobs at the same time.'

During what later became known as 'Third Arakan', 25 Division first enlarged the Maungdaw base, establishing effective superiority over the Japanese in that region, before clearing the Mayu Range down to Foul Point and occupying Akyab Island. Subsequently, with 3 Commando Brigade under command and the Royal Indian Navy in support, 25 Division triumphed at the decisive Battle of Kangaw before outflanking the retreating Japanese through amphibious landings at Myebon and Ruywa. No fewer than four Victoria Crosses were awarded to members of 25 Division as a result of these decisive actions. Stanley reflected: 'It wasn't an enjoyable life, but at times it was great to see the results of our maths. Daresay I used to think back to our nights in the shelters on Southsea seafront. I never thought I'd see home again.' Then there was the money: 'Call-up pay 1 shilling a day; little later 3 shillings a day; sergeant had 6 shillings day. My pay after the school in India: 3 shillings a day plus 3 shillings a day trade pay plus 3 shilling a day Jap campaign money = 9 shillings a day, which was pretty good in those days. Very little was drawn overseas, so we had quite a lot to collect at the end.' Having first been posted overseas in January 1941, Stanley served in Freetown, Sierra Leone; South Africa; India; and Burma, 'where I spent the worst time of my life and the longest'.

222 The Final Curtain: Burma 1941–1945

Stanley and Joan Seymour.

The war had a real impact: 'Due home thank God, picked up PoWs at Borneo, Singapore, Saigon, etc – saw the White Cliffs of Dover towards the end of 1945. I had a wonderful "Welcome Home" in lights everywhere outside "Kelso" – great party later. Not being all that well, nervous state and underweight because of the Burmese campaign, I did not settle down until starting work in September 1946, having spent most of my time on Bognor Sands, weather permitting.' That explains why, despite having been demobbed in January 1946, Stanley did not join the Ordnance Survey for almost nine months. Stanley worked as a surveyor, so his war service stood him in good stead and guided his civilian career in a completely different direction. During the next thirty-three years – until his retirement in 1979 – he worked in Wimbledon,

Chessington, Bognor Regis, Brighton and Littlehampton. In March 1948 in Willesden, Middlesex, Stanley Seymour married Vivien Ivy Witcher and they had two children: Hilary, who was born in March 1952 and Ian (who predeceased his father by six months), who was born in April 1956.

After the death of his second wife, Stanley was invited to a dance and met Joan, with whom – by coincidence – he shared a surname. Stanley and Joan were married at Tottington Manor, Edburton, West Sussex, on 28 September 1999. In the words of Joan's daughter, Sue: 'They really had found true happiness. Stanley always had a smile on his face and, as Mum would say, he was a true gentleman. They blessed every day they had together and both enjoyed good health until, sadly, Stanley had his stroke. They fell in love with Skiathos where they found the perfect hotel in Trolous Bay, which they visited many times and were greeted by staff and locals alike with first names and hugs!!' Having become a life member of the Burma Star Association on 20 July 2004, Stanley and Joan were active supporters of the Brighton branch. He died in Worthing in February 2006 and she died in June 2019. As Sue explained, 'It was Stanley's wish to leave a legacy to the Association, and Mum wanted to make sure she honoured that.' As result, Joan left the association a most generous – and totally unexpected – bequest of £25,000, which will benefit our veterans and also the Burma Star scholars.

126426 Major David Shirreff MC, King's African Rifles

Alexander David Shirreff was born on 29 October 1919 at Naini Tal, Uttarakhand, India, younger son of Alexander Grierson Shirreff, Indian Civil Service, and his wife Dulcie Marion, younger daughter of Lieutenant Colonel Walter Herbert Baxter, Commanding Officer, 1st/4th Battalion, Dorsetshire Regiment, who died of meningitis in India on 18 May 1917 while on leave from Mesopotamia. David Shirreff attended Sherborne School in Dorset, where he was a member of the OTC, recalling, 'We had drill, musketry, map-reading and compass work. Annual Camp was taken quite seriously: we once had to march from Sherborne to Warminster, which was quite a long way. We had quite regular field days in the summer terms and tactical training in the periods that we spent in camp.' Between school and university, he travelled in Germany and Austria, learning to speak German in the process. After completing a year at Exeter College, Oxford, he explained that 'it was quite obvious that war was coming. In fact, I remember feeling that there was no point in considering any career because I was bound to land up in the army one day. I volunteered and was enlisted in the Oxfordshire and Buckinghamshire Light Infantry but, after an interview, I was selected for OCTU at Sandhurst. I never actually served in the ranks and went straight to Sandhurst in October 1939.' At Sandhurst during the 'phoney war' period, 'there were still one, or perhaps two, companies of pre-war 'gentleman cadets', who wore very much smarter uniforms than we did – we were wartime officer cadets'.

Major A.D. Shirreff MC, Dorsetshire Regiment, attached King's African Rifles.

After four months at Sandhurst, he was commissioned into the Dorsetshire Regiment, with which he had family connections, and not only through his grandfather. His uncle, Lieutenant Colonel (later Colonel) Donald Baxter MC TD, managing director of the Sherborne-based family brewing company, was commanding the 4th Battalion when war broke out, and was later honorary colonel of the 4/5th Battalion. Initially posted to the regimental depôt in Dorchester, where he remained for six months, training companies of recruits, he 'volunteered for a number of things to get out of England because there didn't seem any likelihood of anything happening in England for some time. A notice came round asking for volunteers to be seconded to the King's African Rifles and that was the one I was successful in. Two of us from the depôt put our names down; the other chap was David Evans, who was later killed in Madagascar [137354 Lieutenant David Evans MC, Dorsetshire Regiment, a contemporary from Sherborne School, was killed in action on 2 November 1942 and is buried in Diego Suarez War Cemetery].' He sailed from Gourock on the Clyde in the *Winchester Castle*, stopping at Freetown before trans-shipping at Cape Town for the voyage to Mombasa.

The journey lasted a month: 'There were two to three hundred officers and about the same number of British NCOs who were also being seconded to the KAR. We had Swahili classes on board and old Africa hands got up and told us how to treat the African. One man who had obviously been an educationalist with liberal ideas told us to make friends with our troops and one old mining engineer told us, quite seriously, that the best way to treat an African is to beat him when he does wrong and beat him in case he does wrong again, which, I think, probably horrified us at that stage and wasn't very good advice anyway.' At Waterworks Camp, Nairobi, selection took place and Lieutenant Shirreff 'stepped forward' and volunteered to join 5th (Kenya) Battalion, King's African Rifles (5 KAR). He continued: 'We were issued in London with tropical kit which consisted of a pith helmet and shorts and bush shirts, which we found on arrival in Nairobi was totally unacceptable so we jettisoned it and purchased our kit in Nairobi from Indian tailors who knew the sort of kit which the KAR was wearing. Our uniform was a khaki bush tunic with long shorts which came down between your knee and your ankle, which were very practical, with puttees underneath them.

'I was posted to C Company and I was put in charge straightaway of No. 14 Platoon. There was a British company commander, second-in-command, four platoon commanders, a British sergeant major, a British

CQMS and two other British sergeants. The intention was that each platoon should have a British sergeant and an African sergeant but we were never up to that strength. I couldn't talk to my soldiers to start with. I'd learnt a bit of Swahili on the boat but the first essential was to learn Swahili. The sergeant was a Boran called Abdi, who was a very old experienced soldier and a very nice man and he used to speak to me very slowly so that I understood what he said and he was very helpful indeed. I took over from an officer called T.R. King, who was from the Kenya Regiment and knew Swahili well, so I was something quite new to them. There were 35 in the platoon, with three rifle sections, a headquarters section and a grenade section. Within a month, I could just make myself understood in Swahili. They were from a number of tribes: about one-third Kamba, one-third Nandi or allied Kalenjin tribes, and the rest were Somali, Samburu and Luo. The five or six Somalis considered themselves very much superior to the Kenya Africans but they got on reasonably well together. The policy of the KAR then was not to be monolithic by having companies or platoons of one tribe, which was very helpful. The NCOs were all regulars with six or eight years' service and they were well trained in the rifle and Bren gun. They were good shots and had exceptional eyesight. They were very good at drill – they enjoyed drill.

'Their tactical training was fairly limited but the company commander, a Regular Scots Guardsman called David Kimble, was an extremely good soldier and I soon began to realise that he was really training the company extremely well in bush warfare training. The idea was to maintain control of your company in thick bush when, very often, you probably couldn't see a man five yards away and he used whistle and bugle signals. He had a company bugler and he blew various calls which the troops got to know: 'Advance', 'Retire', 'Move to the right', 'Move to the left', 'Fire', 'Cease firing'. That was his method of training and I didn't find it difficult to adapt the tactical training that I had learned in England. We had a 22-set at company HQ, which communicated with battalion HQ; each platoon had an 18-set, which worked after a fashion and was carried by the platoon signallers and we had field telephones. If the radios broke down, then we used to send runners. We also had a heliograph, which we did use sometimes; it had a range of several miles.

'We used to go on route marches and they were used to travelling very long distances: they could certainly do 15 or 20 miles in a day without any trouble at all, carrying their rifle, ammunition and pack. When I arrived, they had just been kitted out with boots for the first time; before then, the KAR had worn rubber tyre sandals, which suited them very much better. The Army had decided that they should have boots because there was some fear that the Italians might use mustard gas. They were unused to their boots, didn't like them very much and were rather heavy-footed. Once they had got properly fitted with the right sized boots, then they got used to them, adapted to them and their marching was just as good as it had been with their previous footwear. We rather expected the Italians to advance down across this vast, open desert to Nanyuki, which they probably could have done but which they never attempted. We were very thin on the ground indeed: there was only one battalion spread out between the frontier and Nanyuki.'

5 KAR took part in the Abyssinian Campaign and David Shirreff was mentioned in despatches on 30 June 1942. Of the concluding phase of an assault on a dug-in Italian battalion position near Mount Fike, 75 miles south of Addis Ababa, he explained: 'We made our way through the bush to the right and emerged on their left flank at the edge of the cleared space in front of their gun positions. We arrived at the edge of this bush pretty well undetected. I think they were concentrating on D Company and we simply formed up, two platoons in front in extended order, two platoons in the rear and the company commander in the middle. His bugler blew the charge and off we went, firing from the hip – we had practised that drill – both with rifles and Bren guns. We charged and I can remember as we went forward seeing the Italians still firing down on D Company to our left and trying to tug their weapons round to meet us. Anyway, we got into them and it was over quite quickly. The Askaris really had got their blood up and they went to work with the bayonet and it was quite a job stopping them. That was the first occasion when I found a cluster of Europeans round me. The Italians made for the European officer to try and save themselves.' After the Abyssinian Campaign had been successfully concluded, 'we had a pet cheetah which we had found chained and manacled in the market so we bought it off this chap and it lived with us in the Mess, it came with us down to Kenya [in December 1941] and stayed with us at Yatta. Eventually, when we went overseas to Madagascar, we arranged for it to be sent home to London Zoo, where it stayed until it died.'

Rumours of overseas service started to circulate: 'At Yatta, we were told that we were going abroad; we didn't know where, but this was where there was some trouble. The first thing that happened was that the whole battalion, apart from the Somalis and the Samburu, sat down on the parade ground and refused to go on parade. They sent a message to the CO to come and see them and he sent a message back that he certainly wasn't going to see them and that they should return to duty. Things were quite tricky for some hours but eventually they were persuaded to go back to duty by the senior NCOs. They went back to duty and two ringleaders – I think both were Luo – were arrested and eventually court-martialled and that was the end of it. ... There were a number of desertions among the Samburu, which was unfortunate; they weren't at all afraid of going overseas but they wanted to be sure that proper arrangements were made for them to get married before they went and quite a number of them pushed off from Yatta and walked home, but they all eventually came back to the battalion. ... We had good reinforcements and when we eventually left Yatta, the battalion was in very good heart again and from there we went to Madagascar. ... The Madagascar operation was undertaken to prevent the Japanese moving in there: Japanese submarines were already operating in the Mozambique Channel.' His first action was unusual: '14 Platoon was to land on Mayotte [one of the Comoro Islands] and capture the French district commissioner and whatever armed troops he had. ... I went myself with a small patrol to the district commissioner's house, following the road by the aerial photographs. We got to the DC's house, gained entry somehow, went upstairs and found the district commissioner in bed with his 10-year-old son, poor chap. The son woke up and started screaming: black-faced soldiers carrying Tommy guns at four o'clock in the morning were rather alarming. ... He was very Vichy and very hostile.'

On 25 October 1942, Lieutenant David Shirreff was recommended for – and subsequently awarded – a Military Cross 'for continuous gallantry in action': 'On 19 October 1942 at Ambositra [in Madagascar], Lt Shirreff was ordered to lead a patrol to reconnoitre the road. Finding no signs of the enemy, he pushed forward to within 200 yards of the enemy's main position. In spite of heavy LMG fire, he directed his own fire with great coolness, causing several casualties to the enemy and forcing them to disclose their positions. It was entirely due to Lt Shirreff's initiative that this important information was obtained. On 20 October 1942, he led his platoon with courage and resource in the main attack at North Ambositra, showing no regard for his own safety. On 28 October 1942, at Ambatolatelo, while in charge of the forward platoon of the company, Lt Shirreff attacked and captured the enemy outpost position before the remainder of the company arrived to support him. Throughout the whole campaign, he has shown a consistently high standard of leadership and courage, and his example has been an inspiration to all ranks.' He said: 'I was standing with Captain 'Chippy' Lewin [OC D Company] and David Evans, the mortar officer, while we were watching our patrols moving forward and Evans was killed by a sniper, who got him through the head. That was really the last casualty we had. ... I think it was very good preparation for going into action in Burma, both for the troops and for the officers, who had started out pretty inexperienced, except for the regulars.'

In the mid-1990s, David Shirreff rediscovered what he entitled *Burma Story*, writing in the postscript: 'This journal, which lay for many years undiscovered in our loft, has been typed exactly as written in 1944 without alteration.' It forms the basis for what follows: 'After the Madagascar campaign the author was promoted captain and took command of B Company, then part of the Tulear garrison, in May 1943. In January 1944, the Battalion returned to Kenya and, after all ranks had had leave, embarked for Ceylon in July 1944, having been asked for by Major General Fowkes as Divisional Reconnaissance Battalion for 11 (EA) Division [11 Division]. After a long journey by sea, river steamer and road, the Battalion reached Palel in Assam in September 1944. The Japanese had been defeated in the crucial battles of Kohima and Imphal and were retreating down the Kabaw Valley. The monsoon was still at its height.

'On September 10, the Battalion marched out of Palel to join 11 Division in the Kabaw Valley. Instead of marching out with B Company, I led the heterogeneous collection of odds and sods in HQ Company. Although I had commanded B Company for eighteen months, because I was only a captain while the HQ Company commander was a major, we were exchanged a few days before we left Palel. The establishment demanded it. I didn't think I had been fairly treated by the CO [49974 Lieutenant Colonel Philip Alfred Morcombe OBE] and have never been quite so depressed in my life. However, such is the Army. We marched fifteen miles the first day, the last seven all uphill. We were soft and it was the first time we had ever carried big packs. A number of my odds and sods fell out. Next day we marched ten, which was easy, but the third day was fifteen again and the worst of all, uphill practically all the way. We had arrived at our first stage, Bulldozer Ridge.

'Here we stayed for about a week, while I tried to sort out my command. On September 25 we marched from Bulldozer Ridge to a few miles short of Tamu. The road, although very rough, was still fairly firm, and marching was not unpleasant. It was very hot and we marched stripped. The next day, we started at 4 am to avoid the heat, but it was not worth it. To start with, we lost ourselves in the dark in the maze of tracks around Tamu and marched further than we needed. Also the road had petered out, it was raining, and we were marching all the time in mud over our ankles. It was a most exhausting march. We camped near a *chaung* and collected some fish with hand grenades, which were a welcome change.

'Next day was worse still, still raining and we were supposed to reach our destination at Tinztin. When we reached Sunle about midday, the *chaung* was in spate and impossible to cross. Several jeeps and trucks were swept away and the bridge was down. We had to camp on the north bank of the Sunle *chaung* on sodden ground. Here our troubles really started. It rained incessantly so that we were never dry. Eventually most of us got fed up with wet boots and slithered about in the mud in bare feet. Our rations ran out and we were extremely hungry for a day until the Adjutant spotted a herd of buffalo. Nine were shot and the first stew was the most delicious meal I have ever tasted (5 KAR got into serious trouble with political officers for shooting tame Burmese buffalo. At company level we never heard anything more about it). We were completely without rations for three days and existed entirely on buffalo meat and soup. This gave most people diarrhoea but it was better than going hungry. On the evening of the third day, we had an airdrop and from then on we were never short of food.'

The following month, 5 KAR were in action against a strong Japanese position at Letsegan: 'The attack was put in on October 22. B Company had to attack frontally while A and D went round behind. I had the inglorious job of sitting at rear Battalion HQ with the odds and sods. B Company moved straight up the hill and gained contact at 0830. They were moving up a narrow spur and were too close together. They were also too early as the mortar barrage had not yet gone down. The first platoon attacked with great thrust and reached some bomb craters thirty yards from the first trenches when they were called back to allow the mortar barrage to be put down. Unfortunately, the mortars fired short and dropped on the middle of B Company and caused fifteen casualties, including the platoon commander and, by ill luck, all the senior NCOs of the reserve platoon. This platoon was without a leader except for a L/Cpl, who carried on very well until he was shot. Thus, one platoon was virtually out of action from the beginning. The Japs kept quiet while the mortars were firing but as soon as they stopped their LMGs and dischargers opened up again. The airstrikes had helped the enemy as they had cleared the trees away in front of a position and they had a clear field of fire for 100 yards. The company commander was wounded in the stomach [91047 Major Richard Peyton Townley died in hospital on 9 March 1945 and is buried in Maynamati War Cemetery in Bangladesh] but the two remaining platoon commanders rallied their men and tried to attack again. They again reached within thirty yards but suffered very heavy casualties and, when the position was made known to the CO, he ordered them to withdraw. Casualties suffered were two officers wounded, five Askaris killed and twenty-nine wounded.

'In spite of the pasting they had had from their own mortars, the troops had behaved extraordinarily well, pressing forward with great determination. The Somalis and Samburu particularly distinguished themselves. Unfortunately, they suffered the heaviest casualties and most of the senior Somali NCOs were wounded. One young Samburu [Pte Landini] had charged the position by himself and was later found dead on top of a Jap bunker. Meanwhile, A and D Companies had been having a rough time on the other side. The position had not been sufficiently recce'd and it was found that there were two separate positions, both equally strong, so that the two attacking forces were fighting separate battles and could not help each other. A Company engaged at 0930, D Company on their left a little later. They both deployed all their platoons without finding a flank to turn, and A Company in particular suffered heavy casualties, two officers wounded, nine Africans killed and thirty-five wounded.

'At last, after nearly four hours of battle with the Japs resisting fanatically from bunkers and treetops, a platoon of D Company [commanded by

WO Kipchoge] turned the left flank and charged from behind. The surviving Japs fixed bayonets, left their trenches and charged down the hill at A Company. They were all shot down. Twenty-four Jap dead were found on this position. After consolidating the first position, the CO sent the 44 KAR company who were in reserve to recce the second position which B Company had attacked. They found that the Japs had escaped from this down the cliff. So ended the battle of Letsegan at 3 pm after five hours' fighting. The cost to the Japs was the loss of a vital position protecting Mawlaik, and thirty-five dead. The cost to us was fourteen killed and ninety-nine wounded in the Battalion, which was about three times the casualties we had in the whole of the Abyssinian campaign.

'The Battalion earned a special word of praise from Fluffy [the divisional commander] who told us that no-one else could have done the job. This was probably quite true, but it was also obvious that we could not afford to have any more equally expensive battles, and that the Japs were quite a different proposition from the Itos and French. The Battalion was greatly weakened and of the casualties a great proportion had been NCOs. From then on, in B Company at any rate, Cpls and L/Cpls were doing Sgts' jobs or even commanding platoons and unpaid

David Shirreff's Samburu orderly, Private Seremon Lendioo, with the Shirreff children. After the war, he would regularly arrive unannounced from his tribal lands in the Northern Frontier District of Kenya to wherever David Shirreff was posted and stay for a few weeks, before returning to his wives and cattle.

L/Cpls were commanding sections. I took over B Company after the battle, which pleased me greatly, but it was a sadly-depleted company, seventy combatants strong.'

David Shirreff's elder son, General Sir Richard Shirreff, wrote: 'I shall never forget attending, as a small boy, 5 KAR's Letsegan Day parade at Nanyuki in Kenya, which commemorated their proudest Burma Campaign battle honour: fine-looking, proud, immaculately-drilled Askaris in khaki, distinctive in their fezes with their officers wearing slouch hats and brightly-coloured hackles.'

After Letsegan, David Shirreff returned to B Company as company commander and 5 KAR continued to lead the 11 Division advance down the Kabaw Valley as divisional recce battalion fighting several battles to dislodge fiercely-held Japanese positions. His account continued: 'A few days later, I took out another patrol to Hamandawa. I was wrong in taking out patrols myself, being a company commander, but at the same time I wanted to satisfy myself that I could do it as I was not very confident of my map-reading in this country, but I found after two patrols that I was adequate. I also found out that you must choose between going off the track, which is slow and exhausting but one hundred per cent safe, or else going along the track, which is fast but asking for trouble if there are Japs about. The Japs, incidentally, always move along tracks, usually chattering with their rifles over their shoulders, but they don't mind being bumped off. I always moved off the tracks, largely owing to the insistence of my orderly [Private Seremon Lendioo]. Very often, when I was tired of going up and down hill bending double most of the time, I would suggest going onto the track, but my orderly always refused to let me. In fact, he really commanded all my patrols. On this patrol we reached Hamandawa on the evening of the first day, having lost our way completely at one time. We slept the night near the *chaung*, crossed over the next morning and found the large Jap position which one hundred Japs had recently evacuated. We pushed on towards Namkaput and met a few Japs just short of the resthouse. They disappeared into the bush before we could fire at them. I got back to Letsegan at midnight on the second night. It was a most exhausting patrol. We had taken no tea or sugar and not very much food. I never made that mistake again. Tea makes a tremendous difference to one's endurance.'

A week or so later, 'Duggie returned from Brigade with rather amplified orders. Our task was to cross over the Chindwin and take over from the Assam Regiment, who were already across. We were then to advance down the east bank keeping pace with 21 Brigade, who were moving down the west bank. This seemed rather a risky job for two weak companies but we were lucky. On the morning of the 14th [November], B Company started crossing. Bob Stille went into hospital with poisoned legs, and Hutch [Lieutenant Hutchinson] went in with fever, which turned out to be typhus. He died three weeks later. We started crossing on rafts made of grass and tarpaulins, which were unwieldy and rather dangerous. The first attempt to carry mules resulted in the mule losing its head, kicking out wildly, and knocking the crew into the water. One Askari was run down by the rescue launch and drowned. The mule swam back to the shore. After that we gave up the idea of taking mules across. At midday an airdrop produced collapsible assault boats, which were a great improvement. All B Company was across by the evening, which was not a bad achievement as the river was over 1,000 yards wide, the current strong, and the Askaris' idea of navigation very rudimentary. Some of the rafts were swept miles downstream before they made land, but they all fetched up safe. Here Romulus Kleen ex-Divisional Scouts [a Swedish volunteer and former Tanganyika white hunter] arrived, and took over 7 Platoon. I put Sergeant Brown in charge of 6 Platoon so still had a European for each platoon.'

A little more than three weeks after crossing the Chindwin, 'on the 7th [December], Anton [Major Anthony Charles Kingston Barkas, OC A Company] took out two platoons to recce the Jap position. He was ambushed and suffered some casualties, including one officer killed [329407 Lieutenant Leslie Robertson, who is buried in Taukkyan War Cemetery]. As a result of this, I was ordered to attack the position and, if possible, capture it, otherwise do as much damage as possible and then withdraw. On the morning of December 8th, I took with me Sergeant Mwangangi from A Company and walked all round the Jap position. Mwangangi took me right up to the position and showed me a Jap sentry leaning on his rifle, smoking a cigar. We could hear them chattering. From the extent of the position, I calculated that there were two platoons of Japs there on a small ridge covering the track and *chaung*. I went back to the CO and told him that I considered it too much for one weak company to tackle. I was told that the Brigadier [Brigadier J.F. Macnab,

Allied cemetery in Burma.

commanding 21 (EA) Brigade] was only prepared for one company to get a 'bloody nose', so I had to get on with it. An airstrike was arranged at 1600 and I was to attack at 1630. I had a Sikh lieutenant from the Indian mountain battery with me.

'We dumped our packs on the ridge two miles from the Japs and waited for the airstrike, sitting around eating and smoking. At 4 pm twelve Hurricanes came over and dropped their bombs. Although the mortar smoke indicating the target was put down in the right place, the Hurricanes dropped their bombs wide and made no strafing runs. I didn't consider that the position had been sufficiently softened up, so asked the gunner for ten minutes' intense fire from 1630–1640. I got the company moving and closed to within half-a-mile of the Japs. The guns put down a very effective barrage and must have shaken the Japs considerably. I had decided to attack the Japs from the rear (south) and as soon as the guns stopped we moved up with 5 Platoon as fire platoon and 6 and 7 following. 5 Platoon were only fourteen strong but all good men. 6 Platoon were numerically stronger but contained several useless men and had the least experienced platoon commander so I kept them in reserve.

'5 Platoon came out of the bush and effectively surprised the first Jap position. Two Japs were killed and the remainder disappeared, leaving about forty packs and a large dump of ammunition. The Japs started fighting back from the second hill near the *chaung*, so I left 5 Platoon as fire platoon and took 7 Platoon round to the right to try and push them off. I left Willie [Captain R.H. Warton, 2IC B Company] in charge with 6 Platoon in reserve. It was now about 6 pm and growing dark. Romulus urged 7 Platoon on energetically and they pressed forwards well enough against fairly heavy small arms and grenade fire. But the strain was beginning to tell on everybody and they were not so keen to go forward as they had been. I was moving on the left of 7 Platoon with my orderly and was crossing a small ravine when a Jap on the other side threw two grenades at me. I was hit in the right arm and back and my orderly was badly wounded. I was now out of touch with Romulus, it was getting dark and John Armitage shouted to me that his men were running out of ammunition. I crawled back to John's hill and tried to appreciate the situation, without much success.

'The Japs were clinging tenaciously to their final position, it was getting dark and we were short of ammunition. Romulus sent back word to say that he was held up and had lost one man killed and two wounded. As my orders were not to capture at all costs but to inflict damage and then withdraw, I decided to recall Romulus. Willie was calmly chatting to the CO over the wireless, and I took over from him and explained the situation. I asked for more ammunition and another company to complete the job. But he told me to pull out. If I had not been wounded myself, I might have put in another attack, but I did not want to leave others to do what I certainly did not relish myself, so I was quite grateful when the CO ordered a withdrawal. We had certainly inflicted casualties on the Japs and they withdrew from the position the same time as we did, but it was a pity that we couldn't finish off the job. If we had had another hour of daylight, we would probably have taken the whole position and killed a lot of Japs, but it was a waste of time indulging in 'ifs' after a battle.

'It was now pitch dark and the Japs started lobbing over a few mortar bombs. Our own mortar ammo was finished, as was most of our SAA, so we made no answer. One man, L/Cpl Ncube, had died of his wounds, so we left him there. Seremon was very weak, but we had no stretcher, so he had to walk. I was beginning to feel rather weedy and my right arm was useless but I could walk well enough. We set off carrying our loot.

In the darkness, platoons were separated but we all eventually arrived at our dump, where the Sikh lieutenant and Battalion MO were waiting for us. I was rather depressed at our failure but was considerably cheered by Romulus, who was not given to enthusiasm and yet considered that we had done a good show. I never heard what the official verdict was on our action. The fun and games were not over for the night. I lay on a stretcher deep in the narcotic semi-consciousness of morphia so did not pay much attention to them. 'Jitter parties' were reported round the Brigade perimeter. Their 3" mortars opened up on fixed lines and nearly blotted a section of Battalion HQ Platoon and an artillery OP, which Willie had sent down near the *chaung* for the night. The artillery *jemadar* and African corporal came back spitting with rage. Willie phoned up Brigade HQ and was told he could safely send back the outpost as the mortars would not fire again. Twenty minutes later, the mortars opened fire again and again the OP was nearly blotted. The *jemadar* took a very dim view of Brigade HQ.

'Next morning, Doc Thompson took me and the other wounded down to the Brigade Field Ambulance. As there was no landing ground in operation at that time, we could not be evacuated until the bridgehead was joined up, so we lay for a week on stretchers under parachute tents. I was quite comfortable but very bored as there was nothing to read. The Battalion went on down to the main Yeu road and remained in the forefront until the bridgehead was finally linked up and 2 Division passed through. B Company was forward company most of the time and did more than its share of the work. John Armitage was badly wounded on a patrol but Willie and Romulus got through safely. The company finished up not much more than sixty-five strong, having had during the campaign over fifty casualties: five officers wounded, eight men killed and forty-one men wounded. Yet when 2 Division passed through, the Askaris did not want to go back and rest. They wanted to go forward and finish the job and then be allowed to go back to Africa.'

In his postscript, David Shirreff wrote: 'In November 1993, I went to Japan with a party of British Burma Campaign veterans at the invitation of the Japanese Burma Campaign veterans and we had a meeting with veterans of the 33 Division (the 'White Tigers'), who had opposed us in the Kabaw Valley. I met a sergeant of 215 Regiment who had been in the position against us on the Ingon Chaung on December 8 1944. He told me that there had been 30 men defending this position, which I found rather galling!'

David Shirreff married firstly, on 23 June 1945, Helen Mary Wingate, a friend of his sister, Anne, at Sherborne School for Girls, daughter of Ernest Winkworth Napper, a tea planter in Ceylon, who retired to Parkfield, Belstone, Devon. They had two daughters. He married secondly, Dione Hilary, only daughter of Dr Bernard Wood-White of The Old Rectory, Falkenham, Suffolk, and his wife Hilary Dorothea Vere (formerly Sparrow, née Denning). Having joined the Colonial Service after the war, he served as a district officer and district commissioner in Kenya. Following Kenyan Independence on 1 June 1963, he returned to England, qualified as a solicitor, settled near Bury St Edmunds and became a partner in Bankes Ashton (solicitors). In retirement, David and Dione lived in a house called Leveretts, at Walberswick in Suffolk. As well as *Bare Feet and Bandoliers*, an account of Orde Wingate's Gideon Force operations during the Abyssinian campaign, he also wrote *The Walberswick Frigate* and co-wrote *Suffolk Memories: Stories of Walberswick and Blythburgh people during World War II*. He became a life member of the Lowestoft branch of the Burma Star Association on 5 December 1991 (membership number S/4382/91). Described in his obituary in *The Daily Telegraph* as 'a modest, courageous and talented man' and 'a keen ornithologist, an enthusiastic fox hunter and devoted countryman', David Shirreff died on 12 July 1999; Dione Shirreff died on 8 October 2016; they had two sons and a daughter.

273680 Captain Gordon Short, Queen's Own Royal West Kent Regiment

Gordon Pickard Short was born on 17 March 1921 at Burrington, North Devon, only son of William Ernest Short, Honorary Alderman of Devon County Council, of Hillcrest, Burrington, and his wife Elsie, elder daughter of Jonathan Pickard, seed and manure merchant and sub-postmaster, of The Post Office, Burrington. Gordon explained: 'James Pickard and his son, Jonathan, used to thresh out the seed, take it back to his farm, clean it up and make up a mixture, before selling it back to the local farmers. J. Pickard & Co (Burrington) Ltd was founded in 1846 and over the years the business grew from a Post Office sideline to a fine example of a rural trading establishment. In 1907 the Earl of Portsmouth sold the Eggesford House estate and a lot of people were therefore able to buy their own farms: Jonathan Pickard bought Forches Farm, which is now known as Homelands, and built a new house, which they called Hillcrest. During the First World War my father was a Transport Officer. He was used to reading the country signs and that skill, allied with some fortunate premonitions, enabled him to save lives on at least two occasions. During the Second World War, he was the Area Officer for the Special Constabulary in North Devon while my mother was an Evacuee Warden. My parents married in 1911 and, when I was born ten years later, someone shouted across the floor of the Barnstaple Corn Exchange: "Congratulations, Bill, did you ever find out who't was?"

'When I was four, I was out for a Sunday walk with my grandfather, Jonathan Pickard, when my legs suddenly collapsed under me and I was stuck in the sitting position. Dr Bush from Chulmleigh was sent for and specialists in Exeter and London consulted. The diagnosis was a form of creeping paralysis – a case of poliomyelitis or polio – and the accepted view was that, when it eventually touched my head, that would be the end of it. My father did not accept this; instead he employed Nurse Garrett, who lived with us at home and tried out a new-fangled massage technique. After six months I was visited by the doctor, who took a pin and stuck it into my foot. When I jumped, he said: "Nurse, you're winning. Keep it up!" By the time I was 8, I could walk again. I attended Wallingbrook School in Chulmleigh, under the headmastership of John Powlesland,

and left at the age of 14 to go to Seale-Hayne Agricultural College. I did a 12-month agricultural course because I needed to know a little bit about the technical side of it so that I could talk to the farmers.

'Including a couple of reservists from the Great War, nine of us from Burrington – Fred Harris, Bill Hanford, Arthur Davey, Arthur Jeffries and his son-in-law Sam Parker, Jim Parkhouse, Herbert Kingdom, and my cousin Roy, and I – all enlisted in the Territorial Army on the same evening in the spring of 1939. We became members of the High Bickington Platoon in the 6th Battalion, The Devonshire Regiment [6 Devon]. The battalion was based in Barnstaple and we attended summer camp near Bulford on Salisbury Plain a few months later. On 1 September 1939, two days before war was declared, there was a radio announcement: "All Territorials report to their unit headquarters tonight." At Torrington there were three medical officers sitting behind a table and we all lined up with our pay books. I had been categorized "B5 – Office work only" but, after a check-up, they upgraded me and my pay book was stamped "A1", which I remained for the rest of the war.

'There was a lot of moving around in the early days. Initially we were stationed at Crownhill Barracks in Plymouth, before moving to Falmouth, for guard duties at the docks. I was a clerk in the quartermaster's department and they made me an acting unpaid lance corporal in case someone came in being a bit awkward. Once, when I was alone in the office doing some typing, an officer came in. He tapped his cane on my desk, saying: "You should stand up when an officer comes into the room." I replied: "I'm sorry, Sir, but if I did that every time someone came to speak to the quartermaster, I would never get my work done." He then looked at me more closely and said: "Don't I recognize you?" "I expect so, Sir," I replied, "you were one of the salesmen in Brinley's Garage when my father bought a new car a few months ago: a Wolseley 14A DV63." "Ah! Short of Burrington," he said. From then on, I could always go to him for a special pass, if necessary. The lads were particularly pleased that I always managed to bring a turkey back with me when I went home.

'Later we moved to Rayleigh in Essex, where Roy met his wife, Millie, before moving to Skegness. I managed to take my little Morris 10 with me and the transport sergeant, who had been one of the mechanics at Brinley's, helped me to hide it away and always made sure that I had enough petrol to get back to camp. The orderly room sergeant had been the clerk at Slee Blackwell, the family solicitors, and he was able to arrange late night passes so the three of us often used to stay out at dances till midnight. We were constantly on the move: from Skegness, we went to Maidenhead, then to Northern Ireland, up to Yorkshire and then back to Shoreham and Weymouth. During the Battle of Britain we were headquartered at Horsham in Sussex, guarding the coastline, while air battles took place overhead.

'One day I had a call from my father: "You had better apply for a commission." He explained that Roy, who was four years older, had already applied for one. I said: "Why do I need a commission when I've got a nice little job in the quartermaster's office?" My father replied: "The war isn't over yet and, if you're both lucky enough to come back safely, then Roy will be a major while you will still be a lance corporal – and you won't be able to tell him what to do." I had already caused a bit of

Second Lieutenant G.P. Short, Devonshire Regiment.

an upset when I said to the CO that I only had to look round the battalion to realise that I could do at least as well as the rest of them. Nevertheless, I was recommended for a commission and, after pre-OCTU at Wrotham in Kent, was sent to 164 OCTU at Barmouth in North Wales.

'I was only there for a few months because they were pushing us through and chucking the pips at people fairly fast in those days. I received a Regular Army Emergency Commission in the Devonshire Regiment on 1 May 1943 and was posted to the 9th Battalion [9 Devon], which had been formed from the 6th Battalion. I was proud to wear my father's old Sam Browne, which he in turn had purchased from an officer who had fought in the Boer War. I still have it at home. One of the first tasks that I was given was organizing a battalion sports day in Dorchester. Although I had no idea at all how to do this, all went well on the day and I suddenly became rather popular. We lived in a tented camp in a wood just outside Dorchester, close enough to walk into town. 9 Devon provided reinforcements for other battalions:

it was milked down, more or less [9 Devon was finally disbanded in August 1942].

'I was selected to go to the Far East as a battle replacement and sailed from Liverpool on 23 October 1943. One evening, I was on deck with a fellow officer, with whom I was sharing a cabin. As we looked back and watched the sun setting in the Strait of Gibraltar, I said: "What a marvellous sight. I hope that when we come home and look at this again, we shall see the sun rise through the same gap." He replied: "You might but I shan't." "Why?" I asked. He answered: "Oh, I'm quite convinced there is a bullet out there for me somewhere and I doubt if I shall come home." On his first tour of duty in the jungle, he put his binoculars to his eyes and was shot by a sniper. He died instantly.

'Our ship had engine problems so we spent more than a month in 147 Transit Camp, on the outskirts of Cairo, waiting for a ship to take us to India. I had my first experience of outdoor latrines: a small canvas awning round a pole, a pit in the sand and your own newspaper to read and use! One evening, a large party of us – mostly lieutenants and captains, but including an Indian major – went to a hotel for a drink. The hotel porter said: "I'm sorry, gentlemen, only white officers are allowed in this hotel." This was our first experience of racial discrimination, even though our Indian colleague was the senior officer present. We simply found ourselves another hotel. Although I didn't see any fighting in the Middle East, I discovered when I was filling in the medal application form after the war that my time spent in Egypt qualified me for the Africa Star.

'Eventually a ship was found, with a British captain, an all-Indian crew, 150 officers and 800 men. The major in charge of troops was a bachelor, with very little experience of mixing with the ladies. This became a problem when, having already embarked the officers and men, he was asked to find room for fifty QA nurses. I was in charge of the baggage while the orderly officer was in charge of administration. He said to the major: "Well, we think the best thing you can do, Sir, is leave it to us. We will organize the troops and Short will take care of the baggage and act as entertainment officer." The nurses were accommodated two to a cabin, in the middle of the ship, surrounded by the officers' cabins. They proved to be extremely popular.

'On New Year's Eve we arranged a ball, and one of the nurses – a very frisky Irish girl – said that she would ask the questions to eliminate an Honesty Dance. The first one was: "Would anyone who is wearing less than three items of clothing – excluding shoes – please leave the dance floor?" The second one was: "If anyone has to knock on their own cabin door before entering, would they please leave the dance floor?" Of course, everybody walked off, leaving the Captain dancing with the Matron, to howls of laughter and a burst of applause. There was another amusing incident. After passing through the Suez Canal, our ship sailed alone, with just a frigate as escort. On Christmas Day, the frigate sent a signal: "Would you please check that someone is actually steering your ship, because you've gone round in circles three times and we can't keep up?" A visit to the bridge revealed that the quartermaster, who oversaw steering the ship, had drunk rather too much rum and had gone to sleep on the floor, and the ship had been left to its own devices.'

Lieutenant G.P. Short in tropical kit.

Instead of joining his own regiment, Gordon was seconded to the 4th Battalion, Queen's Own Royal West Kents (4 RWK), joining D Company, commanded by Major Donald Easten. 4 RWK was the only battalion from 161st (Indian) Infantry Brigade to reach the garrison at Kohima before the sixteen-day siege began. Initially, D Company was in reserve. Gordon explained: 'When I eventually arrived in India, they gave me no jungle training at all – I just went out absolutely green. After travelling by train from Bombay to Calcutta, I went to Comilla and joined the battalion just before the battle of Kohima began. On the evening of 8 April 1944, Donald said to me: "You stay here; I won't give you any troops tonight because we've got to go to the tennis court to have a skirmish. Your turn will come tomorrow." That was the beginning of the "Battle of the DC's Tennis Court". Lance Corporal John Harman, whose family owned Lundy Island, was killed that night. He had already used his Bren gun to good effect, wiping out a Jap machine gun position which had been causing a lot of damage to our front-line troops, and was returning to our lines when he was shot in the back. He was awarded a posthumous VC for his actions. We just had to carry on defending and lost an officer and fifty men during the siege.

'When we began to advance our division, the 5th Indian Division and the 17th Indian Division leapfrogged one another on the way south to Rangoon. We moved down through the hills past Imphal, on the road to Tiddim, sometimes using lorries and jeeps but more often fighting through the jungle, with mules carrying our equipment and supplies. I was appointed Animal Transport Officer and it was a real problem that they used to step on our feet. Mine became pretty bad. We sent out patrols to push the Japs back. My batman had been a professional poacher in Sussex before the war and he was extremely good at reading the signs in the jungle: footprints, broken branches, crushed leaves, etc. On a two-day patrol our mission was to carry out a reconnaissance of a Japanese camp, before two battalions launched a frontal attack. From experience we learned that if you got behind the Japanese they always disappeared. By the time we found the Jap camp, although the billycans were still on the camp fires, they'd got themselves and their kit away safely. My batman then made his way alone back to our own lines in order to prevent the attack from going ahead.

'Having been ordered to attend an anti-tank course in Dehra Dun, I flew from Burma to Calcutta, where I stayed in a hotel reserved for officers. I was sitting in the lounge, enjoying a John Collins, when I heard a familiar laugh. Seated at the next table was my cousin, Roy, who had just flown in from Africa as a member of the advance party of 82nd (West African) Division, which was being deployed to the Arakan. Extraordinarily, we were both staying in that hotel for a single night. On the return journey, a few weeks later, I bumped into Colonel Stocker, who lived at Chulmleigh.

'During the spring of 1945, we were rapidly travelling south, via Mandalay and Meiktila, towards Rangoon. By this time, we had wheeled transport and were using Bedford trucks: they were stripped down and the doors had been removed and replaced by bars and a cloth. The roads were challenging, often with vertical walls on one side and a sheer drop on the other. We were driving in convoy and, concerned that my driver was falling asleep, I gave him a gentle slap. This frightened him so much that he turned the steering wheel too sharply and our truck was left dangling precariously over the sheer drop. There were thirty men in the back, together with all their kit. By the time we had carefully unloaded everything, the front of the convoy had disappeared, while we were blocking the road. So we pushed our vehicle over the side. Eventually, an empty truck came along, with an English driver. We talked and it turned out that he lived in South Molton and before his call-up had worked as a builder's mate for a firm called Sanders, building a new house just opposite our family home in Burrington.

'During the advance south I was ordered to take a patrol to establish the extent of a Japanese position. By this time, we were in the central plain, rather than the jungle, and it was fairly open country. As we came to some rougher country, we came under fire from two machine guns. Although no-one was hit, we could identify the Jap positions by the flash of the guns. Our orders were to retreat at this stage, so we put down a smokescreen, before we returned back through the open fields. I looked down and saw something shiny. My foot was just a couple of feet away from the top of a mine. I ordered my men to not lie down but to keep walking and we all returned safely. We used to dig in every night, deep enough to provide protection from Japanese fire. One of my jobs was to inspect the slit trenches or shell scrapes. In one of our exposed positions, a sniper fired five shots at me: I felt the wind of three of them and saw the strike of the other two. The Japanese were very well trained as snipers. They often climbed trees and would tie anything loose – including themselves, their rifles and their equipment – to the tree. If you hadn't hit him, then he might fire a shot at you from behind.

'We were one of the battalions tasked with attacking Rangoon and I was designated to be one of the first in the battalion to cross the Pegu to establish a bridgehead. It turned out that the city had been evacuated. We found out because some of the prisoners had climbed onto the roof of Rangoon Jail and had written in huge white letters: 'EXTRACT DIGIT – JAPS GONE'. We therefore returned to the jungle to mop up stragglers. Later Captain Watts and I were stationed at Rangoon Jail, looking after Japanese prisoners, for two or three months. It was 24 hours on and 24 hours off. There was one female Japanese prisoner and she remained in our quarters, to keep her away from the other troops. The prisoners slept in the open and we found it necessary to set up Bren guns in the centre of the open-air compound. When conducting our inspections, we were always most careful to stand back-to-back, with revolvers drawn, in case the prisoners attempted to jump us. For the Japanese, it was considered an honour to kill an enemy before being killed yourself.

'After the two atomic bombs had been dropped, I was appointed transport officer and sent back to India, with my new batman, an Anglo-Indian, to identify kit that the battalion had left behind at various depôts earlier in the war. Military equipment was returned to the depôts while personal possessions were sorted in groups: that which belonged to those who had died and that of those who had survived. That in the former category was carefully parcelled up and returned to the next-of-kin. Fortunately I was issued with rail warrants enabling me to travel wherever I wanted in India. When the task was complete, I therefore enjoyed a very welcome break in Srinagar. After returning to Rangoon, the order soon came through for me to return to England, via Calcutta and Bombay, overland through France to Dover and then to Portsmouth Arms station at Burrington, where my father met me.'

A photograph sent to HRH The Duke of Edinburgh, Patron of the Burma Star Association, on his 90th birthday by four members of the North Devon branch who were born the same year: (left to right) Bill Morgan (February), Gordon Short (March), John Squire (April) and Vin Tamlin (May).

On 26 April 1951 in Barnstaple, Gordon married Joyce Doreen, daughter of William Ford, one of Pickard's customers, and his wife Daisy (née Richards). They had three sons: John, Graham and Nigel. Joyce died on 5 May 2020. Hillcrest had both a tennis court and a bowling green but it was the latter pastime which really caught on. Gordon became president of the Devon County Bowling Association in 1993, won the County Triples Championship in the same decade, was a founder member of the England Bowling Association Charity Trust and has toured the world playing his favourite sport. He is also what is generally described as a 'pillar of the community', chairing Burrington Parish Council for more than thirty years – succeeding his father and handing over to one of his sons – and also serving as chairman of the governors of Edgehill College in Bideford, as a governor of Seale-Hayne College, and as a member of the Inland Revenue Appeals Committee. A Methodist Foundation, Edgehill College, which has since merged with Grenville College, was the sister school of Shebbear College, attended by his three sons and five of his six grandchildren. Gordon became a member of the Burma Star Association on 19 July 1989 (membership number S/4190/89), serving as Chairman of the North Devon branch.

3064464 LAC Alan Sier, Royal Air Force

Charles Alan (Alan) Sier was born at 17 Pheasant Street, Worcester, on 5 January 1927, only child of Charles Alan (Charles) Sier, who was then serving with the Black Watch, and his wife Elsie Caroline, younger daughter of James Evans, a signal fitter, also of Worcester. After her husband had been posted to India, Elsie moved back into her family home, joining her parents, her sister and her seven brothers. Though too young to fight in the First World War, Charles joined the army as a boy soldier and served in India, China, German and Ireland. After leaving the army, he worked initially as a steamroller driver working for Worcestershire County Council, before joining Redman Heenan as a long-distance haulage lorry driver. When war broke out, he was living with his boss, William Tibbetts, at 64 Bromfield Road North, Halesowen, while Elsie was a laundress at a power laundry, living at 12 St George's Lane North, Worcester. He later worked for Heenans & Froud, an engineering company, and as a fitter for the Great Western Railway, before ending his working life by managing two ex-servicemen's clubs in Barbourne, Worcester: The Vaults and The Ewe and Lamb. Alan initially attended St George's Roman Catholic School before moving, at the age of 11, to Samuel Southall Secondary Modern, also in Worcester. Known as 'Sammy's' and guided by the headmaster, Bernard Brotherton, the school motto was 'Upright and Thorough'.

Alan explained: 'After leaving school at the age of 14, my first job during the war was also at Redman Heenan, as an apprentice under Mr Wright. I was doing jobs for anti-aircraft guns, submarine cooling systems and also gas fittings. At the age of 15½, I joined the Transport Department of Metal Box, working as a fitter in the garage. Before receiving my call-up papers, I belonged to 187 Squadron

3064464 LAC C.A. Sier, Royal Air Force, at Tengah, Singapore.

ATC, which was based at the rear of Kay's [a mail order company] in Barbourne, until it burned down in May 1941, when we moved to Perdiswell. Everyone who joined the ATC had a number which began 306. I learned to fly in a Tiger Moth, with former Battle of Britain pilots 'on rest', from Perdiswell Sports Ground in Bilford Road. One day in 1942, my mate, Bill Brooker, who lived in Shrubbery Avenue, just up the road, said: "I'm meeting a girl and we're going dancing at Stew's [Dance Academy] in Silver Street. She's got a friend so will you make up a foursome?" And that was how, one Saturday night at six o'clock, I met my future wife, Eileen. She was in the Red Cross and I was doing nights at the Victoria Institute. We met most days: I left my bike at Foxwell Street and rode home afterwards.

'After I was called up on 19 November 1945, I reported to No. 3 Recruit Centre, Padgate for the "duration of present emergency" as a member of the Royal Air Force Volunteer Reserve, with registration number WTB 14075. During my training, which I thoroughly enjoyed, I passed tests to drive cars, lorries, motorcycles and other mechanically-propelled vehicles, before qualifying as a crane operator on British cranes made by Coles Cranes Ltd, and on a 22-ton American crane made by Bay City Crane Inc. I also learned to drive the Bedford OX articulated tractor unit and the three-ton Queen Mary trailer. After being warned off for service overseas, I was given three days' compassionate leave so Eileen and I got married on 7 August 1946 at New St Martin's in London Road. We had a reception at the Co-op in Trinity Street and one day in London for our honeymoon. When I got back from honeymoon, I boarded the *Empress of Australia* and sailed to the Far East. The postal service was good and the happiest memory of my military service was reading a letter from Eileen telling me that I had a baby son and that she was OK.

'We stopped off in Singapore, where we lived under canvas at Tengah, awaiting our posting orders. While we were killing time in Singapore, I was ordered to guard 700 Japanese [JSP] in their camp at Tengah. We were all issued with a .303 with no bullets but they were no trouble. They lived in a large wooden building, with a walkway down the middle. At night our guards used to walk along that walkway. They repaired the runways and some of them did my *dhobi* – in exchange for a couple of cigs. I always thought that the Japanese were small people but some of them were quite large. I was then posted to Burma, initially to No. 42

Maintenance Unit (42 MU), which soon closed down, and then to No. 2 Forward Equipment Unit (2 FEU).

'We arrived by sea in a troopship, SS *Empire Pride*, at the port of Rangoon. Although we didn't know it, the town of Rangoon had no working water system, toilet system or any electricity. Worst of all, the plague – the so-called "Black Death" – was rampant. Before we disembarked, all personnel had to be vaccinated with 3 cc of yellow vaccine to protect them. We all lined up on deck and some of the lads dropped like flies after being vaccinated.

Alan Sier in front of the Shwedagon Pagoda, Rangoon.

Eventually, though, we made it to our new home in Rangoon, which was pretty basic, with wooden billets and a large tank of drinking water. For latrines there was a large pit with a pole to sit on, surrounded by a fence covered with sacking. We only had rain water for a wash and shower, using buckets with holes punched through the bottom. Our working area was an ex-film studio, with an open-air cookhouse. The whole experience was a bit of an eye-opener. Our billets were near the Shwedagon Pagoda and I once climbed the 120 steps up to the platform and struck the large bell.

'The main role of 2 FEU was the disposal of wartime materiel that the RAF had left behind: vehicles, bombs, parts on airfields and downed aircraft, etc. We had six drivers and took it in turns to do jobs on vehicles: jeeps, Leyland Buffalos, Ford 3-tonners, Queen Marys and Chevs. We used a Buffalo to transport unexploded bombs to a place up the Burma Road in the middle of nowhere, where they were detonated. Unknown to us, the Japanese had used the same area and had stored ammunition underground. The lads in charge of detonating the bombs had lined up four 3,000-pounders when – suddenly – the whole place went up. There

The drivers of No. 2 Forward Equipment Unit: LAC Alan Sier (bottom right); Corporal Den Mepham (top centre).

was an enormous explosion and a number of Indian soldiers, two of our lads, the detonation crew and a *charwallah* were killed. It was a great shock to everyone. Another terrible memory was being involved in a vehicle accident on the Burma Road. I was in the rear of a Bedford QL, sitting on the side holding onto the overhead bars. We collided with an oncoming vehicle, my knee was smashed up and I spent six weeks in a field hospital.

'When Burma left the British Empire, the Burmese formed a government. At that time, we were billeted in a nice house in Rangoon, waiting for a ship to take us to Singapore. The head person in the new Burmese government was Aung San and the members were all sat in the Parliament House when a body of men burst in the room with machine guns and killed all the new government members as they sat round the table. The Burmese had finished with the British and we could do nothing – just wait for the troopship home. I understand that the men with guns had come from the north of Burma and they were Reds.' On 7 April

The lying-in-state of assassinated members of Burma's Executive Council, Jubilee Hall, Rangoon, July 1947.

1947, Burma held its first elections, based on universal suffrage, and the Anti-Fascist People's Freedom League recorded a landslide, winning 173 of the 210 seats. Just twelve weeks later, on 19 July 1947, Aung San was chairing a meeting of his Executive Council in the Secretariat Building in Rangoon when three gunmen armed with Sten guns burst in, killing Aung San and killing or mortally wounding six other council members. U Saw, who had been prime minister of Burma before the Second World War and had been detained for four years in Uganda for initiating communications with the Japanese, was subsequently convicted – and executed – for planning the assassinations.

Alan continued: 'We didn't have much contact with the local population, although the Burma police would do guard for us at night. The climate was unpleasant – but predictable. In the morning it was frosty before we started work but, by midday your tropical uniform shirt was ringing wet through. It rained every day at the same time about 3 pm. Try living in a two-man tent in monsoon weather, with a ditch around the tent to catch the rain! My health problems started in Singapore: during the next two years I had tinea, ringworm, slight malaria and prickly heat. Our food was mostly powdered: potato, milk, eggs. We did have a glass of rum every day though, with salt and other tablets. I still miss the comradeship of my good mates. The services certainly opened my eyes to the world and taught me how to treat people. I only saw Lord Mountbatten once. A few days before his arrival, the MTB had struck a submerged object in the harbour, which took one side of it away. When Lord Mountbatten arrived by ship, he boarded the MTB with the good side facing him. I was a member of the RAF guard which received him on the landing stage.

'On being discharged from the RAF on 14 September 1948, I went back to my job at Metal Box, which they had kept open for me. Over the years I became chargehand under Mr Roberts, and when he retired I became foreman, with nine men working for me. We were responsible for the maintenance of 250 'mechanical units': cars, forklift trucks,

Alan Sier after flying in a Tiger Moth on 23 July 2008, Sywell, Northamptonshire.

Alan and Eileen Sier on their seventieth wedding anniversary, August 2016.

power units, artic vehicles, trailers, flatbed units, etc. In all, I worked for Metal Box for 43 years. I received a gold watch and garden tools and was eventually made redundant. I then found a job with the Post Office, driving a 3-ton van and delivering parcels, but I gave that up after twelve months because of getting up and down from the rear of the van by rope. I finished as a volunteer mini-bus driver for the New College, Worcester [which was founded in 1866 for the 'blind sons of gentlemen' and where Edward Elgar was once Professor of Violin]'. Alan's bride was Eileen Muriel May, daughter of Albert Brooker, locomotive engine driver and later station master, of 68 Foxwell Street, Worcester, and his wife Mabel (née Stanley). They had three children: Keith (who was conceived on their one-night honeymoon), Dawn and Chris. Although Eileen died on 16 November 2017, Chris also lives in Worcester and saw his father most days. Alan died on 25 September 2021, following a short illness; however, Chris explained that the family 'would still love to see his RAF experiences in print'.

JX 730343 Telegraphist (S) Ken Tomkinson, Royal Navy

Kenneth Stanley (Ken) Tomkinson was born in Manchester on 18 May 1926, son of George Tomkinson, a decorator who lost his job when war broke out – and subsequently served as a fire fighter and a member of the Local Defence Volunteers – before finding employment with the Prudential Insurance Company when peace returned. Ken was educated at Ardwick Central School, in south-east Manchester, which was temporarily evacuated to Bacup, a textile town in the South Pennines, on 1 September 1939, just two days before war was declared. The new arrivals shared premises with Blackthorn Senior School, which had opened as recently as 20 June 1939, with places for 480 scholars. He returned to Manchester in time for the Blitz: 'Living in Parkside Road, Moss Side, there was bombing most nights. It was far more dangerous being a civilian and I was in more danger then than I was when I was serving. We were blitzed and bombed out at Xmas 1940 but survived. It's a strange thing to say but, as a youth at the time, it was very exciting.' Ken joined the School Training Corps, with the ultimate intention of volunteering for the Royal Air Force, which you could only do when you had turned 18. Ken explained: 'I had a friend, Dougie Tyrer, whose father didn't want him to fight and he was sent down the mines – serve him right! Now I wasn't going down the flipping mines, so I volunteered for the Royal Navy, which you could do at 17.'

After basic training at Skegness, Ken was sent to Brighton, where they were housed in civilian billets, and he was taught International Morse code, followed by the Japanese version, Wabun code. He then went to Eastbourne for specialist training on the use of direction-finding (DF) equipment, before attending a signals school in Plymouth. During Operation Overlord, the Allied invasion of Normandy, there were real concerns that the Luftwaffe might make effective use of their Fritz-X and Hs 293 wireless-guided antiship glide bombs, which employed the same guidance control system. The threat was very real: on 9 September 1943, two Fritz-X bombs struck the battleship *Roma*, flagship of the Italian fleet, in quick succession and she sank, with the loss of 1,393 lives. As a Special Telegraphist, Ken was one of those tasked with bringing electronic countermeasures into effect by using Type 650 transmitters to jam the guidance systems. Based at the Admiralty

Parade on the flight deck of HMS *Vindex*: Ken Tomkinson (the taller of the two) is next to his friend Terry Sawyer, on the inside of the middle row on the extreme right.

Surface Weapons Establishment (ASWE) at Funtington in West Sussex, Ken and his colleagues 'were hoping that we would make a difference by sending out confusing signals. Whether it worked, I don't know. No-one seemed to have any idea what we were doing, even locals who were living in the area at the time, who I talked to later in the local pub – very strange.' The important thing is that, unlike the invasion of Italy nine months earlier, not a single Allied vessel was struck by a German glide bomb off the Normandy coast.

Ken was now posted to RAF Middle Wallop to receive training as a member of the signals component of a Mobile Overseas Naval Airbase (MONAB) team. The communications equipment was stored in former railway carriages and they were taught to erect the 80-foot radio masts. A group of twenty MONAB workers took passage from Liverpool to Sydney in HMS *Vindex*, a former US escort carrier. Just before they set sail, the captain said, not very reassuringly: 'It's going to be serious. There will be a lot of casualties. I strongly recommend that you all make a will.' Ken had also become an expert in the HF/DF role, which enabled vessels equipped with so-called 'huff duff' equipment to identify and track enemy submarines. After arriving in Sydney, he first served in HMS *Armada*, a Battle-class destroyer commissioned on 2 July 1945, before transferring to the almost-equally-new Colossus-class aircraft carrier HMS *Glory*.

The city of Hiroshima in ruins after the dropping of the first atomic bomb on 6 August 1945.

Having accepted the surrender of the Japanese garrison at Rabaul on 6 September 1945, HMS *Glory* assisted with the retaking of Hong Kong: 'As MONAB 8, we were put ashore at Kowloon, along with all the equipment for establishing the Kai Tak airfield again, which did not take long, as it was all contained in railway carriages plus generators. Our HF/DF carriage had a directional aerial sticking out of the roof and, once we had power, we set up a 24-hour watch, all in a matter of two days. In the harbour were a group of American search planes and a supply ship: they invited us on board for a meal in exchange for a few bottles of our saved rum ration. Eventually the RAF kicked us out and we sailed back to Sydney in HMS *Slinger*, a small supply carrier.' A subsequent mission involved visiting Hiroshima to deliver urgent supplies to the stricken Japanese city. Ken said: 'To see all that destruction was terrible. The devastation was awful. I couldn't believe that we had to do that to end the war in the Pacific. I've got a lump in my throat just thinking about it.' On the back of a photograph of Hiroshima he had written: 'Scared us all on board ship – the silence and the smell of death.' During the voyage home, he also visited Singapore and spent a little time at Colombo in Ceylon: 'I had a very lucky time in the

Royal Navy and travelled the world at His Majesty's expense, bless him.'

Back in civilian life after almost four years, Ken settled in Oldham and worked as a transport manager for Vendapac, an American vending machine company, before retiring to Chorley. Ken explained: 'I have been married three times – so I have been busy.' By his first wife, Gladys, daughter of Jack Dyson, who kept a grocer's shop in Salford, he had two children: Michael and Jayne. Ken's third wife, Joan, to whom he had been married for twenty years, died two years ago, but Michael comes over from Rochdale once a week and the two of them go out to the pub together. Until being made redundant at the outset of the Covid-19 epidemic, he had volunteered for the last twelve years in the Endoscopy Ward at Chorley Hospital. When he went, as someone in his nineties, for his vaccination, he explained: 'I couldn't believe the state of most of them. It was very sad. We only live so long because of the pills and potions of the NHS.'

Ken and Joan Tomkinson at the VJ-Day seventieth anniversary commemorations, Horse Guards, 15 August 2015.

On 14 October 1981, Ken joined the Oldham branch of the Burma Star Association (membership number T/1536/81) although he admitted: 'My award of the Burma Star for such a short period of time has always been an embarrassment, after talking to rescued ex-Jap prisoners of war – both Forces and civilian survivors – and listening to stories from my late wife, whose husband, John Cross, served for more than three years' fighting in Burma and whose health was permanently affected and probably resulted in his early death.' At the end of our conversation, Ken, whose memory cannot be faulted, said: 'This has been a very unusual call, I must say.' We subsequently exchanged a number of emails, which he typed in upper case. His delightful sign-off was invariably 'VERY BEST WISHES, I SALUTE YOU.'

579013 LAC Thomas Tuer, Royal Air Force

Thomas (Tommy) Tuer was born on 24 January 1926 in Glue Terrace, Newcastle-upon-Tyne, second son of Joseph Tuer and his wife Minnie, daughter of Thomas Bamford, house painter, of 37 George Street, Newcastle-upon-Tyne. Tommy explained: 'He'd served with the Coldstream Guards in the First World War where he'd had some bad times so worked as a road sweeper for the Cleansing Department of Newcastle Corporation because he couldn't manage anything else.' The family moved to 15 Bracken Place and subsequently to 50 Atkinson Road in Newcastle and Tommy was educated at South Benwell School in Atkinson Road before sitting the Eleven Plus and getting a place at Rutherford College [which became Rutherford Grammar School in 1945 and Newcastle College in 1988]: 'There was a boys' school section and it was a good school although I was one of the poorer ones, which made it a bit awkward. I didn't have a pair of football boots and my father couldn't afford the uniform although he did buy me a school cap. My mother died in 1937 and it was very difficult for my father looking after us. Eighteen months later, he married my stepmother, May, who had an illegitimate child called John. She became a mother for us while my father became a father for her son. My elder brother was called John, so John Neve changed his name to Norman Tuer and it made him one of our family.

'There were five hundred boys at Rutherford College and we were all offered the option of being evacuated to Carlisle: two hundred of us took up the offer. At the age of 16 I took the Matric examination but didn't pass at the higher standard and just got School Certificate, as we called it. In Carlisle with nowhere to live, I also took the examination for a place on the Royal Air Force Apprentice Scheme. Both sets of results came through at the same time and I passed the RAF exams so I went to No. 1 School of Technical Training at RAF Halton. It was normally a three-year course but had been shortened to two years because of the war. I was there from 18 August 1942 to early June 1944. It was the best technical education then available in the world, studying technical drawing, engineering and metalwork. I spent six weeks in the blacksmith's shop and six weeks in the turning shop, which was equipped with lathes and milling machines. There was a tensile machine with which we used to stress metals to see how far we could take them and also a machine used to test hardness, either with a diamond point or with hard steel balls.

'At the end of the course, we were all tested and graded: LACs scored more than 80 per cent; AC1s between 60 and 80 per cent and AC2s between 40 and 60 per cent. It was very difficult and I don't think that we had an LAC on our course. I narrowly achieved AC1 and qualified as a fitter/armourer. Having been trained as an RAF apprentice, I was obliged to sign on for twelve years.' Lord

579013 LAC T. Tuer, Royal Air Force.

Mountbatten later said: 'One thing is absolutely true. The air battles of Burma were won in the classrooms and workshops at Halton; won not just by knowledge and skill of your maintenance crews, it was won by the spirit that Halton has produced.' Tommy continued: 'We were then posted to RAF stations all over the place and you were usually sent to somewhere near your home town. On 18 June 1944, I was posted to RAF Ouston, a dozen miles west of Newcastle on the road to Carlisle [then the home of No. 64 Operational Training Unit]. I was only there for a few months because they had the wrong types of aircraft – Ansons and Oxfords – for my type of training. These were training aircraft and I had been taught about guns, bombs and explosives. Eventually a new officer arrived and said about me: "They've only got bows and arrows for him here." So I was posted to RAF Milfield, also in Northumberland, where they were equipped with Spitfires and Typhoons. On 11 December 1944, I was posted once again, to the Air Fighting Development Squadron (AFDS), which conducted trials and developed aerial tactics, initially at RAF Wittering and later at RAF Tangmere. Not long afterwards, I received an overseas posting order.

LAC Thomas Tuer

'After reporting to Morecambe on 15 June 1945, I sailed from Glasgow to Bombay in HMT *Corfu*. Thousands of us were held in transit camps before we were posted to our squadrons. Having arrived at Worli Transit Camp on 21 July, I was posted to 152 Squadron and, after a week-long train journey across India, eventually reached Calcutta. On 10 August – the day after the second atomic bomb had been dropped on Nagasaki – I arrived in Rangoon. The squadron was still moving south and the first that I saw of them was at Mingaladon, the airfield on the outskirts of the city. Everyone was preparing for the invasion of Singapore so we had to move everything out. When we got to Singapore on 8 September, we were transferred to landing barges. Kallang airfield had been a flying boat station so we landed on the slipway. That was how the Royal Air Force got in! There were about four hundred Allied ships anchored off Singapore – it was a terrific sight. I was on guard duty when they finally surrendered [the official Japanese surrender took place in the Municipal Building, now the City Hall, on 12 September 1945, when General Seishiro Itagaki signed eleven copies of the Instrument of Surrender in the presence of Admiral Lord Louis Mountbatten]. The squadrons based at Kallang were all equipped with Spitfires. The Spitfires belonging to 136 Squadron were crated up and also arrived by sea, so we had to assemble them. Those aircraft which flew in carried the biggest long-range drop-tanks ever used by a Spitfire. Lady Mountbatten was supervising the repatriation of our prisoners of war from Kallang and it soon became so overcrowded that we had to move to Tengah. Singapore was in a filthy state and we took turns in charge of working parties, supervising Japanese prisoners while they cleaned the place up.

'At Tengah they started to sort everybody out, and because I hadn't been overseas for very long, they sent me to Sumatra. On 19 January 1946, I joined 7017 Servicing Echelon, 155 Squadron, which had received replacement Spitfires from 152 Squadron, at Medan in northern Sumatra. We were responsible for looking after the local population until the Dutch returned. We sailed in a hospital ship from Singapore and, on arrival, an announcement came over the Tannoy: "Before you disembark, you will all load your weapons. Five men in a 3-ton vehicle and three men in a 15-cwt. No two men of the same trade to travel in the same vehicle." The convoy set off along a road surrounded by jungle. Every few miles the convoy would stop and a redcap on a motorcycle would check to see that everyone was okay. We could see that many of the trees at the side of the road were cut halfway through their trunks, ready to be pushed over, and then we would be trapped in an ambush. The thought was very frightening and we were just beginning to realise that, in Air Force slang, this was not going to be 'a piece of cake'.

'When we arrived at the airfield, the biggest surprise was to see an armed Japanese guarding the arched entrance. We debussed and went through the entrance which had, on the left, a guardroom and, on the right, three doors close together, which were the cells. Inside the compound were covered concrete walkways leading to long, narrow buildings, which were our billets. Inside there were low, wooden platforms about a foot off the ground which, we were told, had provided accommodation for eighteen Japanese. They were much smaller than us and we had to squeeze in twenty-five people. At night we set up tin cans on the window shutters and doors so that if anyone tried to get in they would clatter to the ground, acting as an early warning system. The cans had lots of holes punched in them so that the 'enemy' couldn't use them to make bombs. Our Spitfires were dispersed along the perimeter track while there were also a few Japanese reconnaissance aircraft, flown by Japanese pilots and marked with green crosses for ease of recognition.

'Guard duties came round every fourth day and the RAF Regiment officer who inspected us insisted that we wore clean 'jungle green' in case we were wounded and contracted infections from our work clothes. As well as our personal weapon, many of us carried a weapon for hand-to-hand fighting. Mine was a twelve-inch bayonet, which I had found on a dump. We always slept with our arms wrapped round our rifle or Sten gun. Guard duty was the usual two hours on, four hours off, until we were relieved the following day. The food situation was not very good: all the food came through the Army and the RAF was at the end of the queue, by which time there wasn't much left. As a result, we supplemented our rations by buying coconuts, bananas and eggs from the natives. The eggs were about the size of bantam eggs and cost the equivalent of 2s 6d, or half a day's pay, each. Our army liaison officer was called Captain Comfort and he used to brief us once a week on what had been going on. He provided 'comfort' by informing us that a headless body had been left at the headquarters one day and a severed head the next; that an army deserter had been killed at a cinema in town; and that a Dutch army armourer had been kidnapped just along the road from our billets.

'One evening, as we were walking to dinner, there was a burst of machine gun fire forty or fifty yards ahead of our group. Although we saw an Indonesian with his insides shot out by Indian troops, we just carried on to the cookhouse because we were pretty hungry and food was scarce. We later moved into tents, and the worst experience was waking up one evening to the sounds of a battle taking place extremely close by. I could hear the screams as people were hacked to pieces by machetes and swords. There was a small radio receiving station about three hundred yards away, guarded by half-a-dozen men from the RAF Regiment. They had been attacked by at least forty Indonesians – said to be Achinese – and the two men on guard raised the alarm. One man ran across to our tented camp to warn us while the others upended their metal *charpoys* to form a barricade. We lost two men that night while other bodies could be seen in the moonlight but had been dragged away by morning. One day while walking in town – we always walked in pairs – there was a burst of fire from a café across the street. An Indian soldier had slung his Sten gun over the back of his chair but knocked it off when he sat down. When it struck the ground butt first, it started firing – such was the temperament of the Sten gun.

'Our padre was a real man. He would come into the canteen so that anyone could talk to him. The men would be drinking their beer ration and singing all the famous rugby songs – *Old King Cole*, *The Good Ship Venus*, etc – but it didn't bother him. One night he came to our guard post but didn't come inside because he didn't want to disturb those who were sleeping. I went out to talk to him and was surprised to see that he was carrying a Mk. 5 Sten gun, the latest version. I asked him why he was carrying it and he said: "This is not war, this is murder and I don't believe in murder." *Merdeka* was a word that became very familiar to us and which was taken very seriously. It means "freedom" in English, and the intelligence was that when "Merdeka Day" arrived the Indonesians would kill all the foreigners: English, Dutch, Indian, Chinese – everyone. When Merdeka Day [17 August] finally arrived, there was a bit of a scramble and all the aircraft were brought from dispersal much closer to the camp. It was a difficult situation because we were surrounded by hundreds of miles of jungle and only held a small area, perhaps three-quarters of a mile by a mile and a half. We would never make it twelve miles through the jungle to Belawan on the coast so the CO decided that we should barricade ourselves in the cookhouse, where we would at least have some food.

'News then came through that 155 Squadron was to be disbanded and we were going to be relieved by a Thunderbolt squadron. I returned to RAF Seletar on 31 August 1946, after seven months at Medan, where I most certainly did not 'enjoy' my time. After a few weeks back in Singapore, I went to No. 22 Personnel Transit Centre in Cairo, before being posted to No. 107 Maintenance Unit at RAF Kasfareet, in the Canal Zone near the Great Bitter Lake, where I remained for a year or so. Next I was posted to 44 Squadron at RAF Wyton in Cambridgeshire, although I soon embarked on a six-month tour of Africa: travelling from Castel Benito in Libya, to Khartoum in the Sudan, to Nairobi in Kenya and, finally, to Belvedere and Bulawayo in Southern Rhodesia. On 26 April 1949 at St James's, Carlisle, I was married to Mary Peat. Just three weeks later, Mary and I left for Canada because I had been seconded – as a civil servant because I wasn't allowed to wear uniform – to conduct cold weather experiments on different types of engines. Although Mary remained in Edmonton, I used to visit Watson Lake in the Yukon Territory for weeks at a time.

'Having completed my twelve years' service from the age of 18, I was 30 when I left the RAF. I returned to Carlisle and worked for three years as a maintenance fitter for Metal Box, before joining the Blue Streak missile project, based at RAF Spadeadam, near Gilsland, twenty miles east of Carlisle. Blue Streak was a British intermediate-range ballistic missile, which was intended to replace the V-bomber fleet in the mid-1960s. I was involved with testing the Rolls-Royce liquid-fuelled engines and stayed with the project until it was scrapped in 1972. I was promoted four times – from tester to leading

Tommy Tuer, photographed at home in Stanwix by Wendy Aldiss.

tester to assistant test engineer and, finally, to test engineer – so I climbed the ladder a bit. It was a difficult time when Blue Streak was scrapped: the economy was in recession and there were no similar jobs available so I took a job in Carlisle City Library, Headquarters of Cumberland Library Services.' Tommy and Mary had five children: Mary, who lived for just a few hours, Michael (who was born in Edmonton), Philip, Peter and Paul. His wife, Mary, died in December 2019. Tommy became a life member of the Carlisle branch of the Burma Star Association on 25 May 1972 (membership number T/986/72).

Footnote

A Hill called Melrose
by Dr Yashwant Thorat

'May I have a light?' I looked up to see a Japanese – more or less my age – with an unlit cigarette in his hand. I reached for my lighter. He lit up. We were on a train travelling from Berne to Geneva in the autumn of 1980. 'Indian?' he asked. 'Yes,' I replied. We got talking. He was an official in the UN and was returning to home and headquarters at Geneva. I was scheduled to lecture at the university. We chit-chatted for a while; he gave me some useful tips on what to see and where to eat in the city. Then, having exhausted the store of 'safely tradeable information', we fell silent. I retrieved my book – *Defeat into Victory*, an account of the Second World War in Burma by Field Marshal William Slim. He opened the newspaper. We travelled in silence. After a while he asked: 'Are you a professor of Military History?' 'No,' I replied, 'just interested. My father was in Burma during the war.' 'Mine too,' he said.

In December 1941, Japan invaded Burma and opened the longest land campaign of the entire war for Britain. There were two reasons for the Japanese invasion. First, cutting the overland supply route to China via the Burma Road would deprive Chiang Kai-shek's Nationalist Chinese armies of military equipment and pave the way for the conquest of China. Second, possession of Burma would position them at the doorway to India, where they believed a general insurrection would be triggered against the British once their troops established themselves within reach of Calcutta. Entering Burma from Thailand, the Japanese quickly captured Rangoon in 1942, cut off the Burma Road at source and deprived the Chinese of their only convenient supply base and port of entry. Winning battle after battle, they forced the Allied forces to retreat into India. The situation was bleak. The British were heavily committed to the war in Europe and lacked the resources and organisation to recapture Burma. However, by 1943 they got their act together. The High Command was overhauled:

Wavell was replaced by Mountbatten and operational control was given to General William Slim, a brilliant officer. Slim imbued his men with a new spirit, rebuilt morale and forged the famous 14th Army, an efficient combat force made up of British, Indians and Africans. The Japanese, aware that the defenders were gathering strength, resolved to end the campaign with a bold thrust into India and a simultaneous attack in the Arakan in Burma.

In the ebb and flow of these large events chronicled in military history, my father, a soldier, played a part – first in Kohima in clearing the Japanese from the Naga Hills, then in Imphal and finally in the deeply forested mountains of Arakan. Destiny took him there. In the blinding rain of the monsoons in 1943, the Supreme Allied Commander's plane landed at Maungdaw where the All-India Brigade, of which his regiment was a part, was headquartered. Mountbatten was accompanied by his chief of staff, Lieutenant General Frederick 'Boy' Browning, who had been my father's adjutant at the Royal Military College in Sandhurst. He and the two other Indian commanders – Thimayya and Sen – were introduced to Mountbatten who made casual but searching enquiries regarding their war experience. Thereafter he was closeted in the 'conference tent' with the senior commanders for a long time. As they came out, he turned to Reggie Hutton, the brigade commander, and said: "All right, Reggie, let your All-India Brigade do it. But, by God, it is going to be tough." Then, turning to the three of them, he said: "Gentlemen, the Japanese are pulling out of Upper Burma. You have been selected to intercept their withdrawal from there into the South. You will concentrate at Akyab, proceed to Myebon by sea, capture Kangaw, penetrate Japanese-held territory and convert the Japanese retreat into a rout. Is that clear?" It was.

My Japanese friend, who had been listening intently, leaned forward and asked: "Did you say your father was in the All-India Brigade?" "Yes," I replied. Our conversation paused for a while as the waiter served coffee and croissants. Later, picking up the threads, he persisted: "Was he a junior officer at the time?" "Not really", I replied, "he was a battalion commander." He digested the information and said: "Which regiment?" "The Punjab Regiment", I replied. His face changed colour. Maybe it was a play of light and shade, or maybe it was just my imagination, but I thought he was going to be ill. "Are you okay?" I queried. He nodded: "Please carry on."

After marching through hostile territory, the brigade finally landed at Myebon. Their disembarkation was not opposed. They proceeded to Kangaw, little knowing that forty-eight hours later they would be locked in a battle which was to last for a fortnight and claim the lives of three thousand men. Mountbatten had been right. The withdrawal route of the Japanese was dominated by 'Hill Feature 170 – Melrose'. It was firmly held by the Japanese and gave them the enormous advantage of having the 'commanding heights'. Worse, intelligence reported that they had two brigades, while the Indians had only one. Brigadier Hutton realised that, if the withdrawal had to be cut, the hills would have to be captured, irrespective of the numerical disadvantage. He took the call. The first attack by the Hyderabadis under Thimayya mauled the enemy but did not achieve the objective. The second by the Baluchis under Sen met a similar fate. It was then that 'Reggie' asked the Punjabis to make a final effort. Artillery and air support was coordinated. The zero hour for the attack was set at 0700 hrs on 29 January 1945.

At dawn, as the leading companies moved forward, the Japanese opened machine gun fire. The artillery provided cover and laid out a smoke screen. The Punjabis began to climb the hill. Safe from amongst well-dug bunkers, the Japanese rained fire on them. The Indian casualties mounted as men began to drop. The air cover, which was a key part of the plan, failed to materialise – bad weather and bad luck. Taking a calculated risk, the commander pushed on. They were hardly a hundred yards from the top when the Japanese threw everything they had at them. In the face of such unrestrained fierceness, the advance faltered, hovering uncertainly on the edge of stopping. For the commander, it was the moment of truth – to fight or flee? As he saw his men being mowed down by machine gun fire, a rage erupted within him. Throwing caution to the winds, he ran forward to be with them. The scales 'tipped'. The troops rallied, 'fixed bayonets' and charged into the Japanese with obscenities and primeval war cries. A fierce hand-to-hand combat ensued. Neither side took or gave any quarter. The Japanese fought like tigers at bay. The conflict went on unabated through the night. The Japanese counter-attacked in wave after wave but the Indian line held firm. Then the last bullet was fired and there was silence.

Many years later, Mountbatten would describe what took place as 'the bloodiest battle of the Arakan' – and correctly so. The price of victory was two thousand Japanese and eight hundred Indians dead in the course of a single encounter. Fifty officers and men would win awards for gallantry. The battalion commander would be decorated with the DSO for 'unflinching devotion to duty and personal bravery'. But all that was to happen in the future.

At that particular moment on the field of battle, the commander was looking at the Japanese soldiers who had been taken prisoners of war. They had assembled as soldiers do, neatly and in order. On seeing the Indian colonel, their commander called his men to attention, stepped forward, saluted, unbuckled his sword, held it in both hands and bowed. The Indian was surprised to see that his face was streaked with tears. He understood the pain of defeat, but why the tears? After all, this was war. One side or the other had to lose. How could the Japanese explain to the Indian that the tears were not of grief but of shame? How could he make him understand what it meant to be a Samurai? Given a choice, he himself would have preferred the nobler course of *Hara Kiri* than surrender. But fate had willed otherwise. The ancestral sword in his hands had been carried with pride by his forefathers. Now he was shaming them by handing it over. All this was unknown – unknowable – to the Indian commander. He came from a different culture and had no knowledge of what was going on in the mind of his adversary. Yet there was something in the manner and bearing of the officer in front of him which touched him deeply. He found himself moved.

Without being told, he somehow intuited that the moment on hand was not merely solemn but personal and deeply sacred. He accepted the sword and then, inexplicably, impelled by an emotion which perhaps only a soldier can feel for a worthy opponent, bent forward and said clearly and loudly in the hearing of all: "Colonel, I accept the surrender but I receive your sword not as a token of defeat but as a gift from one soldier to another." The Japanese, least expecting this response, looked up – startled. The light bouncing from the tears on his cheeks reflected an unspoken gratitude for the Indian's remark. Coming as it did from the heart, it had touched his men and redeemed their – and his – honour. The Punjabis – and Hindus and Muslims – who had gathered around also nodded in appreciation. Battle was battle. When it was on, they had fought each other with all their strength. And now that it was over, there was no personal or national animosity. Maybe the Gods who look after soldiers are different from those who look after other mortals, for they bind them in strange webs of understanding and common codes of honour, no matter which flags they fly.

The moment passed. He looked at the signal officer and nodded. The success signal was fired. Far away in the jungles below, Brigadier Reggie Hutton looked at the three red lights in the sky – and smiled. His faith in his commanders had been vindicated. He would later explain that at stake that night was not only the battle objective but the larger issue as to whether Indians 'had it in them' to lead men in war. There had been sceptics who felt that his faith was misplaced. He looked at Melrose and smiled. Its capture had vindicated his faith.

I looked out of the window lost in my thoughts. Suddenly, I heard a sob, only to find that my Japanese friend had broken down. He swayed from side to side. His eyes were closed and it was clear that he was in the grip of an emotion more powerful than himself. He kept saying "karma, karma" and talking to himself in his own language. After a while, he looked up with eyes full of tears and, holding both my hands, said in a voice choked with emotion: "It was my father who gave battle to yours on Melrose. It was he who surrendered. Had your father not understood the depth of his feelings, he would have come back and died of shame. But, in accepting our ancestral sword in the manner that he did, he restored honour to our family and my father to me. That makes us brothers – you and I."

The train pulled into Geneva station. We got down. What had to be said had already been spoken. He bowed. "Goodbye," I said, "keep in touch. Incidentally, would you like me to restore the sword back to your family?" He smiled, looked at me and said: "Certainly not. The sword already rests in the house of a Samurai." That was the last I saw of him.

Usha tells me that the probability of our meeting defies statistics. She should know. She studied economics and statistics. There was a world war going on. Good. My father was in the Indian Army; his father was in the Japanese Army; perfectly okay. They fought in the same theatre of war – Burma; understandable. They fought in the same battle; difficult but believable. The war finished, they went back to their families; plausible. But that their sons grew up in two different lands, happened to go to Berne at the same time, board the same train, get into the same compartment, share coffee and cigarettes, have a conversation on something that had happened four decades ago, discover their fathers had fought on opposite sides in the same battle – that undoubtedly is insane.

Personally, I do not believe that there are outcomes in life which are necessarily bound to happen. Yet, sometimes I am not so sure. You can never connect events by looking into the future; you can only connect them by looking at the past. Maybe it is comforting to believe that, because the dots connect backward, they will connect forward also. I don't know. Perhaps in the end you have to trust in something. The sword has a pride of place in our home. Whenever I see it, my mind goes back to the jungles of Arakan where in the midst of the madness of war, two soldiers were able to touch each other and their compatriots with lasting humanity.

<u>Note</u>: Major Drogo Montagu fought with 2/2 Punjab at 'Melrose' during the successful assault while Captain Stuart Guild RA was wounded by shellfire during an O Group before the assault.

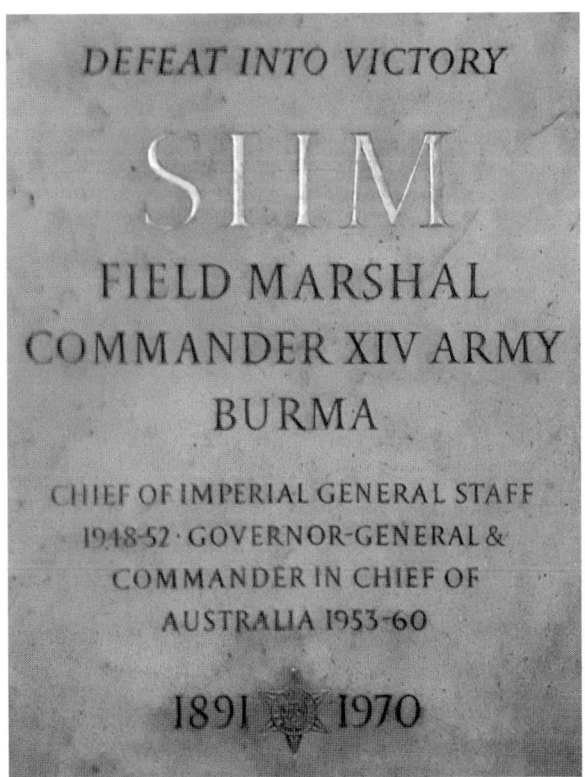

Memorial inscription in St Paul's Cathedral.

Index

Abbottabad, 8
Abdi, Sergeant, 226
Abeokuta, Nigeria, 188
"Aberdeen" *see* Chindits (Special Force): Strongholds
Abyssinia, 227, 232, 238
Accra, Gold Coast, 77, 80–2, 114
Adjetey, Sergeant Nii, 80–1
Admin Box, Battle of the *see* Battles, Engagements and Operations: Ngakyedauk Pass
Agra, 116–17, 168–9, 210
Ahmednuggur, 53, 93, 97
'Aid to the Civil Power', 81, 85, 93, 117, 136, 213–14
Aircraft, Allied:
  Avenger, 2
  B-24 Liberator, 19–22, 135, 184
  Barracuda, 2
  Blenheim, 35
  Corsair, 2
  Dakota, 10, 14, 21, 34, 56, 88–9, 94, 104, 128–31, 135, 139–40, 169, 190–3, 217
  Firefly, 2
  Harvard, 208
  Hellcat, 2
  Hurricane, 205–208, 235
  Seafire, 2
  Spitfire, xv, 59, 112, 260–2
  Sunderland flying boat, 89, 129, 218
  Thunderbolt, 264
  Tiger Moth, 249, 253
  Typhoon, 260
  Vengeance, 32–4, 208
  Waco CG-4A glider, 87–8, 128–30, 139
  Walrus, 19
  Wildcat, 2
Aircraft, German:
  Dornier 217, 99
  Heinkel 111, 134
  Heinkel 177, 134
  Ju-87 Stuka, 145
Aircraft, Italian:
  Savoia-Marchetti SM.79, 146
Aircraft, Japanese, 33, 39, 95, 122, 124, 206
  Mitsubishi Ki-57 Topsy, 112
  Zero, 94
Aitken, Petty Officer Harry, 1–4
Akyab Island, 41, 68, 155, 221, 267
Alexandria, Egypt, 134–5
Amositra, Madagascar, 228–9
Arakan, xvii, 33–4, 41, 80, 96, 100, 121–2, 135, 189–90, 208, 221, 244
  see also Battles, Engagements and Operations: Arakan, 1st campaign; Arakan, 2nd campaign; Arakan, 3rd campaign; Cox's Bazar; Donbaik; Kangaw; Ngakyedauk Pass; Prome
Armed Forces, Allied:
  see also Royal Air Force and Royal Indian Air Force; Royal Navy and Royal Indian Navy
  Armies
    8th Army, 135
    14th Army, xv–xviii, 10, 61, 71, 75, 101–103, 110, 155, 166–72, 201, 267
    Territorial Army, xvii, 5, 92, 186, 240
  Corps
    IV Corps, 52, 104, 168
    XV Corps, 168
    XXXIII Corps, 168
    Burma Corps, xvi, 197
  Divisions
    1st (Burma) Division, xvi
    2nd (British) Infantry Division, 47, 102, 135
    5th (Indian) Infantry Division, xvii, 101–103, 111, 244
    11th (East African) Division, 107–8, 124, 229–37

Index

17th (Indian) Infantry Division, xvi, 155, 159–61, 199–202, 244
19th (Indian) Infantry Division, 104
20th (Indian) Infantry Division, 9–11
23rd (Indian) Infantry Division, 11, 27
25th (Indian) Infantry Division, 155, 193, 221
36th (British) Infantry Division, 95, 142
70th (British) Division, 213–14
80th (British) Division, 165
81st (West African) Division, 77–8
82nd (West African) Division, 77–9, 114, 188–93
Brigades
   2nd (West African) Infantry Brigade, 77, 188–93
   3rd Commando Brigade, 221
   3rd (West African) Infantry Brigade, 138, 142
   14th (British) Infantry Brigade, 94, 96, 141
   14th (Indian) Airlanding Brigade, 77
   51st (British) Infantry Brigade, 156
   16th (British) Infantry Brigade, 94
   21st (East African) Infantry Brigade, 108, 234–7
   71st (Indian) Infantry Brigade, 75
   77th (Indian) Infantry Brigade, 128, 139–40
   80th Brigade, 13
   111th (Indian) Infantry Brigade, 129
   123rd (Indian) Infantry Brigade, 100
   161st (Indian) Infantry Brigade, 243–6
   All-India Brigade (51st (Indian) Infantry Brigade), 267–8
Regiments and Corps
   2nd Punjab Regiment, 70, 154–7, 267–71
   3rd Carabiniers (Prince of Wales's Dragoon Guards), 50–3, 92–7
   5th (Royal Inniskilling) Dragoon Guards, 93
   7th Rajput Regiment, 193
   9th Jat Regiment, 101
   10th Baluch Regiment, 156, 196–203, 268
   13th (Lancashire) Parachute Battalion, 73
   18th Royal Garhwal Rifles, 74–6
   19th Hyderabad Regiment, 70, 116–18, 156, 268
   26th Hussars, 93–6
   152nd Regiment, Royal Armoured Corps, 50
   Artists' Rifles, 212
   Bedfordshire and Hertfordshire Regiment, 212–18
   Black Watch, 95, 217
   Border Regiment, 158–62
   Burma Rifles, 95
   Devonshire Regiment, 5–16, 117, 150–3, 202–203, 240–3
   Dorsetshire Regiment, 225
   Gold Coast Regiment, 77–82, 188–94
   Gordon Highlanders, 74, 124
   Gurkha Rifles, 11, 13, 68, 97, 128–9, 221
   Highland Light Infantry, 183
   King's African Rifles, 107–109, 224–38
   King's (Liverpool) Regiment, 127–32, 159, 178, 184
   King's Own Scottish Borderers, 182–5
   King's Royal Rifle Corps, 46
   Lancashire Fusiliers, 176–81, 128
   Leicestershire Regiment, 95
   Life Guards, 92
   Nigeria Regiment, 137–43, 188
   Northamptonshire Regiment, 186–7
   Royal Norfolk Regiment, 70, 191–5
   Queen's Own Royal West Kent Regiment, 55–6, 110–13, 239–47
   Queen's Royal Regiment, 55–7
   Royal Army Medical Corps, 101, 117, 170
   Royal Army Service Corps, 187–91
   Royal Artillery, 25–8, 66–73, 121–6, 220–3
      8th Field Regiment, 68, 220–1
      27th Field Regiment, 66–73
      44th Light Anti-Aircraft Regiment, 121–6
      59th Anti-Tank Regiment, 220–1
      114th (Sussex) Field Regiment, 73
      208th Field (SP) Regiment, 27
      455th Independent Light Battery, 26–7
   Royal Berkshire Regiment, 127

Royal Corps of Signals, 164–75, 208
Royal Engineers, 84–91, 95, 128, 133–6, 192, 216
Royal Garhwal Rifles, 74–6
Royal Indian Engineers, 116–17
Royal Scots Dragoon Guards, 52
Royal Sussex Regiment, 137, 142
Royal Welch Fusiliers, 45–8
South Staffordshire Regiment, 128
Suffolk Regiment, 98–106
Wiltshire Regiment, 151
Armed Forces, Japanese:
  Japanese Army, xvi, 199, 214
  15th Japanese Army, 10, 101, 160
  215th Regiment, 197, 237
  33rd Japanese Division, 197, 199
Armitage, John, 236–7
Asansol, 32, 122
Assam, 33, 40, 94–5, 128, 139, 151, 198, 229, 234
Atherton, Eric, 51
Atomic Bombs, 22, 35, 42, 56, 72, 97, 112, 135, 152, 157, 171, 184, 246, 261
Attipoe, Corporal Patrick, 81
Auchinleck, Field Marshal Sir Claude, 103
Aung San, 251–2

Bamford, Fusilier Robert Eric, 179
Bangalore, 34, 52, 90, 116–17, 155, 196, 214
Bangkok, Thailand, 56
Barkas, Major Anthony Charles Kingston, 224
Barua, Pradeep, 156
Bassein, 194
Bastone, Sergeant George, 5–16
  Mentioned in despatches, 14
Battles, Engagements and Operations:
  Battles
    Arakan, 1st Campaign, xvii
    Arakan, 2nd Campaign, xviii, 100–101
    Arakan, 3rd Campaign, xviii, 66–71, 114, 156, 189–93, 221, 267–70
    Hill 60, 142
    Imphal, xviii, 9–13, 33, 50, 52, 96, 101–103, 110, 151–2, 159–61, 199
    Ingon Chaung, 234–8
    Kangaw, 69–71, 156, 190, 221, 267–70
    Kawkareik Pass, 197–9
    Kohima, xviii, 2, 33, 50, 96, 101–102, 110, 159–61, 229, 243
    Kyunsanlai Pass, 141
    Letsegan, 230–3
    Mawlu, 140, 217
    Meiktila and Mandalay, xviii, 96, 103–104, 110–11, 152, 199–200
    Ngakyedauk Pass, 100
    Nippon Hill, 9–11, 151
    Nunshigum Ridge, 52
    Pegu Hill, 200
    Pinhmi Bridge, 180
    Prome, 96, 184, 193
    Pyabwe, 161
    Rangoon, 34–5, 78, 112, 244–6
    Sittang Bridge, xvi, 161, 197–9
    Tennis Court, the, 243–4
  Engagements
    Cox's Bazar, 122
    Donbaik, 122
    Hill 1106, 190–3
    Ukhrul Road, 11–12
  Operations
    Operation Capital, 103–104
    Operation Dracula, 71, 75
    Operation Ha-Go, 100
    Operation Husky, 146
    Operation Iceberg, 2
    Operation Longcloth, 128, 214
    Operation Overlord, 255
    Operation Pedestal, 145–6
    Operation Python, 131
    Operation Thursday, 128–30, 214–18
    Operation U-Go, 10, 100–101, 160–1
    Operation Zipper, 157, 221
Baz, Subedar Moghal, 202
Behagg, LAC Fred, 17–24
Belgaum, 154
Bengal
  Bay of, xvii, 2, 68, 85
  East, 20, 21, 122
  Famine, 123
Bevan, Gunner Alan, 25–8
Bhopal, 135, 207
Bishenpur, 102, 161, 199
'Black Cats' *see* Armed Forces, Allied: Divisions, 17th (Indian) Infantry Division
Black Death *see* Diseases, Infections and Vectors

Index 275

"Blackpool" *see* Chindits (Special Force): Strongholds
Bombay, 7, 20, 25–6, 31, 40, 47, 55, 60, 66, 93, 99–100, 105, 110, 121, 127, 135, 151, 159, 166, 183, 207, 209, 213–14, 218, 243, 246, 261
Brahmaputra River, 33, 56, 60, 94, 116, 161
Braun, Major, 8–9
Brighton *see* Battles, Engagements and Operations: Kangaw
British Red Cross, 151
Britten, Regimental Sergeant Major, 137
"Broadway" *see* Chindits (Special Force): Strongholds
Broome, Captain Jack, 2
Brown, Sergeant, 234
Browning, Lieutenant General Sir Frederick 'Boy', 267
Bulldozer Ridge, 230
Bullock, Corporal Neil, 29–37
Burma Road, xvi, 251, 266
Burns, Sir Alan, 80
Buthidaung, 78, 155

Calcutta, xvii, 21, 26, 32–5, 60, 71, 100–103, 110–11, 126, 135–6, 151, 155, 169, 196, 213–14, 243–6, 261, 266
see also Rest and Recuperation: Leave
Calvert, Brigadier Mike, 128–9, 139–40, 178
Cape Town, South Africa, 25, 31, 207, 225
Capelli, Captain Carlo, 146
Carfrae, Major Charles, 139–42
Military Cross, 140
Cayley, Bill, 197
Cemeteries *see* War Graves
Ceylon, 3, 5, 8, 23, 62, 77, 114, 146, 168, 229, 238, 258
Chakrata *see* Rest and Recuperation: Leave
Chin Hills, 199, 214
Chindits (Special Force), xvii, 85–90, 94–6, 127–30, 138–43, 214–18
Strongholds
"Aberdeen", 94, 140, 214–15
"Blackpool", 88, 129
"Broadway", 86–8, 128–30, 178–9
"Piccadilly", 130
"White City", 139–40, 179–80, 217
Chindwin River, 13, 103–104, 108, 123–4, 169, 234

Chittagong, 26, 33, 41, 67, 70, 100, 104, 122, 135
Chittagonian Inland Water Transport, 68
Civil Disturbances *see* 'Aid to the Civil Power'
Climatic Conditions, xvi, 10, 12, 33, 52, 58, 64, 94, 102, 111, 114, 117, 140, 155, 167–9, 193, 197–8, 200–201, 208, 217, 229–30, 252, 267–8
Colombo, Ceylon, 8, 23, 258
Comfort, Captain, 262
Comilla, 101, 166–8, 183–4, 243
Communications:
  Postal service, 60, 65–9, 112, 122, 167, 193, 249
  Wireless and signals, 19, 25–7, 56, 61–3, 68–73, 78, 96–7, 128–9, 154, 159–61, 165–75, 177, 184, 205–10, 212–14, 226, 255–7, 263
  see also Morse Code
Conder, Lieutenant Colonel Henry, 184
Construction and Engineering:
  Airstrips, 87–8, 128, 139–40, 215, 217
  Bridges, 94–5, 102, 135
    Kalewa, 13, 123–4
  Roads, xvi, 135, 192
Convoys, 20, 25, 31, 50, 55, 69, 144–6, 150–3, 207
  JW61B, 145
  KMF22, 127
  KMF25A, 99
  KMF26, 100, 133–4
  KMF29A, 2
  Operation Pedestal, 145
  PQ17, 2
Cook, Major Arthur, 117
Cornaby, Captain Peter, 51
Coward, Noël, 167
Cox's Bazar, 26, 33–4, 85, 100, 122, 208
Craddock, Squadron Sergeant Major William, 52
Creasy, Sir Gerald, 80
Crete, 100
Crockett, Lieutenant, 79

Dacca, 122, 207
Dakar, Senegal, 187
Darjeeling *see* Rest and Recuperation: Leave
Davis, Corporal Eric, 38–44
Day, Fusilier Richard, 45–49

Delhi, 74, 103, 121, 130, 168–9, 213–4
  see also Rest and Recuperation: Leave
Delhi Belly see Diseases, Infections and
  Vectors
Deolali, 14, 66–7, 100, 105, 110, 127, 135,
  151, 159, 177
Diamond, Sergeant, 138
Digri, 33
Dimapur, 123, 135, 159, 169
Din, Naik Fazal:
  Victoria Cross, 199
Discipline and Punishment, 5, 95, 159,
  171–2, 189, 216
Diseases, Infections and Vectors:
  Abscess, 218
  Diarrhoea, 56, 121, 200, 207, 230
  Dysentery, 10, 32, 101–102, 116–18, 135,
    152, 179–80, 184
  Heatstroke, 117
  Impetigo, 66
  Jaundice, 112
  Jungle sores, 12, 112, 218
  Malaria, xvi, 34, 95, 101, 103, 116, 121–2,
    140, 152, 161, 184, 195, 218, 252
  Malnutrition, 161
  Meningitis, 205, 224
  Mosquitos, 12, 155, 166
  Plague, 250
  Pneumonia, 52
  Polio, 239
  Prickly heat, 252
  Renal colic, 10
  Ringworm, 252
  Septic infections, 129, 234, 262
  Tinea, 252
  Tropical sprue, 161
  Typhus and scrub typhus, 9, 218, 234
  Venereal disease, 173, 194
Docherty, John, 124
Donbaik, 122
Downs, Lance Corporal Ted, 50–4
Duffy, Sergeant Major, 102
Dunn, Pat, 197
Durban, South Africa, 7, 85, 93, 220
Dyer, Lieutenant Colonel Jerry, 197

Earle, Major, 153
Easten, Major Donald, 243
Edwards, Eddie, 21
Ellicott, Lance Corporal Mervyn, 55–7
Entertainment see Rest and Recuperation:
  Entertainment

Equipment, Allied:
  Amphibious craft
    Assault boats, 86, 234
    Z Lighter, Z-5 or 'HMS *Enterprise*',
      67–71
  Armoured Fighting Vehicles
    Bren gun carrier, 51, 85, 98–101
    Churchill tank, 50
    M3 Lee tank, 50, 93, 96–7
    Matilda tank, 50
    Sherman tank, 27, 52
    Stuart tank, 52
  Artillery
    Oerlikon 20mm cannon, 165
    QF 25-pdr, 18, 69, 193, 220–1
    QF 3.7-inch mountain howitzer, 26
  Mortars
    2″ mortar, 70, 154
    3″ mortar, 111, 154, 193, 199–200,
      231
  Personal weapons
    .303 Lee-Enfield rifle, 46, 88, 147,
      189, 226, 249, 262
    Bren gun, 5, 8, 14, 160, 226–7, 244,
      246
    Carbine, 88, 129
    Colt .45, 93
    Lewis gun, 8
    Smith & Wesson .38, 129
    Sten gun, 27, 40, 64, 189, 252, 262–3
    Thompson sub-machine gun, 69, 228
    Vickers machine gun, 197
    Webley pistol, 81
  Radios
    18-set, 71, 226
    22-set, 69, 128, 226
    48-set, 184
    399 radio transmitter, 168
Evans, David, 225–9
Evans, Lieutenant General Sir Geoffrey,
  103

Faisalabad, 90
Fields, Gracie, 56
Fletcher, Ron, 86–90
Forgotten Army see Armed Forces, Allied:
  Armies, 14th Army
Foster, LAC Brian, 58–65
Fowkes, Major General Charles
  Christopher, 229

Freetown, Sierra Leone, 31, 187–8, 221, 225

Gibbs, Captain, 27
Gibraltar, 20, 99, 187, 206, 242
Gibson, Perla, 7, 93
Giffard, General Sir George, 77
Goa, 26
Greenwood, Bill, 196–8
Guild, Captain Stuart, 66–73, 271
  Territorial Decoration and bar, 73

Hall, Major Nobby, 142
Halsey, Admiral William F 'Bull', US Navy, 10
Hamandawa, 233
Hamilton, Jock, 65
Hamilton, Major Patrick, 74–6
  Mentioned in despatches, 76
Hammond, Private Joseph, 77–83
Harman, Lance Corporal John:
  Victoria Cross, 244
Harvest, Lieutenant Colonel Gerard Augustine de Vere, 10
Haynes, Captain Pip, 141–2
Heppell, Corporal Peter, 84–91
Hilder, Captain Richard, 54, 92–7
Hill 170 *see* Battles, Engagements and Operations: Kangaw
Hmawbi, 34
Holden, George, 197
Home Guard, 6, 15, 18, 66, 110, 127, 164, 255
Hong Kong, 147, 257
Hooghley River, 100
Hukawng Valley, 95
Hutchinson, Lieutenant, 234
Hutton, Brigadier Reginald Antony, 156, 267–70
Hyderabad, Maharajah of, 34

Imphal, 41, 60, 108, 135, 168–9, 197–8, 229, 267
  see also Battles, Engagements and Operations
Imray, Superintendent, 80
Indaw, 94, 216–18
Indawgyi Lake, 89, 129, 217–18
Indian Air Force *see* Royal Air Force and Indian Air Force

Ingon Chaung *see* Battles, Engagements and Operations
Inya Lake *see* Rest and Recuperation: Recreation, Sailing, Lake Victoria
Irrawaddy River, 13, 78, 88, 104, 135, 199, 216
Ismailia, Egypt, 136
Itagaki, General Seishiro, 261

Jakarta, Java, Dutch East Indies, 63
Jamshedpur, 122
'Jankers' *see* Discipline and Punishment
Japanese Surrender, 27, 35, 62, 73, 76, 112, 125–6, 147, 157, 161, 180, 257, 261
Japanese Surrendered Personnel *see* Prisoners of War: Japanese
Java, Dutch East Indies, 72
Jefford, Wing Commander C.G., 33
Jenkins, Sir Evan, 118
Jenkins, Vernon:
  Military Medal, 51
Jervis, Jake, 197
Jessore, 20–1
Jhansi, 86, 94, 127–8, 214
Johari, 34
Jones, Private Idris, 98–106
Jullundur, 8, 117–18, 154
Jutogh, 118

Kabaw Valley, 108, 229–38
  see also Battles, Engagements and Operations: Engagements, Ingon Chaung
Kaduna, Nigeria, 138
Kalewa, 13, 50, 123–4
Kallang, Singapore, 261
Kalutara, Ceylon, 8
Kalyan, 34, 183
Kamaing, 129
Kangaw, 69–71, 156, 190, 221, 267–8
  see also Battles, Engagements and Operations
Kantu, Sweeper:
  Mentioned in despatches, 201
Karachi, 7, 9, 31, 35, 105, 131, 135–6, 162, 189, 204, 207
Kawkareik Pass *see* Battles, Engagements and Operations
Kellett, Tommy, 183
Ken River, 86, 94

Kennedy Peak, 159–60
Kenya, 225–38, 264
Kettle, Colour Sergeant Maxmos, 107–109
Khyber Pass, 31, 52, 184
Kiff, Lance Sergeant, 14
Kimble, David, 226
Kindaungyyi, 79
King George VI, 80, 97
King, Lieutenant, 68
King, T.R., 226
Kinnmargon, 34
Kipchoge, Warrant Officer, 232
Kleen, Romulus, 234–7
Kluang, Malaya, 73, 152–3
Knibb, Sergeant Vic, 110–13
Knowland, Lieutenant G.A.:
    Victoria Cross, 70
Kohat, 208
Kohima, 44, 49, 60–1, 135, 159, 267
    see also Battles, Engagements and Operations
Kuala Lumpur, Malaya, 65, 73, 153–7, 172–3
Kudowor, Lance Corporal Wisdom, 114–15
Kumbhirgram, 33
Kyauktauga, 201
Kyunsanlai Pass, 217
    see also Battles, Engagements and Operations

Labu, 95
'Lady in White' see Gibson, Perla
Lagos, Nigeria, 138, 188–9
Lahore, 104–105
Lalaghat, 128–30, 139
Lamptey, Private Odartey, 81
Landini, Private, 231
Lansdowne, 74
Lashio, xvi
Latham, Francis, 152
Leach, Major 'Slogger', 100
Leeches, 12, 140, 189
Leitch, Neil, 141
Lendioo, Private Seremon, 232–6
Letsegan see Battles, Engagements and Operations
Lewin, Captain 'Chippy', 229
LILOP see Rest and Recuperation: Leave
Llango, 161
Local Defence Volunteers see Home Guard

Long, Johnny, 87
Longley, Major, 129
Lucknow, 5, 180
Luscombe, Lieutenant Ted, 116–20
    Indian Independence Medal, 118
Lynn, Vera, 90, 101

MacDonald Fraser, George, 161
Macgregor, Captain K.W., 67–70
McInnes, Bombardier Neil, 121–6
Macnab, Brigadier John Francis, 108, 234–5
Machin, Private Sid, 127–32
Madagascar, 225–9
Madigan, 33
Madras, 22, 52, 90, 142, 171, 177
Malaya, 48, 56, 73, 108–109, 152, 157, 167–8, 172, 203, 206
    see also Post-War Operations: Malaya, planned invasion of
Malta, 145, 205–206
Mandalay, 14, 50, 125, 244
    see also Battles, Engagements and Operations: Meiktila and Mandalay
Manipur, 102, 197
Massey, Sapper Arthur, 133–6
Maubin, 78
Maungdaw, 66, 100–101, 221, 267
    see also Battles, Engagements and Operations: Arakan, 3rd Campaign
Mawlaik, 232
Mawlu see Battles, Engagements and Operations
Mays, Bill, 65
Mayu Range, 101, 122, 221
Medals and Citations:
    Distinguished Service Order, 6, 129, 140, 156
    Indian Independence Medal, 118
    Mentioned in despatches, 14, 76, 142, 149, 156, 201, 227
    Military Cross, 102, 111, 147, 152, 172
    Territorial Decoration, 73
    Victoria Cross, 70, 97, 199, 221, 244
Medan, Sumatra, Dutch East Indies, 63–5, 261–4
Medical Services, xvii
    see also Medicines
    Battlefield evacuation, 52, 70, 79, 89, 101, 129, 135, 161, 183, 191–2, 218, 237

Index   279

Hospitals
  Asansole, CMH, 32
  Bangalore, CMH, 32
  Bangalore, Convalescent Depôt, 52
  Burma, Field Hospital, 251
  Calcutta, 135
  Chindit Field Hospital, 141
  Comilla, 101
  Dacca, 62nd Indian General Hospital, 122
  Delhi, Garrison Hospital, 103
  Jullundur, Garrison Hospital, 118
  Karachi, Field Hospital, 9
  Madras, British Military Hospital, 52
  Meerut, 129
  Mogaung, Field Hospital, 180
  Poona, 79
  Ranchi, 184
  Secunderabad, 135
  Shillong, 198
  Trimulgherry, 161
  Royal Army Medical Corps, 101, 117, 170
  Voluntary Aid Detachment nurses, 66
Medicines:
  Ascorbic acid, 189
  Chlorine tablets, 10, 189
  Mepacrine, 95, 140, 152, 187, 194
  Quinine, 101, 218
  Saline drip, 117
  Salt tablets, 26, 189, 253
  Vaccinations, 187, 250, 258
Meerut, 129–30, 157
Meiktila, 14, 42, 61, 161, 169, 202, 244
  see also Battles, Engagements and Operations: Meiktila and Mandalay
Melrose, 70, 156, 266–70
  see also Battles, Engagements and Operations: Kangaw
Mercer, Major Charles, 137–43
  Mentioned in despatches, 142
Mercer, Hugh, 197
Messenger, Robert, 21
Mhow, 166, 171
Milford see Battles, Engagements and Operations: Kangaw
Military Police, 93, 103, 167, 202, 262
Miller, Warrant Officer Roy, 144–9
  Mentioned in despatches, 149
Mingaladon, 112, 261

Mock, Corporal Victor, 150–3
Mogaung, 88–9, 95, 142, 180
Mombasa, Kenya, 3, 225
Montagu, Major Drogo, 154–7, 271
  Mentioned in despatches, 156
Monteith, Major David John, 178
Monywa, 61, 169
Moore, Captain Sir Tom, 83
Morcombe, Lieutenant Colonel Philip Alfred, 229
Morgan, Major Doris Carswell, 118–20
Morib Beach, 157
Morse Code, 19–21, 25, 56, 177, 184, 205, 255
Mount Popa, 96
Mountbatten, Lady, 261
Mountbatten, Admiral Lord Louis, later 1st Earl Mountbatten of Burma, vi, xvi, 26, 68, 71, 156–7, 178, 253, 260–1, 267–8
Muar, Malaya, 73
Mundu, Yeli, 142
Murphy, Sergeant Vincent, 158–63
Murray, Bob, 141
Mussoorie see Rest and Recuperation: Leave
Mustard gas, 25, 84–5, 227
Mwangangi, Sergeant, 234
Myebon, 68–9, 221, 267–8
  see also Battles, Engagements and Operations: Kangaw
Myingyan, 34, 42
Myitkyina, 95, 142, 179, 217

Naga Hills, 267
Nagpur, 207
Namkaput, 233
Napier Barracks, Lahore, 104–105
Ncube, Lance Corporal, 236
Nera Camp, Poona, 93
Newall, Private Benjamin George, 152
Newland, Signaller Dennis, xvii, 164–75
Ngakyedauk see Battles, Engagements and Operations: Ngakyedauk Pass
Nightingale, Freddy, 165
Nippon Hill see Battles, Engagements and Operations
Niven, Ian, 176–81
Norton, Lieutenant John, 81
Nunshigum Ridge see Battles, Engagements and Operations

Okey-doke Pass *see* Battles, Engagements and Operations: Ngakyedauk Pass
Ondal, 32
Ootacamund *see* Rest and Recuperation: Leave

Pahok, 142
Pakokku, 104
Palel, 161, 229
Pandaveswar, 32
Pegu, 22–3, 42, 61, 161, 200–201, 245
Percy-Hardman, Major Cecil George, 6, 9
Perkins, Sergeant, 142
Peshawar, 154, 184
Philippeville, Algeria, 99, 150–1
Phillips, Squadron Leader, 208
Phyu, 125
"Piccadilly" *see* Chindits (Special Force): Strongholds
Pinhmi Bridge *see* Battles, Engagements and Operations
Poona, 27, 77, 79, 85, 93, 183
Pope, Captain, 151
Port Said, Egypt, 127, 135–6, 183
Post–war operations:
    Disposal of wartime materiel, 186
    Japan, occupation of, 47–8
    Malaya, planned invasion of, 42, 52, 62, 72, 171
    Sumatra, 63, 76, 261
Potsangbam, 161
Powers, Private Lawrence 'Lawrie', 182–5
Prisoners of War:
    Allied, 15, 22, 38, 57, 62–4, 197, 208, 222, 245, 258, 261
    German, 162, 182
    Italian, 169, 207
    Japanese, 12, 47, 56, 63, 73, 140, 147, 152–3, 245–6, 261, 269–70
Prome, 96, 184, 193
Pyabwe *see* Battles, Engagements and Operations

Quetta, 31–2
Quinlan, Sergeant Alf, 173

Racial Tensions, 31, 93, 117
Radar, 59–64, 210
Ramree Island, 75

Ramsay, Captain Maurice, 186–95
    Military Cross, 191
Ramu, 122
Ranchi, 9, 27, 47, 184, 189, 198–9, 213
Randle, Captain John, 196–203
    Military Cross, 199
Rangoon, xvi, xviii, 8–9, 23, 42, 51–2, 56, 60–5, 71–2, 75, 87–90, 96, 125, 152, 161, 170–1, 184, 250–2, 261–6
    see also Battles, Engagements and Operations
Ratnap, 208
Rawalpindi, 97
Razabil, 101
Red Cross *see* British Red Cross
Red Hill, 199
    see also Battles, Engagements and Operations: Imphal
Red Sea, 20, 23, 99, 126, 165
Rest and Recuperation:
    Leave
        Calcutta, 110
        Chakrata, 32
        Darjeeling, 122–4
        Delhi, 103
        Home, 135, 161–2, 173
        LILOP, 131
        Mussoorie, 118
        Ootacamund, 21–2, 34, 171
        Shillong, 27, 198
        Simla, 27, 116, 198–9
        Srinagar, 246
        Survivors' leave, 100
    Entertainment
        Cinema, 170, 184, 209
        Concerts
            Elsie and Doris Waters ('Gert and Daisy'), 89, 172–3
            Gracie Fields, 56
            Noël Coward, 167
            Vera Lynn, 90, 101
        Dancing, 103, 122, 243
    Recreation
        Climbing
            Dobbabetta Peak, 171
            Garhwal Himalaya, 75
        Football, 117, 169–70, 177
        Sailing, Lake Victoria, 62
Rice, Sergeant George, 204–11
Rice, Leonard, 204–206

Rice, Fusilier Louis, 177
Richards, Brigadier Collen, 77
Riggs, Captain John, 212–19
Risalpur, 52, 208
Robertson, George Currie (Robbie), 178
Robertson, Lieutenant Leslie, 234
Royal Air Force and Indian Air Force, xv, 17–24, 29–37, 38–44, 58–65, 75, 85, 128, 139, 182, 204–11, 216, 248–54, 259–65
  Air Training Corps, 38–9, 41, 58, 158, 182, 184, 249
  RAF Regiment, 263
  Royal Air Force Volunteer Reserve, 249
  Squadrons
    2 Forward Equipment Unit, 249–51
    6 Indian Air Force Squadron, 207–208
    42 Maintenance Unit, 249
    110 (Hyderabad) Squadron, 30–5
    124 Repair and Service Unit, 40–2
    136 Squadron, 261
    152 (Hyderabad) Squadron, 260–1
    155 Squadron, 261–4
    206 Squadron, 194
    357 (SD) Squadron, 20–1
    938 (Balloon) Squadron, 30
    Air Fighting Development Squadron, 260
Royal Commonwealth Ex-Services League, 83, 107
Royal Indian Navy *see* Royal Navy and Royal Indian Navy
Royal Navy and Royal Indian Navy, xv, 1–4, 144–9, 221, 255–8
  British Pacific Fleet, 2, 147
  Fleet Air Arm (1832 Squadron), 2
  see also Ships: Combat ships
Rupkund Massacre, 75
Rust, Commander H.T., 145
Ruywa, 71, 191–2, 221

Saigon, French Indo-China, 72–3, 222
Salween River, 197
Santer, Dickie, 6–7
Saunders, Wing Commander, 34
Scott, Lieutenant Colonel Walter, 128–30
  Distinguished Service Order, 129
  Military Cross, 128
Secunderabad, 8, 96, 135, 159–61, 171

Sen, Lieutenant Colonel Lionel Protip 'Bogey', 156, 267–8
  Distinguished Service Order, 156
Seymour, Gunner Stanley, 220–3
Shadazup, 89
Shenam Pass *see* Battles, Engagements and Operations: Nippon Hill
Shillong, 27, 55–6, 198
  see also Rest and Recuperation: Leave
Ships:
  Combat ships
    HMS *Argus*, 204–206
    HMS *Ark Royal*, 206
    HMS *Armada*, 256
    HMS *Begum*, 2
    HMS *Bramble*, 144–5
    HMS *Codrington*, 116
    HMS *Devonshire*, 148
    HMS *Eagle*, 146
    HMS *Formidable*, 147
    HMS *Furious*, 206
    HMS *Glory*, 257
    HMS *Illustrious*, 147
    HMS *Implacable*, 147
    HMS *Indefatigable*, 147
    HMS *Indomitable*, 144–7
    HMS *Kenya*, 116
    HMS *Manxman*, 1
    HMS *Nelson*, 147
    HMS *Prince of Wales*, 206
    HMS *Slinger*, 257
    HMS *Unicorn*, 2
    HMS *Victorious*, 147
    HMS *Vindex*, 256
  Troopships
    Alcantara, 27
    Almanzora, 218
    Athlone Castle, 20
    Capetown Castle, 90
    City of London, 135
    Corfu, 261
    Derbyshire, 151
    Devonshire, 171
    Dominion Monarch, 157
    Duchess of Richmond, 126
    Duchess of York, 7
    Duke of Roxburgh, 183
    Dunnottar Castle, 159
    Empire Pride, 250
    Empress of Australia, 127, 249

Johan van Oldenbarnevelt, 30–1
Louis Pasteur, 93
Maloja, 165
Marnix van Sint Aldegonde, 99, 150
Mooltan, 116, 118, 159
Orduna, 23
Orontes, 131
Queen of Bermuda, 55, 173, 189
Ranchi, 133
Rohna, 134
Samaria, 65
Santa Elena, 99
Stirling Castle, 14
Strathaird, 40
Strathnaver, 66
Tabinta, 47
Talma, 171
Tierra del Fuego, 60
Winchester Castle, 127, 225
Shirreff, Major David, 224–38
  Mentioned in despatches, 227
  Military Cross, 228
Short, Captain Gordon, 153, 239–47
Shwebo, 104
Sier, LAC Alan, 248–54
Silchar, 33, 40–1
  Silchar Track, 161
Simla *see* Rest and Recuperation: Leave
Singapore, 35, 42–3, 47, 56–7, 62–5, 74, 152, 171–3, 203, 207, 219, 221–2, 248–52, 258, 261–4
Singh, Squadron Leader Mehar, 207
Sittang Bridge *see* Battles, Engagements and Operations
Sleet, Bombardier, 70
Slim, General Sir William 'Bill', later 1st Viscount Slim of Yarralumla and Bishopston, vi, xvi–xviii, 120, 129, 169–70, 172, 201, 266–7
Srinagar *see* Rest and Recuperation: Leave
Stille, Bob, 234
Stilwell, General Joe 'Vinegar Joe', US Army, 95, 217
Stocker, Colonel, 244
Suez Canal, 20, 23, 99, 110, 133–4, 151, 159, 189, 243
Sungei Petani, Malaya, 56
Sunle, 230
Supplies and Provisions:
  Air resupply, xvii, 10, 61, 67, 72, 78, 95, 102, 124, 129, 140, 146, 173, 175, 190–1, 230, 234

Provisions
  Food, 6, 10, 26, 30, 32, 35, 41, 47, 68–9, 78, 90, 93, 95, 99, 102, 107, 111–12, 123, 128–9, 137, 161, 170, 182, 188–94, 200, 202, 207, 216, 230, 233, 252, 262–4
  Water, 10, 34, 69, 111, 151, 187, 189–93, 216, 218, 250
Surrendered Japanese Personnel *see* Prisoners of War: Japanese

Tactical doctrine, Allied:
  'Boxes', 61, 100, 191–3, 199
  Patrols, 9–13, 27, 47–8, 56, 85, 88, 93–6, 101–102, 151–2, 155, 160, 189, 197, 201, 216–18, 228–9, 233, 237, 244–5
Tactical doctrine, Japanese:
  Artillery, 51, 69–70, 96, 101, 155, 190–3, 200, 271
  Infiltration, 61
  'Jitter parties', 9, 11, 27, 190, 193, 237
  Kamikaze, 2, 147
  Punji stakes, 13
  Roadblocks, 13, 51
  Snipers, 61, 78, 142, 161, 242, 245
Takoradi, Gold Coast, 79–80, 194
Tamlyn, Lieutenant Colonel C.F., 191
Tamu, 103, 124, 230
  Tamu Road, 9
Taungup, 193
Tengah, Singapore, 249, 261
Tennis Court, Battle of the *see* Battles, Engagements and Operations
Thimayya, Lieutenant Colonel Kodandera Subayya, 156, 267–8
  Distinguished Service Order, 156
Thompson, Doc, 266
Thorat, Lieutenant Colonel Shankarrao Pandurang Patil, 70, 156–7, 266–71
  Distinguished Service Order 156
Thorat, Dr Yashwant, 266–71
Tiddim, 159, 199
  Tiddim Road, 102, 160, 244
Tideswell, Sergeant Bill, 179
Tinztin, 230
Tomkinson, Telegraphist (S) Ken, 255–8
Toothill, Captain 'Toots', 197
Townley, Major Richard Peyton, 231
Training:
  see also Training Establishments
  Amphibious landings and river crossings, 26, 86, 90, 94, 138, 152, 157

Index   283

Armoured fighting vehicles, 50, 93–4, 98
Basic training, 2, 25, 30, 38, 46, 50, 58, 66, 77–8, 84–5, 92–4, 98, 107, 110, 116, 121, 127, 133, 137–8, 150, 158–9, 165, 177, 183, 198, 255, 260
Bush warfare, 226
Chemical warfare, 84
Construction and engineering, 85, 114, 133, 259–60
Driver and vehicle maintenance 39, 66, 77–8, 98, 107, 121–2, 249
Jungle warfare, xvi, 47, 56, 67, 75, 108, 114, 128, 135, 138, 151, 154–5, 159, 178, 183, 189, 198, 214
Language, 117, 138, 154, 169
Mountain warfare, 8, 189
Muleteer, 94
Officer training, 66, 116, 131, 137, 186–7, 196, 224
Radar, 59
Weapon and gunnery, 5, 39, 46, 122, 144, 146, 165
Wireless and signals, 19, 25, 56, 165–6, 177, 184, 205, 255–6
Training Establishments:
  Aberdeen, Scotland, Depôt, Gordon Highlanders, 74, 183
  Agra, Indian School of Electrical & Mechanical Engineers, 168–9
  Ahmednuggur, India, Fighting Vehicle School, 93
  Ballykinler, Northern Ireland, 183
  Bangalore, India, Officers' Training School, 116–17, 196
  Barmouth, Wales, 164 OCTU, 241
  Blackpool, Lancashire, 19
  Blackdown, Surrey, RAC OCTU, 93
  Bradford, Yorkshire, 25
  Brecon, Wales, 46
  Bridgnorth, Shropshire, 39
  Bridlington, Yorkshire, RAF Equipment Training School, 30
  Brighton, Sussex, 255
  Bury St Edmunds, Suffolk, Depôt, Suffolk Regiment, 98, 165
  Carlisle, Cumberland, Depôt, Border Regiment, 116, 133, 158
  Castle Martin, Wales, 50
  Catterick, Yorkshire, 156 Training Regiment, RAC, 50
  Catterick, Yorkshire, 123 (RA) OCTU, 66
  Chichester, Sussex, Depôt, Royal Sussex Regiment, 137
  Colchester, Essex, 127, 150
  Cranwell, Lincolnshire, RAF Electrical & Wireless School, 205
  Dorchester, Dorset, Depôt, Dorsetshire Regiment, 241
  Dymchurch, Kent, 163 OCTU, 212
  Eastbourne, Sussex, 255
  Eastchurch, Kent, 9
  Filey, Yorkshire, RAF Basic Training Centre, 30
  Formby, Lancashire, Primary Training Wing, 6
  Halton, Buckinghamshire, RAF No. 1 School of Technical Training, 259
  Invergordon, Scotland, 39
  Lincoln, Lincolnshire, 59–60
  London, RAF Air Crew Receiving Centre, 39, 59
  Lynmouth, Devon, 84
  Maidstone, Kent, Depôt, Queen's Own Royal West Kent Regiment, 55
  Malvern, Worcestershire, HMS *Duke*, 2
  Padgate, Yorkshire, RAF No. 3 Recruit Centre, 30, 182, 249
  Penrith, Cumberland, 50
  Plymouth, Devon, 255
  Portsmouth, Hampshire, HMS *Excellent*, 144
  Sandhurst, Berkshire, 161 (Royal Military College) OCTU, 137, 154, 156, 224
  Shorncliffe, Kent, 46
  Shotley, Suffolk, HMS *Ganges*, 144
  Shrewsbury, Shropshire, 20 Infantry Training Centre, 110
  Skegness, Lincolnshire, 255
  Southend-on-Sea, Essex, 202 (RASC) OCTU, 187
  Stockton, Yorkshire, 150
  Wakefield, Yorkshire, 25
  Warrington, Yorkshire, 19
  Winterbourne Gunner, Wiltshire, 2nd Chemical Warfare Group, 84
  Wrotham, Kent, pre-OCTU, 66, 116, 187, 241
Transport
  Air, xvii, 14, 21, 35, 56, 61, 87, 89, 94–5, 104, 112, 128–9, 131, 142, 152, 161, 183, 208, 214, 244, 261
  see also Supplies and Provisions

Animals
  Elephants, 94–5, 216
  Mules and Ponies, 8–9, 26, 94–5, 100, 128–9, 139–140, 151–2, 178–9, 191, 214–16, 218, 234, 244
  Rail, 21–2, 32–4, 56, 60, 94–5, 103, 105, 111, 123, 130, 135, 139, 159, 170, 179, 213–14, 216–17
  Road, xvi, xvii, 14, 32, 34, 41–3, 60–1, 64, 67–8, 77–8, 90, 94–5, 97, 101–104, 112, 124–5, 135, 139, 159–60, 166–71, 177, 191–4, 201, 207, 213, 229–30, 237, 244–5, 250–1, 261–2, 266
  Water, xvii, 7, 14, 23, 27, 30–1, 33–5, 40, 47, 55–6, 60, 62, 65–6, 68–70, 77, 85–6, 89–90, 93–4, 99, 107, 114, 116, 118, 126–7, 131, 133–5, 142, 147, 150–1, 153, 157, 159, 161, 165, 171, 173, 183, 187, 189, 206–207, 209, 213, 218, 225–6, 229, 234, 242–3, 249–50, 261
  see also Ships: Troopships
Tuer, LAC Thomas, 259–65
Tynan, Lieutenant Colonel Peter, 117

Ukhrul Road *see* Battles, Engagements and Operations

VE-Day, 71, 117, 169
VJ-Day, xiii, xviii, 3–4, 114, 149, 162, 174, 202, 209, 211, 219, 258
Vaughan, Lieutenant Colonel Peter, 139–42
  Distinguished Service Order, 140
Victoria Cross, xv, xvii, 70, 97, 199, 221, 244
Victoria Point, xvi
Voluntary Aid Detachments *see* Medical Services: Voluntary Aid Detachment nurses

War graves:
  Diego Suarez War Cemetery, 225
  Madras War Cemetery, 177
  Maynamati War Cemetery, 231
  Sahmaw Cemetery, 179
  Taukkyan War Cemetery, 44, 87, 152, 234
Warton, Captain R.H. ('Willie'), 236
Waters, Doris, 89, 172–3
Waters, Elsie, 89, 172–3
Watts, Captain, 245
Wavell, Field Marshal Archibald, 1st Earl Wavell, 103, 152, 267
Waw, 161
Weather *see* Climatic Conditions
"White City" *see* Chindits (Special Force): Strongholds
'White Tigers' *see* Armed Forces, Japanese 33rd Japanese Division
Wilson-Williams, Gunner, 71
Wingate, Major General Orde, 128–9, 138, 217, 238
Wishart, Crawford, 128–9
Women's Voluntary Service (WVS), 187, 210
Wongara, Sergeant Major Mammadu, 189
Worli, 20, 208–209, 261
Wright, Maurice, 201

Yelahanka, 34
Yeu Road, 237
Yomas Hills, 193
Yunnan, China, xvi
Ywathit, 140